THE HIDDEN
IRELAND

*A Study of Gaelic Munster in the
Eighteenth Century*

DANIEL CORKERY

GILL AND MACMILLAN

Published in Ireland by
Gill and Macmillan Ltd
Goldenbridge
Dublin 8
with associated companies in
Auckland, Delhi, Gaborone, Hamburg, Harare,
Hong Kong, Johannesburg, Kuala Lumpur, Lagos, London,
Manzini, Melbourne, Mexico City, Nairobi,
New York, Singapore, Tokyo
0 7171 0079 0
First published 1924, fourth impression 1956
This edition published 1967, eighth impression 1989
Print origination by Cahill & Co. Ltd
Printed in Hong Kong

Contents

Introduction

I

Years before I settled down to this book I was keenly aware of the need for it. At the same time I held back, fearing that I was not the man to write it, that I had neither the scholarship nor the leisure. In the wrestling of those two thoughts was a discomfort that in vain I tried to lay aside with a " but "—" but no one else thinks it worth while to write it " —that is, the book I had already in my mind's eye.

Another thought tempted me. The whole movement for the revival of the Irish language, I felt, had been allowed to drift almost entirely under the guidance of grammarians. For the learning of such men, and their care for accuracy, I have the deepest respect. But (O blessed word!) there are too many of them about, I said; they have lost the sense of proportion; and because of this the conditions have become too meticulous, hard, and acrid for that wayward crop, literature, to throw out those promiscuous spurts of growth which are the very routine of youth. This book is a study of some of the Munster Gaelic poets of the eighteenth century. It is perhaps the first serious attempt made to understand them. It cannot be said, however, that those poets for some years past have been neglected; contrariwise they have been studied, almost entirely from the grammarian's point of view, though, and not from any other, literary or even human. Not their works have been studied so much as their words; their prepositions and particles rather than their visions!—a hard fate to befall a set of men who not only were poets but lyric poets, whose lives moreover, whose whole period indeed, was a living agony. How they must thank me if, even in a blundering way, I throw open their songs to more kindly eyes!

Among the grammarians I do not, of course, include the historians of the literature—men like Professor Bergin, Professor O'Donoghue, Professor O'Rahilly, Professor Douglas Hyde, Father Dinneen, Mr Robin Flower and others whose words I quote so often in the following pages. To those I am well content to play the not unnecessary part of *vulgarisateur*.

All those as well as their students will, of course, find numerous errors after me, if they care to look. There are, however, errors and errors. Lord Morley held history to be an epic art—and the propulsive course of epics is not to be hindered by even shoals of errors. And if this opinion be not cover and shield enough for me and my faults I add to it that saying of Goethe's: The best that history has to give us is the enthusiasm which it arouses.

II

Such errors as are to be found in this book will not prevent it from lighting up the period it deals with;—not only that, but subsequent periods of Irish history will, let us hope, be a little the clearer for it, even that very terrible phase from which we have not yet quite emerged. It will not, in any way, replace Lecky's study of the same century; that book it will rather supplement, inasmuch as its province is that side of Irish life, the Gaelic side, which to him and his authorities was dark. He must have thought the Gaelic language a wayside *patois*, clearly not one of the permanent forces of the nation. In the preface to his *History of England in the Eighteenth Century*, of which book his chapters on Irish history, of course, form part, he explains that his aim was not to write a history year by year or to give a detailed account of battles or of the minor political incidents, but " to disengage from the great mass of facts those which relate to the permanent forces of the nation or which indicate some of the more enduring features of national life."

From his own pages one would never feel that the soul of the Gael is one of the more enduring features of our national life. Yet this very fact becomes daily more evident, and all future historians will more and more have to wrestle with it. Far from disengaging for us the urge of that soul he would have us consider as complete an analysis of Irish life in which it is not referred to. The soul of a people is most intimately revealed, perhaps, in their literature; the Gaelic people in that period were possessed of much literature, were, moreover, constantly adding to it, for they had many poets; yet of this literature, of these poets, Lecky knew nothing.

He enlightens us on the attitude of those historians among whom he wished to stand: "What characterises these writers is that they try to look at history, not as a series of biographies, or accidents, or pictures, but as a great organic whole; that they consider the social and intellectual condition of the world at any given period a problem to be explained, the net result of innumerable influences which it is the business of the historian to trace."

To the social condition of both the Gaelic people and the Ascendancy he gave close study; to the intellectual movements among the Ascendancy he gave the same earnest thought; but at similar movements among the Gael, also, just as surely, the net result of innumerable influences, he gave not even one single glance! The inference is that there were none, or that, being there, they were not matter for such historians as he. In his biography it is written: "Survivals of the old national life in a country always interested him particularly, and in Holland he had exceptional opportunities of seeing these." But the survivals of national life among the Gaels made no appeal to him. He wrote : "To destroy the prestige and position of Trinity College would be to drive the ablest Irishmen more and more to the English Universities, and thus more and more to denationalise the talent of Ireland." He had but little idea how denationalised his own

7

mind was; he could describe himself quite seriously as the latest successor of the Four Masters!

Nevertheless, his book is a noble work, packed with knowledge. What it lacks, however, was the very life of the building. If his account of Ireland were the whole truth, the subsequent history of Ireland must have been very different from what it actually has been. That subsequent history is a rough story of a national ideal grimly pursued; it is perhaps the best illustration in the world's history of how strong and indeed terrible a force nationalism comes slowly to be when tempered in the fires of adversity and smithied in the forge of persecution. Mr Stopford Brooke some years ago took the mass of poetry written by Irishmen in the English tongue. He searched it for its distinctive elements. In the end he marked out three—Nationality, Religion, and " what England calls Rebellion."[1] Nationality, Religion, Rebellion! Now, if this be the finding of a competent critic with regard to that poetry, practically all of which was written in the nineteenth century, what would we say of a historian of that century who had never given a thought to that mass of literature or its writers? If his work gave one to understand that none such existed, that consequently the desire that would crave such utterance either did not exist, or else, so weakly as not to find expression for itself—surely it would not be too severe a condemnation of such a work to say that whatever of good it held in it, the life of the building was not in it? Now, one goes only a little way into the Irish poetry of the eighteenth century when one comes on the same three notes, the same, yet how vastly different! How much deeper, louder, stronger, fiercer!

Lecky, however, telling his tale of that century, omits all reference to this body of literature, almost all of which may be spoken of as explicitly or implicitly historical.

It is when his shortcomings are known that his book

---

[1] Introduction to *A Treasury of Irish Poetry (In the English Tongue)*.

becomes of great value; for one turns to it then for what it contains,—for information on the material conditions of the country or for the story of the Dublin Parliament, that noisy side-show, so bizarre in its lineaments and so tragi-comic in its fate, to which he gave such attention. His account of the life of the country as a whole needs many supplementary books, not one. Some indeed have already appeared; and this book aims at being simply one other.

III

Lecky's attitude towards Irish would not matter if similar views did not still exist in the country. It would be well for all outsiders who would understand Ireland and its tragic history, or indeed any phase of it, always to keep before them the fact that the Ascendancy mind is not the same thing as the English mind.[1] The English mind we can fairly come upon in the literature of the English people; but how astray would he be who would make himself an image of the English, as we in Ireland have known them, from the study of that literature! As well think to find in it the English of India! The first article in an Ascendancy's creed is, and has always been, that the natives are a lesser breed, and that anything that is theirs (except their land and their gold!) is therefore of little value. If they have had a language and literature, it cannot have been a civilised language, cannot have been anything but a *patois* used by the hillmen among themselves; and as for their literature, the less said about it the better. In the course of time the natives become tainted with these doctrines; and cry approval when the untruths of the Ascendancy are echoed from some distant place, as if at last a fair judgment has been pronounced, not recollecting that the Ascendancy have had for hundreds of years possession of the ear of the world and

[1] How well old Spenser understood this! See in his *View of the State of Ireland* the passage beginning: " Lord, how quickly doth that country alter men's natures!"

have not failed to fill it with such opinions as were opportune. What pains one is to come upon an Irishman who cannot speak either of the Irish language or Irish literature or Gaelic history except in some such terms as the Ascendancy in Ireland have taught him. In his case the Ascendancy have succeeded; they have created in him the slave-mind. They have won his thoughts and affections from his native country. " We dare say," wrote Sir Samuel Ferguson, " we dare say, had it been the policy of any party in ancient Greece to win the thoughts and affections of the Greeks from their own country, so as to make them a safer provincial dependency of some earlier civilised neighbouring nation—Syria, say, or Egypt—this sort of argument or expostulation would have been very often employed by them : Where is the use of tracing back the barbarous traditions of the House of Atreus? . . . . Why waste your time on idle enumerations of the pedigrees of Inachus? . . . . Turn your thoughts to Egypt. . . . . The glorious actions of Sesostris are something indeed worthy of the study of men of enlightenment. The sources of the Nile, and the causes of its overflow, you may investigate with profit and delight . . . . indulge no more the idle dreams of being Greeks—North-west Egyptians, methinks, would sound more proper."

Even today, here in Ireland, we are aware of thousands who must have been seduced by some such accents; the prejudice against the language is insensate; yet a nationality that has been toughened in whole centuries of foul fortune will not easily give up that tongue in which alone the desires of its heart have been uttered in their truest, deepest, and most beautiful forms. That this is so cannot be gainsaid. Why then seek any other argument for keeping it alive?

To revive Irish, cry the Progressives—Progressives!—is to stay the wheels, to put the hands of the clock back. They are filled with a vision of whirring wheels, glistening belts, flying argosies,—a mechanical world, its speed ever accelerating, its output ever increasing! One can indeed imagine a multiplicity of languages as making for confusion among barbarian

10

peoples; but if we, with all those mechanical aids to boot, cannot carry on smoothly under such conditions as did not ever in the world's history entirely prevent commerce and traffic—surely all our pains to invent have been in vain? After all, all that aptness in mechanism means control of force; it is all in the economy of nature; it is natural. What is not natural is that "progress" should spell "uniformity." If those whose very dreams have become mechanical still see any use for the arts, it can only be that they pay lip-service to old saws. How anyone who cares for literature can bear to see a language, any language, die is a thought beyond us. Even an old outworn language digged out of the earth—who can measure its latent power or forecast its influences? Fragments of stone have been picked out of the ground by field labourers: they have so shaken, so disturbed, so inspired, so coerced the whole art-mind of Europe ever since, that one sometimes regrets that ever they were awakened from their dreams!

But it is comforting to know that even during the very period that those "Progressives" look upon as having been ruled by their own modern and efficient ideas, several dead and half-dead languages have been quietly recovering their powers of speech! Perhaps this, too, is in the economy of nature; is not without purpose.

IV

Reading those re-discovered poets day after day, I was more and more struck with the extent to which the modes of Mediæval literature survived in them. At first I felt merely curious; but somehow becoming aware that the whole trend of modern literature was towards those self-same long dis-carded modes, I grew to think that here was such a justifica-tion for reviving the language as overshadowed all others.

In this place it is not feasible, even if one were able, to take such a wide or penetrating view of modern literature as would show whether or not Renaissance moulds are being flung aside as no longer of use. One must be satisfied to sketch out roughly certain lines of thought which give us to feel a great struggle going on in modern literature between the dying spirit of the Renaissance and the re-discovered spirit of Nationality. It is not to-day nor yesterday that this fight began. What is every Romantic movement, every *Sturm und Drang* movement, but a skirmish in it? Does not every such movement begin by an increased consciousness that the breadth, movement, colour of life, the romance of it, cannot be poured into classical moulds? (Of course, the moulds are not really Classical at all; they are only Classical at second-hand; they are Renaissance.) It is the surface-movement, the surface-flush of life that at first seems to protest against the inflexibility, the too-regulated shapeliness, the too-restricted colouring that those Renaissance modes insist upon, for all their size and grandeur. Then the pageantry of the past, where surface-movement, surface-colour, are less mixed with other elements, joins in the protest and clamours for expression. But it does not matter to the argument which of the two comes first; the thing to insist upon is that every Romantic movement is a national effort to discover for present needs forms other than the Classical forms.

It has to be insisted upon that Renaissance standards are not Greek standards. Greek standards in their own time and place were standards arrived at by the Greek nation; they were national standards. Caught up at second-hand into the art-mind of Europe—thus becoming international, their effect was naturally to whiten the youthfully tender national cultures of Europe. That is, the standards of a dead nation killed in other nations those aptitudes through which they themselves had become memorable. Since the Renaissance there have been, strictly speaking, no self-contained national cultures in Europe. The antithesis of Renaissance art in this regard is national art. To some it must seem as if the Renaissance has justified itself in thus introducing a common strain into the art-consciousness of all European countries. That common strain was certainly brilliant, shapely, worldly-wise, strong, if not indeed gigantic, over-abounding in energy, in life! Yet all the time there was a latent weakness in it, a strain, a sham strength, an uneasy energy, a death in life. It always protested too much. Dissembling always, it was never simple-hearted enough to speak plainly, and so, intensely. It therefore dazzles us rather than moves us. If it has justified itself, then should we swap Rheims cathedral for St Peter's and Rouen for St Paul's! " One would, however, swap Dante for Shakespeare?"—Yes, but what did Shakespeare's native wood-notes wild know of the Unities? Happy England!—so naïvely ignorant of the Renaissance at the close of the sixteenth century. Unhappy France!—where even before Shakespeare was born they had ceased to develop their native Christian literary modes, had indeed begun to fling them aside for those of Euripides and Seneca. The edifice they built up in after years upon these borrowed alien modes is both noble and vast, perhaps even great, but it is not either a Rheims or a Rouen: its appeal to the spirit has less in it both of magic and depth. The Renaissance may have justified itself, but not, we feel, either on the plane of genuine Christian art or genuine pagan art. It is not as intense or as tender as the one, nor so calm, majestic and wise as the other.[1]

A Romantic movement is not usually thought of as a violent effort to re-discover the secret power that lay behind Greek art; yet in essence that is what every Romantic movement has been. The personal note, the overweening subjectivity, that marks such movements is a protest against the externality of

---

[1] When writing this I had forgotten that Wilde had more brilliantly said the same thing: " To me one of the things in history the most to be regretted is that the Christ's own Renaissance, which has produced the Cathedral at Chartres, the Arthurian cycle of legends, the life of St Francis of Assisi, the art of Giotto, and Dante's *Divine Comedy*, was not allowed to develop on its own lines, but was interrupted and spoiled by the dreary Classical Renaissance that gave us Petrarch, and Raphael's frescoes, and Palladian architecture, and formal French tragedy, and St Paul's Cathedral, and Pope's poetry, and everything that is made from without and by dead rules, and does not spring from within through some spirit informing it."—*De Profundis*.

Renaissance moulds. The local colour, the religious *motif,* the patriotic *motif,* these are an adventure in rough life rather than in the pale meadows of death. That is, every Romantic movement is right in its intention: it seeks to grow out of living feeling, out of the here and now, even when it finds its themes in the past, just as Greek art, which also looked for themes in its people's past, grew up out of the living feeling of its own time and place. The Renaissance would hold by a dead age and a dead land.

There is perhaps no tongue in Europe that has not had its Romantic movement, or movements. If we are destined to see no more, it is simply that the Old Man of the Sea has been flung from our backs, that the Renaissance is dead.

The Renaissance, artificial from the start, rootless, had sometime to die. Dead, what could succeed it except a return to national standards? Whether or not we feel that every literature in Europe is doing this may be a question of knowledge. But it is not necessary to take them in turn and observe their courses. Let us rather ask ourselves: What language in Europe since the French Revolution—which outburst, for all its Classicism, really meant the overthrow of the Renaissance—has done the greatest work in literature? The answer is the Russian. That literature, born too late to share deeply in the wares of the Renaissance, is at once the most national and the most significant of all modern literatures. A memorable and comforting fact—pointing out the way of light and freedom.

Note again, the influence that other late comers in the field of world-literatures, such as Danish, Norwegian, Swedish, are having on the world of letters. It is the literatures of these countries that are really the pathfinders of to-day. Note again, how impossible it would have been for America to make any progress in literature if Whitman had not arisen to slay the New Englanders. Still further observe the huge extent to which dialect is entering into the stuff of modern literature in almost all countries. Imagine what Racine would say to Eugene O'Neill! Dialect is the language of the common people; in

14

literature it denotes an almost overweening attempt to express the here and now, that, in its principle is anti-Renaissance.

If one confined his attention to English, it would be interesting to show how truly modern is A. E. Housman's *Shropshire Lad,* how old-fashioned Francis Thompson: Housman, the Saxon, the Nationalist; Thompson, the Latinist, the child of the Renaissance. Again, an interesting contrast could be made between Hardy, the delineator of a rural parish, and Shaw, whose country is the world, though, of course, Shaw is anything but pure Renaissance. He is not old-fashioned through and through.

But indeed in a hundred different ways it could be shown that in every live country, literature is creeping back to the national hearth, as if it would there find a mother tongue in which to express its judgment on such human souls as most deeply move its affections.

If another line of argument be necessary, one could institute an interesting comparison between the art which Renaissance standards have most tongue-tied and that which fortunately has never known them—Sculpture and Music. What a difference! It is almost the difference between Life and Death. The value of this argument is that it sufficiently answers those to whom Europe without the Renaissance is unthinkable. One certainly does not hold that Music has not been influenced, and deeply influenced, by the Renaissance spirit, but the question all through is not one so much of ' spirit ' as ' mode ': in music we have, happily, clear evidence that modern Europe could invent art-forms when put to it—all out of its own head! If only it could have done so in Sculpture! Music is really the one triumph of modern Europe in art.

This aspect of the value of Irish poetry—how it brings the mind right into the stream of modern literature, as far at least as expression is concerned—struck me more and more while reading these forgotten poets, although, of course, the tradition in which they lived failing more and more, they are the least Gaelic of Gaelic poets. Indeed it seems to me that nearly all modern poets in English are trying, never, however, with

15

the same triumphant success, to write lyrics in the manner of Keating's "A Bhean Lán de Stuaim." When they succeed in doing so the Old Man of the Renaissance will have been flung from the shoulders of our civilisation.

V

In these following pages only one aspect of the Hidden Ireland is delineated: the literary side. To fill out the vision of that land, so dark, so scorned, yet so secretly romantic to those who know it, one would need to have as well a full account of the Irish adventurers of that century, of such men as Morty Óg O'Sullivan and Art O'Leary—to take two of many figures so different, so very different both from " Barry Lyndon "—the " Irishman " of fiction and Barrington's " Irishmen " of history.

One also needs an adequate account of the wandering priests and friars moving hither and thither between this country and the Continent, suffering so deeply, striving so gallantly to keep the institutional side of the Church from utterly fading away. Finally, with a comprehensive study of the folk-poetry—the most precious heritage of all produced by the Gaels in that century—as well as of the folk-music then composed, we should feel that we had fairly explored the riches of that starving people. Until those other avenues are also opened up one cannot have any deep idea of their hidden lives.

I desire to thank Mr John O'Toole, Mr Séumas Ó hAodha, M.A., and Br Senan, of the Capuchin Order, for help and advice. My thanks are also due to Professor Bergin for permission to use some of his translations of bardic poems.

CHAPTER I

THE HIDDEN IRELAND

I

In the latter half of the eighteenth century, whether Catholics should be free to enlist in the British Army was warmly debated by the ruling caste in Ireland. It was, of course, the Penal Laws that stood in the way: according to these, no Catholic could do so, for it was not thought wise that Catholics should learn the use of firearms. However, Townshend became Viceroy, and took a new view of the matter. " He argued that ' as the trade and manufactures of Ireland are almost totally carried on by Protestants, the number of whom is very small in proportion to the number of Papists,' it was of the utmost importance that Protestants should not be taken away for foreign service, and he proposed that Papists, and Papists alone, should be enlisted. 'A considerable number of able men might be raised from amongst them in a short space of time in the provinces of Leinster, Munster, and Connaught.' Rochford answered that the arguments of Townshend had convinced the King of the impropriety of drawing off a number of Protestants from those parts of the country where the chief manufactures were carried on; that he could not without a special Act of Parliament order the recruiting agents to restrict themselves to Roman Catholics, but that in the present very pressing exigency he authorised them to make Leinster, Munster, and Connaught their recruiting grounds."[1] In this manner, adds Lecky, the Catholics were silently admitted into the British Army. (1771.)

A few years later, among the Catholics who took advantage of this hoodwinking at the Law was a poor Munster peasant, a labourer, a wild rake of a man, named Eoghan Ó Súilleabháin. He had misbehaved himself whilst in the service of the Nagle family, whose place was not far from Fermoy, and enlisting in the Army was his way of escaping the consequences. From Fermoy he was sent to Cork, transferred to the Navy, and straightway flung into England's battle-line, thousands of miles away.

If one dwell on the incident, a great deal of Irish history, Irish history in any century, may be realised. Townshend, the Viceroy, the representative of Law, rough-rides over it when it suits him. The penalised Catholic, living from day to day, is callous whether his act is thought lawful or unlawful, if only it helps him here and now. In between English Viceroy and Gaelic peasant, strongly contrasted types as they are, we have the Nagle family, not greatly surprised, it is likely, at all this, they having seen what they had seen.

If one could, with imaginative assurance, enter first the life of the Townshend circle, and explore it; enter then the life of the Nagle family—a house where Irish was spoken to their Kerry labourers and English to their visitors from Dublin—and absorb it; and from this circle pass on and make one's own of the world of the labourer—that hidden, teeming and ragged world that threw him up, a genius!—then one should be qualified to tell the story of Ireland in the eighteenth century. As yet, unfortunately, no historian of it has been so qualified.

The story of the Townshend circle has been shredded out patiently enough by the historians, to be again woven into something like coherency and shapeliness. Novelists have dealt

---

[1] Lecky, *History of Ireland in the Eighteenth Century.*

with such houses as that of the Nagles, chiefly Maria Edgeworth; and writers of history have discovered interesting matter in the memoirs such families have, in rare instances, left behind them. But neither novelist nor historian has dealt with that underworld which threw up the silver-voiced labourer, Eoghan an Bheóil Bhínn—Owen of the Sweet Mouth—as his own people named him then, as they name him still, affection warming the soft Gaelic syllables—for with that hidden land neither historian nor novelist has ever thought it worth his while to deal.

Lecky imagined he had dealt with it! Not without pity for them, he wrote of the people of that darkened land as an almost countless mob—plague-stricken, poverty-stricken, shiftless, thriftless, desperate. He numbered them, as best he might, and traced their sufferings to the causes—and what else remained to be told? Of a mob, what else is there to tell?

This book, too, must touch on their sufferings, their degradation; but afterwards will move on to hint, at least, that all the time much else remained to be told. If only one could do it with as much patience, with as much learning, as Lecky did his share of the work! But even to dream of that, much less to attempt it, is not the task for the day. The immediate task is to show that Lecky presents us, for all his industry and learning, with only a body that is dead and ripe for burial; to show that this is far from being the truth; that all the time there was a soul under the ribs of this death; that the music which was the life of that soul had strength and beauty in it; and that to remain a clod to that music is for us not only to misunderstand the period, but unnaturally to forego our happiness and our privilege.

To that Hidden Ireland of the Gaels, then, we turn our faces.

II

To reach it one must, leaving the cities and towns behind, venture among the bogs and hills, far into the mountains even, where the native Irish, as the pamphleteers and politicians loved to call them, still lurked. "The savage old Irish," Swift named them; and Berkeley wrote of them as growing up "in a cynical content in dirt and beggary to a degree beyond any other people in Christendom." So far down in the depths were they that to the law of the land, though three times more numerous than all the others, they had no existence at all! In times of peace even, they were referred to as "Domestic enemies." "The phrase 'common enemy' was, in the early part of the eighteenth century, the habitual term by which the Irish Parliament described the great majority of the Irish people."[1] And elsewhere Swift wrote (1720): "Whoever travels through this country and observes the face of nature, or the faces and habits and dwellings of the natives, would hardly think himself in a land where either law, religion, or common humanity was professed."[2] "Torpid and degraded pariahs," is the epithet of the balanced Lecky, speaking for himself; and Chesterfield, a mind still more balanced, said: "The poor people in Ireland are used worse than negroes by their lords and masters, and their deputies of deputies of deputies," while Madden spoke of all Ireland as "a paralytic body where one half of it is dead or just dragged about by the other," which, perhaps, is the unforgettable phrase.

The Hidden Ireland, then, the land that lies before us, is the dead half of that stricken body; it is the terrain of the common enemy, ruled by deputies of deputies of deputies, and sunk so deep in filth and beggary that its people have been thrust, as torpid and degraded pariahs should, beyond the household of the law.

This Hidden Ireland we will first look at and see as the travellers who dared to open it up beheld it; that is, we shall see its face rather than its heart; its body, but not its soul. It will be only a glance; for the historians, Lecky especially,

---

[1] Lecky, *History of Ireland in the Eighteenth Century.*
[2] *A Proposal for the Universal Use of Irish Manufactures.*

have made their own of this aspect of it, and their books are there for the reading. But that glance given, we shall make on for thresholds that they never crossed, in hope that what we shall further discover will not only complete the picture they have given, but frankly alter it, as a dead thing is altered when the spirit breathes upon it and it speaks.

III

The Hidden Ireland was in a sense coterminous with Ireland itself, bounded only by the same four seas. Even the children of the Cromwellians who themselves, hardly fifty years before, had come to live in it, could not now speak English.[1] Into the very heart of the Pale, into Dublin itself, this Gaelic-speaking Ireland flowed in many streams. The nobility, coming from their big houses in the provinces, spoke Irish to their servants. Those society people were not Gaels either in blood or feeling, and many of their descendants have become bitterly anti-Irish, yet it is certain that the Colthursts of Blarney and the Lord Kenmare family in Kerry, were at this time speakers of Irish; it was necessary for them to be so, for otherwise they could not direct their workmen, who often knew no English; and those two families may be taken as typical of the county class. Among such people the new-born child was put out to nurse with a neighbouring peasant woman, and the intimacy thus established was frequently maintained in after years. It may also be taken as certain that the hangers-on about these large houses—the land stewards, agents, bailiffs, were frequently ignorant of English. We hear of a " well-bred boy " in the County Down as speaking no language but Irish in 1744;[2] while in the lives of the Gaelic poets we may note that many of them went into the

[1] J. R. Green, *Irish Nationality.*
[2] John Stevenson, *Two Centuries of Life in Down, 1600-1800.*

cities and settled down in them, still singing their songs. Donnchadh Ruadh Mac Conmara (MacNamara) completed his education in the city of Limerick; there in Mungret Street Seán Ó Tuama (O'Twomey) lived for a good many years; while Brian Merriman died there, in Old Clare Street, in 1805. Domhnall Caoch Ó Mathghamhna (Daniel O'Mahony the Blind, died 1720), lived in Cork city, as also did Father William English, a witty poet, whose songs are still favourites among Gaelic speakers. And Father English had scarcely died there, in 1778, when another Gaelic poet, Micheál Ó Longáin, settled in it for some time. These poets, unlike the Colthursts and the Browns (the Kenmare family), were of the Hidden Ireland; but we do not need such evidence to show that its Gaelic waters reached everywhere, either in occasional streams or concealed floodings. Into all these cities, as into all the towns, there was a never-ceasing flowing of the country people, an intercourse that was then far more human and intimate than it is to-day. The roads were always alive with traffic, for country produce was brought in on horse-back or, though not so frequently, in wagons and carts; and arriving at all hours of day and night, and stopping at a hundred different warehouses and inns, the trafficking kept up a chatter and bustle and give and take of mind and wit that similar commerce in our own day knows but little of. Even in Dublin those traffickers were Irish speakers, if necessary; while in places like Cork and Limerick and Waterford their business was very often carried on in that language, as it is in Galway to this very day.

Young, who made his tour in 1776-78, says he found the English language spoken without any mixture of the Irish language only in two places, in Dublin and in the baronies of Bargie and Forth in County Wexford[1]—a statement easily

---

[1] " The inhabitants of the Barony of Forth, near Wexford, are the descendants of the first followers of Strongbow. They have never mixed with the Irish, and still speak a singular language, which is more akin to Flemish than to modern English." *A Frenchman's Walk through Ireland* (1796-7).

credible when one thinks of the children of the Cromwellians themselves having had to make it their mother tongue.

For all this widespread use of their language, however, the Gaels never made their own of the cities and towns: many of them trafficked in them, lived in them, yet were nevertheless little else than exiles among the citizens. Gaelic Ireland, self-contained and vital, lay not only beyond the walls of the larger cities, if we except Galway, but beyond the walls of the towns, if we except Dingle, Youghal, and a few others in Connacht and Donegal. For Irish Ireland had, by the eighteenth century, become purely a peasant nation. Indeed not only did it lie beyond the walls of cities and towns, but its strongholds lay far away beyond all the fat lands, beyond the mountain ranges that hemmed them in. History had seen to that: the rich lands had been grabbed from the Gaels centuries before by successive swarms of land pirates who, in a phrase written by one of themselves (an Elizabethan Brown of Killarney) "measured law by lust, and conscience by commodity." In the softer valleys those land pirates had built their houses, and Irish Ireland withered in the alien spirit that breathed from them. Even to-day we come on the remains of this Gaelic Ireland only in places where there have been no such alien houses for some hundreds of years.

Irish Ireland, then, while in a sense coterminous with Ireland itself, had its stronghold in sterile tracts that were not worth tilling. The hard mountain lands of West Cork and Kerry, the barren Comeraghs in Waterford, hidden glens in the Galtee and other mountains, the wild seaboard of the South and West, the wind-swept uplands of Clare, the back places of Connemara, much of Donegal—in such places only was the Gael at liberty to live in his own way. In them he was not put upon. Big houses were few or none. Travellers were rare; officials stopped short at the very aspect of the landscape; coaches found no fares, the natives being home-keeping to a fault: "They seem not only tied to the country, but almost to the parish in which their ancestors lived," Arthur Young wrote of the Catholics, who had not yet learned to emigrate. Among themselves they had a proverb: "Is maith an t-ancoire an t-iarta" ("The hearth is a good anchor").

The eighteenth century was everywhere a time of violence and hard-drinking for the rich, and for the poor a time of starvation and brutality. If that period was hard on the poor who tilled the plains of France, the rich lands of England, the golden soils of central Ireland, we may conceive how it must have been with the Gaels, whose only portion was rock and bog and wind-swept seashore!

It is only weakness to sentimentalise away the filth, the degradation, the recklessness that go with hardship, starvation and tyranny, when these are continued from generation to generation. If we would realise both the staunchness of the martyr and the blossom-white beauty of his faith, we must understand the rigour of the trial that tested him. In that dreadful century our forefathers were tested as never previously; and one cannot but think that Dr Sigerson is justified in writing: "For a time, Anti-Christ ruled in Ireland. Cromwellian cruelty looks mild, and the pagan persecution of the early Christians almost human when compared with the Penal Code."[1] The test that they underwent we will realise, as we learn of the ways of their daily lives, only if we keep in mind that the insult that went, and will always go, with poverty was the bitterest thong in the manifold lash. Illiterate peasants still keep in mind, as if they thought the lines worth remembering, a certain quatrain, which they attribute to that Eoghan of the Sweet Mouth, that wild rake of a man we have already come upon:

Ní h-í an bhoichtineacht is measa liom,	'Tis not the poverty I most detest,
Ná bheith síos go deó,	Nor being down for ever,
Ach an tarcuisne a leanann í,	But the insult that follows it,
Ná leighisfeadh na leóin.	Which no leeches can cure.

[1] *The Last Independent Parliament of Ireland.*

24

All that has been written about rural Ireland in that century, whether by contemporaries like Young, Miss Edgeworth and Barrington, or later writers like Carleton, O'Neill Daunt or Lecky, leave us with the impression of a land of extraordinary slatternliness—slatternliness and recklessness: while sorrowing, one could not help laughing. There were brighter spots, but these were due to chance or to individual effort. A landlord happened to be a philanthropist, or some tract or other fell out of the memories of the officials and began to fruit of itself. That these very infrequent cases were due to personal efforts speaks plainly enough for the slatternliness of the rest of the country. And it was a striking slatternliness, as common to the rich as to the poor: the typical Big House was as ill-cared for as the cabin—as untidy in its half-cut woods, its trampled avenues, its moss-grown parks, its fallen piers, its shattered chimney stacks, as the cabin with its dung-pit steaming at the door, its few sorry beasts gathered within doors for the night, its swarm of scarce-clad children running wild on the earthen floor. The slatternliness of the Big House was barbaric: there was wealth without refinement and power without responsibility. The slatternliness of the cabin was unredeemed, unless one looks into the soul of things. And between high and low there was, all authorities agree, no middle class; and consequently a dearth of the virtues for which that class stands. Domesticity must have seemed disparate to the very genius of the time. Anti-Christ governed the Catholic poor, not without difficulty; but the Lord of Misrule governed everything; and did so with merely a reckless and daring gesture: at his behest it was that everyone lived well beyond his means.

It is with the state of things after the Union that Miss Edgeworth's book, *The Absentee,* deals: the appearance of the countryside, however, changed but little in all the years of misery between 1690 and 1881—indeed much later than 1881 one could discover whole landscapes—in the Congested Districts of Connacht and Kerry, for instance, where little or nothing had changed: in Miss Edgeworth's book, then, when we find this description of what was called a town, "Nugentstown," we may take it as equally true of the Nugentstown of the eighteenth century:

This *town* consisted of one row of miserable huts, sunk beneath the side of the road, the mud walls crooked in every direction; some of them opening in wide cracks or zig-zag fissures, from top to bottom, as if there had just been an earthquake—all the roofs sunk in various places—thatch off, or overgrown with grass—no chimneys, the smoke making its way through a hole in the roof, or rising in clouds from the top of the open door—dung-hills before the doors, and green standing puddles. . . .

This I take for a quite true description of the small towns and villages of that period. Considering everything, they could not have been otherwise. Who was there to keep order, to set a model? If one reap and reap and never restore to the ground what it loses in each harvest, one should be as careful and as wise as were the rulers of the soil of Ireland in those days.

The larger towns were tidier, for their Protestant inhabitants enjoyed those rights of property that were denied to the Catholics of places like Nugentstown.

But of Irish Ireland it is, perhaps, better to realise the cabin as a thing in itself, than any hamlet, however small; for being then a peasant nation, the cabins, as might have been expected, were the custodians of its mind.

When Michael Doheny was an outlaw in 1848 on the mountains near Glengariff a rainstorm forced him to shelter in a hut which he thus describes in his book, *The Felon's Track:*

The cabin was ten feet square, with no window and no chimney. The floor, except where the bed was propped in a corner, was composed of a sloping mountain rock, somewhat polished by human feet and the constant tread of sheep, which were always shut up with the inmates at night. The fire, which could be said to burn and smoke, but not to light, consisted of heath sods, dug fresh from the mountain. A splinter of bog-wood, lurid through the smoke, supplied us with light for our nightly meal. The tea was drawn in a broken pot, and drunk from wooden vessels, while the sheep chewed the cud in calm and happy indifference. They were about twelve in number, and occupied the whole space of the cabin between the bed and the fire-place.

Elsewhere in the same book he describes a " cabin in the hills " near Kenmare:

> In the house where I slept—as indeed in every house of the same character in the country—the whole stock of the family, consisting chiefly of cows and sheep, were locked in at night. Such was the extreme poverty of the people that they would not be otherwise safe. . . . . There was a slight partition between the room where my bed was and the kitchen, where there were three cows, a man, his wife and four children. It is impossible to convey any idea of the sensations which crowd upon one in such a scene. I fell asleep at last, lulled by the heavy breathing and monotonous ruminating of the cows. Never was deeper sleep.

Catholic Munster certainly was no poorer, if indeed not richer, in 1848 than in 1748, and from these passages we learn how things then were. Doheny himself was sprung from the poorest class of Irish farmers, and followed the plough in his youth, yet it is clear that these cottage interiors surprised him: they would certainly not have surprised the son of any Catholic farmer in 1748, a hundred years before, for, as we know from Young's pages, such cabins might have been met with right up to the gates of Dublin. In 1915, near Ventry, in West Kerry, I found a windowless, one-roomed cabin which could be described in lines taken from Brian Merriman's poem, *Cúirt an Mheadhon Oidhche (The Midnight Court)*, written in 1780:

Bothán gan áit chun suidhe ann,	A cabin with no place to sit down,
Ach súgh sileáin is fáscadh aníos ann,	But dripping soot from above and oozings from below,
Fiadhaile ag teacht go fras gan choímse	No end of weeds growing riotously,
Is rian na gcearc air treasna scríobtha,	And the scrapings of hens across it,
Lag ina dhrom 's na gabhla ag lúbadh	Its roof-tree sagging, its couples bending
Is clagarnach dhonn go trom ag túirlint.	And brown rain falling heavily.

27

Brown rain, because it had come through the soot-impregnated thatch.

These cabins were thrown up anyhow and almost in any place. In the time of the Land League, when evictions were frequent, exactly the same kind of huts were often thrown up in a few hours in the shelter of a ditch, to house the suddenly dispossessed family: though not meant for permanent abodes, some of them were still being lived in forty years after—which should teach us how slowly a landscape wins back to comeliness after a period of disturbance, and enable us further to realise something of the slatternliness of that period in which there had been not even the beginning of recovery.

The cabins of the eighteenth century were sometimes built of stone, mortared or unmortared, but far more frequently of sods and mud. They were thatched with bracken, furze, fern or heath; and must have been often indistinguishable from the bogland, perhaps with advantage. Usually there was but one room, sometimes divided by a rough partition; and often a sort of unlighted loft lay beneath the roof. Chimney there was none, but a hole in the roof allowed portion of the smoke to emerge when the interior had become filled with it. The smoke was often seen to rise up like a cloud from almost every inch of the roof, percolating through as the thatch grew old and thin. The soot that in time came to encrust the walls and thatch within was occasionally scraped off and used as manure.

Between the absence of windows and the ever-present clouds of smoke, the people dwelt in darkness: it did not make for health, nor for quick convalescence when sickness broke out; quite commonly it led to blindness; though one must not forget to add the many prevalent fevers and plagues if one would understand why in any list of the poets of these days one comes so frequently on the word " Dall " (blind)— Tadhg Dall Ua h-Uigín, Liam Dall Ua h-Ifearnáin, Seumas Dall Ua Cuarta, Donnachadh Dall Ua Laoghaire; Carolan might also have been called " Dall," while Donnchadh Ruadh Mac Conmara (MacNamara) became blind in his old age.

Blind poets, blind fiddlers, blind beggars of all kinds were to be seen tapping their way on every road in the country, from fair to fair, from house to house.

Without as within, the hut had a haphazard appearance. Seldom was there a lease, either of house or land; and to improve either led to an increase of rent, perhaps to eviction. No attempt was, therefore, made at tidiness. A hundred years later, in 1838, Lady Chatterton, a lady with a taste for sketching, wrote in charming simplicity of mind: " The only thing I miss in Ireland is my favourite rural scenery; I mean by rural, the neat honey-suckled cottages with their trim little gardens and bee-hives." She would have missed them still more had she come sooner. Every hut had its dung-pit in front of the door, with a causeway of boulders giving passage through it; not far away stood a rick of turf; and practically nothing else: no barns, no sheltering plantations, no market garden, no orchard—and yet it might be a farmer's house.

In appearance the inmates were one with their cabin. Both man and woman usually went barefoot, were scantily clad, and what they had of clothing was some other person's cast-off, patched and re-patched.

The life about the hearth was one with the cabin and its people: it could not be further simplified. House and dress were so miserable that food was almost the only expense; and it was computed that £10 was more than sufficient for the whole annual expense of the family: yet even one bad year brought starvation.

The food consisted almost entirely of buttermilk and potatoes. Morning, noon and night, their dish was the self-same:

Prátai istoidhche,	Potatoes by night,
Prátai um ló,	Potatoes by day,
Agus dá n-eireóchainn i meadhon oidhche,	And should I rise at midnight
Prátai gheóbhainn !	Potatoes still I'd get.

Towards the end of summer their stock of potatoes ran out; and then they went hungry. Conditions improved again

29

in the autumn, and if at this time a person showed any sign of giddy vigour in him, the others said mockingly: " There's flour in the potatoes "—it was breaking out in him as in the tubers. In the winter when the milk was scarce they ate the potatoes with a kitchen made of salt and water, or with a herring, or even a pinch of a herring: " From time to time each one of the family nipped with finger and thumb a little bit of the herring; to give a flavour to his potato."[1] An old peasant, living beyond Dingle, told me that the fishermen, unlike the landsmen, were not so badly off in 1847—the time of the Great Famine—they had the periwinkles! Scraps of food, like periwinkles, all through the eighteenth century were reckoned essential foodstuffs along the coasts.

In some places, Donegal and Kerry, to name two, when everything else had failed, they had the habit of bleeding the cattle, " which they had not the courage to steal," says a contemporary account: mixing sorrel through it, they boiled the blood into a broth, and " Kerry cows know Sunday " became a proverb, for it was to provide the Sunday dinner that they had to suffer.

In the winter months, when the work of the farm could be done in a few hours, the whole family, by rising late and going to bed early, managed to survive on two and sometimes on one meal in the day.

Some corn, some vegetables, a little poultry, were also raised on the farms, which were always small, but these were sold to pay the rent, as also were the live stock, if any, the family knowing the taste of meat only at Christmas and Easter, if even then.

Archbishop King tells us that " one half of the people of Ireland eat neither bread nor flesh for one half of the year, nor wear shoes or stockings."[2]

When life struggled along thus, on its hands and knees, so

---

[1] Le Fanu, *Seventy Years of Irish Life.*
[2] King, to the Lord Bishop of Carlisle, 3rd Feb. 1717.

to speak, there could have been no reserves of goods, food-stuffs or gold. Nor were there any, for whenever, after a prolonged season of rain, famine swooped on them out of a black mist, the poor souls went down like flies. The world rang with the havoc of 1847, but no one hearkened to the periodic famine cries in the eighteenth century. In the famine of 1740—that famine which set Berkeley ruminating on the virtues of tar-water—400,000 are said to have perished. One writer says that the dogs were seen to eat the dead bodies that remained unburied in the fields. Another contemporary wrote: "Want and misery are in every face, the rich unable to relieve the poor, the roads spread with dead and dying bodies, mankind the colour of the dock and nettles they feed on, two or three sometimes on a car going to the grave for want of bearers to carry them, and many buried only in the fields and ditches where they perished."[1]

"I have seen," wrote still another contemporary, "the labourer endeavouring to work at his spade, but fainting for want of food, and forced to quit it. I have seen the aged father eating grass like a beast, and in the anguish of his soul wishing for dissolution. I have seen the helpless orphan exposed on the dung-hill, and none to take him in for fear of infection; and I have seen the hungry infant sucking at the breast of the already expired parent."[2]

And if we move either backward or forward from this midmost period of 1740, things are found to be no better. In 1720 Archbishop King writes: "The cry of the whole people is loud for bread; God knows what will be the consequence; many are starved, and I am afraid many more will."

Bishop Nicholson, an Englishman, tells how one of his carriage horses, having been accidentally killed, it was at once surrounded by fifty or sixty famished cottagers struggling

---

[1] *The Groans of Ireland,* a pamphlet published 1741.

[2] Letter from a Country Gentleman in the Province of Munster to His Grace the Lord Primate. Dublin, 1741.

(For these quotations, and much other evidence, see Lecky *History,* I)

desperately to obtain a morsel of flesh for themselves and their children. In Swift's terrible pages—his *Modest Proposal* was published in 1729—the temper of the time looks out at us: we shudder at Swift's self, we imagine, but the only thing then wrong with Swift was that he had a large heart and a seeing mind. . . . And if instead of backwards we go forward twenty years from 1740 we are entering the period of Whiteboyism—evidence enough that the sufferings had come to a head and broken out.

A new harvest might delay the distress of hunger, but the consequences remained in fevers, fluxes, blindness, insanity, demoralisation. Even in a love lyric one comes on lines like these:

'S gurab í do phóigín thabhar-
    fadh sólás
Dá mbeinn i lár an fhiabhrais.

And 'tis your little kiss would
    comfort me
Were I in the midst of fever.

while the crowds were thinned at Art O'Leary's funeral (1773) by the small-pox, the black death, the spotted fever:

Mura mbéadh an bolgach
Agus an bás dorcha
'S an fiabhras spotuighthe
Bhéadh an marc-shluagh borb san
'S a srianta d'á gcrothadh acu,
Ag déanamh fothraim,
Ag teacht dod shochraid,
A Airt an bhrollaigh ghil.

Only for the small-pox,
And the black death,
And the spotted fever,
That mounted spirited troop,
With their bridles clattering
And making a noise,
Would be coming to your
    funeral,
O Art of the white breast.

And to the Gall, Seán Clárach Mac Domhnaill (MacDonnell) wished

Piannaid is fiabhras dian i dteas
    na dteinteadh.

Torment and gripping fever in
    the heat of hell fire.

But indeed from any one of the poets of that time a collection of such phrases as these—phrases that touch the life of the folk so intimately—might easily be gathered.

As hinted, the conditions of life were such as worsened every plague striking a countryside: the very huts themselves seemed to grip the wandering disease, to hug it, to keep it, until indeed its venom had entirely outworn itself. The cabins were crowded with life, yet, as a rule, contained only two beds, the father and mother sleeping in one, the children in the other, lying heads and points, the boys at one end, the girls at the other. There were no candles nor lamps: at night the family sat and talked around the turf fire, and if anything had to be searched for they lit a rush-light (the pith of rushes, dried and drawn through melted grease or oil), or else a splinter of bog-fir.

Such, then, was the life that went on in and around each of these cabins, if anything so poverty-stricken, so fever-plagued, so uncomely, could be called life.

V

Let us now give a swift glance at the country—the fields, the roads, the woods, the landscape in general. Agriculture was in a poor state, as might be expected when the cottiers were mostly tenants at will. Ploughs were scarce—often only a half-dozen of them in a parish; and these were hired out, as is done today in the case of a huge threshing engine. A *meitheal,* a gathering of the neighbours, assisted in the plough-ing; and two, three, or even four horses, all abreast, were attached to the plough: the process had not become the lone-some task it is to-day. In the early part of the century, the plough was sometimes hitched to the horses' tails—a custom not peculiar to Ireland alone. But the bulk of the crops were raised by spade labour, and not by ploughing. These labourers earned from twopence to fivepence a day; Eoghan Ruadh Ó Súilleabháin, one of them, threatens in one of his poems to go down to Galway, a fat land where the daily wage was sixpence; and there were always complaints and bickerings over the accounts as between middlemen and tenants; the tenant by all sorts of dodges being defrauded of the cash, if not indeed of his earnings: the chronic shortage of small

33

coin, by leading to elaborate systems of barter, conduced towards this everlasting pilfering. " A great number of the peasantry in Ireland," we read, " know perfectly well that for the same work they would receive in England two shillings, and in Ireland only sixpence. And further, they would be much more sure of getting their two shillings in the one country than their sixpence in the other."[1]

All the farm gear was as primitive as the plough. Carts or any sort of wagons were rarely owned or used by the landsmen; and any rough contrivances employed as such had solid wheels beneath them.

The roads were better than might have been expected, and the bye-roads often superior to the highways, for there was a system of local contract labour which gave the Big House care of the bye-roads about it, and a chance of making money into the bargain.

The roads were, of course, the only highways; and vast crowds of beggars, many of them blind, swarmed upon them. In 1742, it is calculated, 30,000 of them were moving from place to place; they were for ever coming between the wind and the nobility—that nobility that Young spoke of as " vermin." Berkeley thought out a scheme by which these vagrants might be set to work, loaded with chains; between them, however, and the cottiers—who never knew when they themselves would also be out on the roads—a great spirit of camaraderie existed, and the footweary found it easier to obtain a lodging for the night than he would to-day along the same roadsides. But there were others as well as beggars upon the highways—pedlars, packmen, horses laden with goods, wagons, carriages, coaches—and occasionally highwaymen.

Everywhere the giant woods were being cut down—the woods that like a magic cloak had sheltered the Gael in every century. The undertakers, the land pirates, not ever quite sure of their standing in so strange a country, were selling the

---

[1] *A Frenchman's Walk through Ireland* (1796-7).

timber on the estates at sixpence a tree—they were rifling the ship they had boarded. "Trees to the value of £20,000 were cut down, soon after the Revolution, upon the single estate of Sir Valentine Brown in Kerry."[1]

An English lawyer named Asgill, who had married the daughter of Sir Nicholas Brown, and bought the estates of the attainted family, was responsible for this. Aodhagán Ó Rathaille, who was born not far from Killarney, sorrowed with the Browns—" Is díth creach bhur gcoillte ar feóchadh " ("Woe, your woods withering away"). But indeed all the poets lamented the vanishing woods: the downfall of the Gaelic or even the Gall-Gaelic nobility, the downfall of the woods—these two went together in their verses. One of our most beautiful lyrics, mourning over the ruin that had come upon the Butlers of Kilcash, begins:

Cad a dhéanfaimíd feasta gan adhmad,	What shall we henceforth do without timber,
Tá deire no gcoillte ar lár.	The last of the woods is fallen.

And in a lyric of about the same time we have:

Anois tá'n choill dá gearradh	Now the wood is being cut,
Triallfaimíd thar caladh.	We will journey over the sea.

This destruction was taking place all over Ireland: it was as if the undertakers had suddenly recollected Spenser's words: "goodly woods fit for building of houses and ships, so commodiously as that if some princes in the world had them, they would soon hope to be lords of all the seas, and ere long of all the world." It was just then that the English were indeed becoming lords of all the seas, for the industrial revolution had begun, and markets needed to be established all over the world. The English adventurers in Ireland, the Bishop of Derry, the Bishop of Kilmore, to name only two, were, as always, in want of ready money; and so between one thing and another the Isle of the Yellow Woods was stripped of its beauty.

---

[1] Lecky, *History,* I.

These half-felled woods were to be seen everywhere, even in the farthest places; there was, for instance, a great clearance made at Coolmountain in West Cork, a place where even to-day a stranger's face is hardly ever seen. Some evil genius, it might seem, was labouring to harmonise all things into an equal slatternliness. The country, moveover, was speckled with ruins—broken abbeys, roofless churches, battered castles, burnt houses, deserted villages, from which the inhabitants were being cleared to make room for beasts; and these ruins were, for the most part, still raw, gaping, sun-bleached, not yet shrouded in ivy nor weathered to quiet tones.

.　　　.　　　.　　　.　　　.　　　.

Such, then, was in general the face of Ireland, such, more particularly, the face of Irish Ireland—that hidden land whose story has never been told. Poverty was its only wear—poverty in the town, the cabin, the person, the gear, the landscape. Civic life was not only broken, but wiped away. Institutions, and the public edifices, ceremonies, arts into which the institutional blossoms in home-centred countries, had ceased to exist. Life did no more than just crawl along, without enough to eat, unclothed, fever-stricken, slow: how could it have a thought for anything beyond mere existence from day to day!

VI

The facts here gathered are the commonplaces of the social history of eighteenth century Ireland; and the political history of the period explains the causes of the whole frightful disorder: for the better understanding, however, of the remaining chapters of this book, as well as for the completion of this, it may be as well to touch upon the immediate causes here.

The rack-rents, that had so much to do with the poverty and the instability of the time, were, of course, themselves the result of the Middleman system, or, as Chesterfield stigmatised it, the deputy of deputy of deputy system of land-tenure. That system worked like a screw-press: the increase in the rent of any farm at the close of any half-year might be small, but the screw still went on revolving, the pressure increasing until, at last, human nature could no longer endure it: agrarian outrages burst out; and on these the man-hunt followed, the noble lords blooding their young dogs. That system one may simplify thus: The landed proprietor—the undertaker or the undertaker's descendant—would let his estate or portion of it, ten thousand acres perhaps, to a middleman: having done this, the noble lord went away to the delights of London or Bath. The middleman, renting a large house in Dublin, then became one of the crowd of place-hunters who, in the phrase of the day, spent their time in Ploughing the Half Acre—that is, the Castle yard—keeping their eyes open, pushing their children forward, and periodically petitioning the King, through the subservient Parliament in Dublin, not to grant relief to the Catholics. The middleman usually acted as agent to a number of noble lords: impossible to oversee his far-flung and scattered acres, he in turn had recourse to men living in the various districts. These local agents, these under-agents, squireens, or stewards, usually kept an office in or near the local town. They in turn again employed bailiffs to collect the rents. These bailiffs were, in many cases, renegade Gaels and renegade Catholics; they were, indeed, the actual torturers, the actual headsmen under the horrible system. It was with them, and with the next nearest circle above them, the squireens, that the peasant came in contact; and the poets, who were, of course, peasants themselves, make us bitterly aware of what that contact meant for the harried people. But these poems will be glanced at later; here it may be better to see these squireens as Young saw them: "This is the class of little country gentlemen, tenants who drink their claret by means of profit rents, jobbers in farms, bucks, your fellows with round hats edged with gold, who hunt in the day, get drunk in the evening, and fight the next morning—these are the men among whom drinking, quarrelling, fighting, ravishing, etc., are found as in their native soil, once to a degree that made them the pest of society."

There was no trick of squeezing money or value out of their tenants at will that these creatures did not know and make use of—from the canting of farms, without a day's warning, to the cadging of poultry from the farmyards, or the juggling with figures at the end of the half-year.

The peasant had to wring from the soil the gold that supported this huge and artificial superstructure—the bailiff in the village, the steward in the town, the agent in Dublin, the lord in England. Living from hand to mouth, with no reserves, the cottier was at the mercy not only of winds and rains, but of every change, and even threat of change, in the body politic, the body economic. It happened that just as the Industrial Revolution had begun to open up new avenues of wealth to the big landowners in England, to woo them into the ways of commerce, disease on a large scale broke out among the herds of cattle in England; and the remedy shows the new direction that men's thoughts had taken: Ireland began to be envisaged as England's feeding ground of the future. A beginning was made by the raising of the embargo on Irish cattle, whereupon vast herds of Irish bullocks were set upon the roads towards the Irish ports. Then followed huge clearances: the landlords became suddenly aware that continuous cropping impoverishes the soil; moreover, no tithes needed to be paid on pasture: in what way they justified their grabbing of the commons is not very clear: the result of all was that herds of dispossessed human beings, as well as the herds of beasts, began to darken the roads. To know with any sufficiency what it meant one must take up some such book as MacKenzie's *Highland Clearances*. Needless to say, "crime" followed, the Whiteboys swooping headlong across the countryside in the dark nights.

Such economic-political storms were, it would seem, as frequent as the famines, which indeed were so often their aftermath. Every such storm stretched the peasant out longer on his rack of torture; and yet the whole tale is not yet told, for one cannot omit mention of the Penal Laws. Only for certain of them the Gael might, by becoming an owner of land, win beyond the rack-renting, and only for those others that forbade him the professions, he might occasionally win away from the land altogether; but no, there was to be no way out: those Penal Laws that denied him ownership, that forbade him education, that closed the professions to him—those laws were as so many nails that held him fast in the bondage where half a century of warfare had left him—a hewer of wood and a drawer of water—" to his conqueror," as Swift significantly added. And this, of course, was the purpose of those laws; and this the Gael knew and felt; so that in picturing to ourselves his condition in that wretched time—his town, his hut, his poor farm-gear, the dismal landscape—all one in misery—let us not forget to realise also that darkness which a mind in which hope is extinguished throws not only on the surrounding fields, but on the very heavens themselves—to picture the Gael's way of life in those days is to feel that one has gone away from the human lands and wanders in a dream which must presently break. And as yet no word has been said about the laws against his religion, the one retreat where his heart might have eased itself of its stifling emotions. The Gael's sufferings had not begun with the eighteenth century, nor was it then for the first time that his religion had been attacked; his cathedrals, his abbeys, his churches, had long since been stolen from him or destroyed. But there was a great difference between the old and the new assaults on his ancient faith. The old assault was open, and had indeed something of manliness in its hot-tempered violence. The new assault, on the other hand, was all lawyer-like with cunning—temptations, rewards and penalties. The children were to be bribed to barter faith for wealth and authority—over their own parents. They were to be wheedled into the luxurious service of God. " All this will I give thee if . . . ." There were no longer any cathedrals to be battered down or monasteries to be dispersed; what remained to be done was the crushing of private devotions, of even the smallest gatherings for religious practices. Not a relic, not a ceremony, not a memorial of the faith was to be allowed. The bells were silenced. The holy wells deserted. The priests banished, a certain number of them bought by gold. The dead must not be laid with their fathers in the abbey grounds. Mass could be said only in secret rock-clefts, with sentries posted on the hilltops; if said in some hidden garret in the town, then a curtain had better be hung between priest and people, so that the flock might afterwards truthfully swear, if put to it, that they knew not who the cele-brant was. And this flock had better bring no prayer-books with them, and if they need a beads, let its appearance be disguised and its pendant any shape but a cross!

. . . . . .

We have now glanced at the state of Catholic Ireland in the eighteenth century, viewing first the appearance of the land and then, very briefly, inquiring into the economy of life which had led to this dire aspect. " But this much," one hears whispered, " we knew before; and why do you speak of the *Hidden* Ireland?" So much, and indeed much else, is known before, to all, it would seem: and were nothing further to be revealed of that unique people, one could not make the complaint that their story had never been told. Implicitly, if not explicitly, Lecky says that nothing else was to be revealed; and the novelists of that period bear him out. And yet this is not so, for a whole world, the world of mind and spirit, remains still be be unveiled. Yes, one might take the facts we have gathered and add life to them, vividly showing those peasants as grubbing their bit of rock-strewn land, " breaking the hill," as the Irish phrase has it, the mists and sea-winds about them, or as cloud-swarms of beggars wander-ing from fair to fair, or, maddened at last, as converging to a churl's fields of a night-time and reaping and carrying off his harvest before the dawn, or as being dragged before the land-bailiff for daring to gather brosna in the woods, or as

40

dying of starvation in their cabins, their mouths green with the munge of nettles;—and over against all this, one might, vividly again, evoke the wine-flushed revelry of the alien gentry, the hunting, the dancing, the drinking, the gambling, the duelling, with the Big House itself in the background, its half-felled woods hanging like dishevelled garments about it—one might do all this, as to the life, and still leave the secret of that land and people unrevealed. The truth is, the Gaelic people of that century were not a mob, as every picture given of them, whether by historian or novelist, would lead one to think. They were mob-like in externals; and one forgives the historians if those externals threw them out, but how forgive the novelists? If not a mob, what then were they? They were the residuary legatees of a civilisation that was more than a thousand years old. And this they knew; it was indeed the very pivot of all they did know, and the insult that followed on their poverty wounded them not only as human beings but as " Children of kings, sons of Milesius!" (" Clanna righthe, maca Mileadh "). With that civilisation they were still in living contact, acquainted with its history; and such of its forms as had not become quite impossible in their way of life, they still piously practised, gradually changing the old moulds into new shapes, and, whether new or old, filling them with a content that was all of the passing day and their own fields. What of art they did create in their cabins is poor and meagre if compared with what their fathers had created in the duns of kings and grianans of queens; yet the hem matches the garment and the clasp the book.

Here hinted, then, what the historians scanted; and scanting the soul and the spirit of a people, what of that people have they profitably to speak? But history has belied the historians, for that people, if they were but a mob, had died, and their nationality died with them: instead of which that nationality is vigorous to-day, not only at home, but in many lands abroad—" translated, passed from the grave."

CHAPTER II

THE BIG HOUSE

I

Irish Ireland had become in the eighteenth century a peasant nation, harried and poverty-stricken, with the cottier's smoky cabin for stronghold. But this does not mean that there were no longer any Big Houses, as we may call them, nor well-to-do families in these Gaelic-speaking countrysides. Both the stories of the poets' lives and the songs they have left us save us from such an idea. Froude tells us that nine-tenths of the land was in 1703 held by Protestants of English or Scotch extraction, an estimate that is probably correct; yet here and there, and especially in Munster, certain big Gaelic Houses had escaped destruction; and only for they had, the story of Irish literature in that century would be very different from what it is, as gradually we shall come to realise.

Through sheer luck, it might be said, these houses had come to survive. They represented hardly ever the main branch of any of the historic families; they were rather the minor branches, far-removed, and not too well known to the authorities in Dublin. Those city-bred, sometimes English-bred, lawyers and statesmen had often only shadowy ideas of the boundaries of the lands they were confiscating. They were not quite sure when their work was done, either in seizing a property or re-parcelling it out among the adventurers. In Cork, in Kerry, and elsewhere, certain old Gaelic families survived not only as landowners but as local magnates right through all the confiscations and penal laws that followed on

42

1641 and, later, on the Boyne. They had succeeded in holding or getting back small portions of the lands from which their ancestors had been driven; and in many cases they must subsequently have quietly enlarged the property, however they had established themselves in it.

For such houses, in obscurity lay their chance of safety. The less that was known of them, especially in Dublin, the better their chance. Inquiry into the family's history, or into the leases, would often have meant extinction; and how well they knew this, an anecdote told of the O'Connells of Derrynane—a house we shall often have to mention—will fix in our mind. Dr Smith, the eighteenth century historian of Cork and Kerry, penetrated into the mountains beyond Cahirciveen, and there partook of the O'Connells' hospitality: we can imagine them as only gradually becoming aware of the Doctor's interest in all that concerned their far places. Nothing could be so little to their taste. It is said that the historian, having set his eye on a pony of good shape, hinted that in exchange for the animal he would give the house honourable mention in his forthcoming work. They at once presented him with the pony, but only on the condition that his history was to be barren of their name. On a subsequent visit, they are said to have kicked him down the stairs.

II

In the invaluable book[1] that tells the story of this family, we find their eighteenth century house in South Kerry thus described:

It must have resembled the House of the Seven Gables. It resolutely turned its back on sea and sunshine, and looked into a walled court-yard planted with trees. It had dark parlours with deep wainscoted window-seats at either side of the hall-door. It was three stories high, and had gables and dormer windows in the roof. Out-offices formed one wing abutting on the courtyard, and there were kitchens and

---

[1] M. J. O'Connell, *The Last Colonel of the Irish Brigade.*

servants' quarters at the back. A bridle-road ran along outside the courtyard wall, and a beautiful garden lay beyond, where a mulberry tree, erroneously said to have been planted by the old monks, still exists.

The house was typical of its class. It was only seldom that a house was then built on an open hillside: a wide prospect was not reckoned adequate compensation for the lack of shelter; nor did a magnificent outlook on the sea make up for the south-west storms that drove in from it. A nook on the lee-side of a bluff, or a nest in a valley bottom, if a road had been laid in it, was preferred to open situations, however charming or healthy. But other considerations also helped to determine both site and style. The difficulty of transport, for instance, forbade the use of any except local materials; and in handling these the neighbouring workmen followed the traditions of the place, nearly always with happy results. The local stone was availed of, sandstone or limestone; and the building was weather-coated with slates, heavy and thick, from the nearest quarries: whether grey, green-grey or purple, the house quietly harmonised with its surroundings of bush, rock and heather. In the building of Derrynane, we may be sure, many bullocks were sacrificed, for without their blood to mix with the lime a substantial mortar could not be had.

Scores of those old houses remain to us: rarely, however, do the courtyard walls still hide away the sunlit country round about. These walls have been removed; and larger windows let into the parlours; for all that, one does even yet find something in those sunken parlours which recalls the cabin of an old-world sailing ship—dark, snug, and stuffy, their atmosphere a part of themselves.

Our interest does not, however, lie so much in the style of building as in the fact that each of these houses, whether roofed with slate or thatch, or built of limestone or sandstone, was the centre of life in its district. As much might be said, perhaps, of all the big houses in Europe at that date—of those in England, France, Germany. In no European country, however, Russia, perhaps, excepted, can such houses have been so entirely the heart of the district as in Ireland. Only in these two countries did they, without avowing as much, rule absolutely. Evidence of this, as far as Ireland is concerned, is overwhelming. In the county of Carlow there was the house of " King " Bagenal, for instance, speaking of whom, O'Neill Daunt[1] says, " no monarch was ever more absolute " within the bounds of his extensive estates. Young, in his travels, came to hear of the " Prince " of Coolavin, although the Prince was then reduced to comparative poverty; while Maria Edgeworth called Richard Martin ("Humanity Dick") the King of Connemara; and such princes and kings were common in the landscape—their sway not always dependent either on their wealth or stretch of acres. The O'Connells in South Kerry were kings as much as the Bagenals or the Martins; and yet, at this very time, the O'Donoghues of Glen Flesk and the O'Mahonys of Dunloe, two other Kerry families, probably looked on them as having let slip the bulk of their ancient Gaelic privileges. Indeed, whether Gael or Gall, there was not a big house in Ireland that did not rule as well as manage its domain.

Within Connemara the Martins, from father to son, reigned with a sway that was absolute and supreme, they being not alone the owners, but also the only magistrates resident within its borders. The keep of a ruined castle on an island within Ballinahinch lake served during many years as prison for the district, and was known as " Mr Martin's Jail." Offenders brought before " Humanity Dick," he would sentence to a week, or fortnight, or three weeks' imprisonment, according as the heinousness of their misdemeanour merited. They were forthwith ferried over to the island, and there being no possibility of their escape thence had even to remain till their time of durance expired.[2]

" Lord of all the lives of the people," is Miss Edgeworth's description of this " Humanity Dick "; and on his Lordship's being once asked if it were true that the King's writ did not run in Connemara, he replied: " Egad, it does, as fast as any

---

[1] *Eighty-five Years of Irish Life.*
[2] J. M. Callwell, *Old Irish Life.*

greyhound if any of my good fellows are after it!"[1] While of his kinsman, Robert Martin, Colonel Eyre, commander of the troops in Galway, wrote to Dublin Castle (1747) that he was able to bring to the town of Galway in twenty-four hours "800 villains as desperate and as absolutely at his devotion as Cameron of Lochiel."[2] And Kennedy, quit-rent collector in Kerry, says of Donal O'Mahony of Dunloe and his 3,000 persons, all of the Pope's religion: "So it may please you, Excie and Lopps, the said Mahony and his mob of Fairesses are so dreaded by his mighty power that noe papist in the Kingdom of Ireland hath the like."[3] The owner of the Aran Islands ruled them as despotically as the Martins ruled Iar-Connacht, only his jail was larger: "When any of his islanders were found guilty of any offence, he would say sternly, speaking in their native Irish: 'I must transport you to prison in Ireland for a month.'"

In the south-west of County Cork there is a village called Leap, because it stands near the wide ravine that opens out into Glandore Harbour; the district beyond this ravine is called Myross, and of this hinterland it used to be said: "Beyond the leap, beyond the law." Now, when occasion served, there were not many parts of Ireland in that century that were not as much beyond the leap as Myross itself. Big landowners like Dick Martin, who, magistrates as they were, played fast and loose with the law of the land, were to be found in every county. Sylvester O'Sullivan—a Kerry informer—states in a memorial which he styles "depositions ready to be sworn," that Archdeacon Lauder, who sat among other magistrates to hear his complaint, spoke as follows in a great "huff and fury": "How now, you rogue! Do you think to get any justice against the County Kerry gentlemen, who are all in a knot, and even baffle the very judges on the circuit? Nay, you are mistaken; our bare words are taken and

---

[1] *Ibid.*

[2] Cf. Froude, *The English in Ireland in the Eighteenth Century.*

[3] *Poems of Egan O'Rahilly,* edited by Rev P. S. Dinneen, M.A., and Prof. Tadhg O'Donoghue.

46

preferred before the Government before the depositions of a thousand such evidences who have no friends to back 'em. This is not France, that severe country where the King's interest is so strictly maintained. No, this is Kerry, where we do what we please. We'll teach you some Kerry law, my friend, which is to give no right and take no wrong."[1] Whether the Archdeacon did really in his huff and fury speak in this strain or whether Sylvester the informer simply made him do so, it is certain that both of them in their hearts knew that the words exactly described the state of things, not only in Kerry, but everywhere else as well.

As for putting the law aside, the Gaelic families, like the O'Connells, had to be more circumspect. They preferred to live outside it; not to invoke it was for them ever the safer way; and when they had actually to appear in court, their plan was to declare only as much or as little of their own circumstances as could not be concealed if the case were to be won. Moreover, the Martins, the O'Connells, and indeed every other big family as well, Gall or Gael, along the sea-board, were professional smugglers, and as such had their own ideas of the true functions of the law and its officers. It was only seldom that they failed to bring these officers to recognise at least the convenience, if not the righteousness, of these inbred views—a task that does not seem to have been very difficult when undertaken, with no lack of smuggled sherry and port, in one of those dark and cosy parlours in a district remote and unvexed of regulations and prying officials. When a Captain Butler in 1782 swooped down on the O'Connells in the act of running in a heavy cargo, Hunting Cap, the chief of the O'Connells of that day, submitting to the inevitable, civilly invited the officer to breakfast, and this invitation Captain Butler was pleased to accept. In some such way the good work was begun, usually to end in the officer's agreeing to take henceforth for himself, as a mere perquisite, a percentage of all cargoes successfully run in. In this case, the

---

[1] Cf. *Poems of Egan O'Rahilly*.

47

breakfast over and the Captain desiring to return across country to his headquarters at Waterville, Hunting Cap, aware of the anger of his people at having had to yield up a valuable cargo, bade one of his nephews to accompany him, and, " In Captain Butler's presence, he handed the crooked knife to his nephew."[1] The crooked knife was an old pruning hook of no value except as a symbol of the chief's authority. " A tenant would walk out and give up his holding at the bidding of the bearer of the crooked knife."[2] So long as any of the O'Connells, the chief's nephew or his most abject menial, bearing the knife, accompanied the Captain there was no fear of his being molested; and, as a matter of history, he was not set upon and beaten until he had himself persuaded the knife-bearer to leave him and return home.

To read of such happenings is gradually to understand that these houses stood for a patriarchal view of life; and the more fully we go into the details of the story the more assured we are of this. In the homeliest practices of hall and kitchen it was patriarchal, as well as in the larger aspect of authority and outlook. " The O'Connells were prosperous people, though their affluence consisted rather of flocks and herds and merchandise than of hard cash. The small mountain tenants mostly paid their rents in labour or kind. Little money changed hands, unless on special occasions."[3] At the house of the Martins of Ross, in Galway, a sheep was killed every week and a bullock once a month; what was not eaten was salted down in huge stone pickling troughs. The country round about provided the fare in such a house—meat, fowl, game, rabbits; the rivers and the sea furnished salmon, trout and other fish. The wines, laces, tea, tobacco, as well as the fineries of household ware, such as mirrors, carpets, velvets, etc., were all smuggled in. The raw materials, if one may so name them, were prepared for use on the spot. The corn grown on the

---

[1] *The Last Colonel of the Irish Brigade.*
[2] *Ibid.*
[3] *Ibid.*

surrounding hillsides was threshed in the adjoining barns, winnowed by hand on the winnowing crag, and ground by women folk in the quern. The kitchen walls contained huge cavernous ovens in their thickness: in these ovens turf fires were kindled and allowed to burn away to ashes, which in turn were swept out that the batch of loaves might be thrust in to bake in the afterheat. The flax and wool were carded and spun under the mistress's eyes. In autumn there were vast slaughterings and saltings of beeves; and every labourer attached to the house received a salted hide to make himself two pairs of brogues. Of the fat and tallow, mould candles were made for the parlour and " dips " for the kitchen. " Add to this the ordinary toil of the laundry, the dairy, the kitchen, and you get some idea of the gangs of people an old-fashioned Irish lady had to rule over."[1]

Such a house reckoned among its menials many a quaint calling that is now no more—the turf-boy kept the turf boxes filled with sods from the stack in the yard, the pump-boy kept a supply of water at hand. There were, besides, cow-boys, drovers, and thatchers. There were smiths, carpenters, weavers, ploughmen, tinkers—and all these had their own workshops and meeting-place. Before the dawn had risen, the farmyard was loud with activity; and when darkness had fallen, lanterns went swinging across it, over and thither, from byre to shed, and from shed to barn.

Every one of those trades was, like the house it ministered to, a little world in itself, the centre of manifold activities. A weaver's shed then was very different from what it afterwards became; and a country carpenter's shop was not merely a place where wheels, carts, gates and coffins were roughly fashioned, as it now unfortunately is. Of the difference in this matter between then and now we become aware if we look at that poem of Eoghan Ruadh Ó Súilleabháin's " A Ghaibhne Chláir Fodla, mo Chómhairle Anois Déanaidh " (" O Smiths of Fodla's Plain, do now my Bidding "). From it we know that then in a smith's shop were made or repaired—plough-shares,

---

[1] *Ibid.*

coulters, surveyor's chains, shovels, pikes, spades, rakes, trowels, reaping hooks, horse shoes, spurs, bits, stirrups, fishing hooks, compasses, wrenches, anchors, screw-pins, thimbles, scissors, guns, pistols, swords, bolts, springs, knives, spits, scythes—and a crowd of other wares that the ordinary country smith never handles now. In like manner every other trade extended itself to every region of its own sphere, whether its sway was over iron, wood, or yarn.

Besides all these work-people and menials, there were, in the words of the Last Colonel himself, "the multitude of our followers and our fosterers." Miss Edgeworth knew English as well as Irish life, but it is an Irish house she is describing in her novel, *The Absentee*, when she says that 104 persons sat down every day to dinner in Lord Kilpatrick's house.

Indeed it would be hard to state in what those houses differed from the castles of the Middle Ages—each a centre of teeming life, a citadel, as one might say; and this we shall more truly realise if we turn to the contemporary evidence in the Irish poets.

III

The keen that Eibhlín Dubh, one of those O'Connells, made over her murdered husband, Art O'Leary, has already been mentioned. In the opening lines she recollects how she had fled with him and how he had received her in his mansion:

> Do chuiris gan dearmhad
> Párlús d'á ghealadh dham,
> Rúmana d'á mbreacadh dham,
> Bácús d'á dheargadh dham,
> Bríc d'á gceapadh dham,
> Rósta ar bhearaibh dham,
> Mairt d'á leagadh dham,
> Cóir mhaith leapthan dam
> Codladh i gclúmh lachan dam,

which, literally translated, gives us:

> You did not forget
> To have parlours brightened for me,
> Rooms decked for me,
> Ovens heated for me,

Loaves fresh kneaded for me,
Roast on the spits for me,
Beeves slaughtered for me,
The comfort of a fine bed for me,
Sleep in the down of fowl for me,

and the swift lines, without straining, evoke to our very eyes the antique bustle and plenty of such a house as O'Leary's was. Far richer, however, is Aodhagán Ó Rathaille's picture of the O'Callaghans at Clonmeen, County Cork. The poet places the words in the mouth of Cliodna, one of the fairy queens of Ireland:

Do dhearcas, ar sí, 'n-a ríoghbhrogh ceolmhar,
Síodaidhe breaca, is bratacha
sróill ghlain,
Cuilg dá ngormadh, othair ag ól
miodh,
Is laochra ag imirt ar fidhchill
na fóirne.

I beheld, said she, in his musical,
princely mansion,
Speckled silks, and garments of
pure satin,
Swords being whetted, invalids
quaffing mead,
And warriors playing at *fidhchill*
of the chessmen.

Cuilte dá ndeargadh ar maidin 's
am nóna,
Córughadh cleiteach ag bairr-
fhionnaibh óga,
Fíon ar briseadh dá ibhe, agus
mórtas,
Feoil ar bhearaibh, is beathuisce
ar bhórdaibh.

Coverlets being prepared, morn
and even,
Young maidens engaged in arranging down,
Wines, newly-opened, being
drunk, and jollity,
Viands on spits, and uisquebagh
on tables;

Dronga ag taisteal gan mhairg
don nósbhrogh,
Dronga ag tuitim 's a gcuisleanna
breoidhte,
Dronga ar meisce gan cheilg don
chomhursain,
Dronga borba ag lobhairt go
glórach.

Companies coming to the famous
mansion without sorrow,
Companies falling down with
feverish pulse,
Companies inebriate without offence to their neighbours,
Companies of pride discoursing
uproariously.

Boltanus cumhra dlúth ag coimh-
rith,
O anáil bhaeith na cléire cóirne,
Gaotha luatha buana as srónaibh,
Na saoithe chasnamhadh mach-
aire an chomhraic.

A fragrant odour issuing in
strength
From the tender breath of the
trumpeting band,
Swift, continuous currents from
the nostrils
Of the nobles who were wont to
hold the battle field.

51

Puirt ar chruitibh dá seinm go ceolmhar,
Startha dá léigheadh ag lucht léighinn is eoluis,
Mar a mbíodh trácht gan cháim ar órdaibh,
Is ar gach sloinneadh dar geineadh san Eoruip.

Dóirse gan dúnadh ar dhúntaibh ómrach,
Céir dá lasadh ar gach balla agus seomra,
Caisc dá mbriseadh dhon bhfuirinn gach nóimeat,
'S gan trághadh lachta ag teacht san ól soin.

Eich dá mbronnadh aca ar ollamhnaibh Fódla;
Eachra garbha ar leacain ag coimhrith,
Troightheacha i n-iorghuil, iomarca beorach
I gcornaibh aithleaghtha d'airgead ró-ghlan.

Ba mhinic san chluain seo fuaim na ngleostoc,
Tromgháir sealg i sleasaibh na gceochnoc,
Sionnaigh dá ndúscadh chúcha is crónphuic,
Míolta as mongaibh, cearca uisce, agus smólaigh.

Luin na seilge ag sceinnim le fórlucht,
Is cearca feádha go fánach glórach,
Connairt an ríogh 's a shaoithe tóirseach
D'éis a reatha i n-aghaidh sleasaibh na gceochnoc.[1]

Airs being played harmoniously on harps,
The wise and learned reading histories,
In which an account was faultlessly given of the clergy
And of each great family that arose in Europe.

The doors wide open on enclosures bright as amber,
Waxlights blazing from every wall and chamber,
Every moment fresh casks being opened for the multitude,
With no ebb in the liquid coming to that drinking feast.

Steeds being bestowed on the *ollamhs* of Fodla,
Strong steeds in teams racing on the hillside,
Foot soldiers contending, abundance of *beoir*
In goblets of wrought silver, of great purity.

Often in that plain was heard the sound of war-bugles,
The loud cry of the chase on the sides of the misty hills,
Foxes and red bucks were being wakened for them,
Hares from the mead, waterhens, and thrushes.

The birds of the chase starting up with great force,
With pheasants dispersed and wildly screaming;
The prince's hounds and his men fatigued
From their pursuit up the slopes of the misty mountains.

These lines were written on the death of Daniel O'Callaghan in 1724, that is, fifty years before Eibhlín Dubh wrote her keen. If we had not made some preliminary study,

---

[1] *Poems of Egan O'Rahilly.*

we might think it wise of the poet to speak through the mouth of a fairy queen, thus baffling our criticism; but our study, slight as it has been, leaves us aware that the poet scarcely took even poetic licence with the facts, as is the manner of Irish poets. He invented nothing; he hardly even heightened the tints: the clear vision in his mind of the house at Clonmeen was, if anything, already too full and too rich. The whetting of the swords, the invalids drinking mead, the young girls stripping the feathers with their slender fingers, the laden tables, the heavy drinking, the harpers, the scanning of the genealogies, the crowds coming and going, the rewarding of the poets, the racing on the hillsides, the fox-chase along the misty slopes, the fowling—it is all flung out at us, as it were, with swiftness, with energy, as if the reason for thus recalling the glories of Clonmeen was all the time so urgent in the poet's thoughts, that hastening towards it, he could not bear to dally on the arranging of his picture or to linger on its choicer features. The theme was a favourite with him; he was of the old order, and held that a poet's trade was to sing the deeds of a patron while living, and to raise a keen for him when dead. Twenty-eight years before, in 1696, he had written thus of the house of Diarmuid O'Leary of Killeen, near Killarney:

Monuar, a thighthe go sinnil san bhfóghmhar,
Gan ceol cláirseach, fáidh ná eolach,
Gan fleadh, gan fíon, gan bhuidhean, gan chóisir,
Gan scoil éigse, cléir ná óird bhinn!

Mar a mbiodh gasra chearrbhach chomhfhoclach,
Fíonta fairsinge i n-eascaraibh órdha,
Laochra gaisce, is buidhean mheanmnach mhodhmhar
Ag rinnce ar halla tighe th'athar le ceoltaibh.

Alas! his dwellings are lonely in the Autumn,
Without the music of harps, without seer, or learned man,
Without a banquet, without wine, without company, without a festive gathering,
Without a poetic meeting, without clergymen or musicians!

Where there used to be a multitude of talkative gamblers,
Abundant wine in golden goblets,
Champion warriors, and a high-spirited, courteous band
Dancing to music in the hall of thy father's house.

Mar a mbiodh éigse, cléir, is geocaigh;
Mar a mbiodh dáimh, is báird na gcóige;
I ríoghbhrogh th'athar cois Gleannamhair Eoghanacht.
Mo scíos 'n fhaid mhairfead, fé leacaibh mo leoghan.

Where the learned, the clergy, and strollers were wont to be;
Where the poets and bards of the country were
In the princely mansion of thy father beside Gleannamhair of the Eoghanacht.
My woe while I live, that my hero lies beneath a stone!

Buidhne dhíobh nár chlaoidhte ón gcóisir
Ag aithris grinn gach líne romhainne,
I starthaibh Gaoidhilge ar ghaois na leoghan,
Clanna Baoiscne is Ghuill mhic Mhórna.

Companies of them, not fatigued by the revel,
Rehearsing the witty compositions of past generations,
In Gaelic tales about the wisdom of the heroes,
Of Clanna Baoiscne, and Goll mac Morna.

Here, as one would expect from the earlier date, the lineaments are more Gaelic, for those big houses were, of course, becoming less and less Gaelic as the years passed. About this long poem, the whole consisting of 229 lines, it is interesting to learn that the greater part has been found " alive " on the lips of " illiterate " peasants in Kerry in our own days.

A house that had fallen from the hands of the MacCarthys into those of a man named Warner we find described in O'Rahilly's poem on Castle Tochar:

Feoil de bhearaibh is éanlaith ón dtuinn
Ceolta, is cantain, is craos na dighe;
Rósta blasta, agus céir gan teimheal,
Conairt is gadhair is amhstrach.

Meat on spits, and wild fowl from the ocean;
Music and song, and drinking bouts;
Delicious roast meat and spotless honey,
Hounds and dogs and baying.

Drong ag imtheacht, is drong ag tigheacht,
Is drong ag racaireacht dúinn go binn,
Drong ar spallaibh úra ag guidhe,
'S ag leaghaidh na bhflaitheas go ceannsa.

A company going, and a company coming,
And a company entertaining us melodiously,
And a company praying on the cold flags,
And meekly melting the heavens.

54

For us the point lies in the praise given to the new owner—the Planter—for maintaining in the house the Gaelic traditions of the former owners, the MacCarthys, maintaining them so unimpairedly that the poet cries out:

Do mheasas im aigne is fós im chroidhe,
An marbh ba mharbh gur beo do bhí.

I thought in my soul and even in my heart
That the dead who had died was living.

Not to be depending entirely on this one poet's testimony, it may be well to take a fragment from another poet of the first half of the eighteenth century: Seán Clárach Mac Domhnaill's account of the household of Thomas Greene of Gort an Tochair, in the county of Clare:

Is gnáth go síor i dtigheas mo mharcaigh
Buidhean go seascair súgach,
Is sásta síothach a bhíd na sagairt
Chríost le sleasaibh búird ann;
Bradán ó'n linn, is caoirigh is ealtain,
Saill na mairt is úire,
Biotáille bríoghmhar thigheann tar lear
De dhruím na mara is lionnta;
Ol is imirt, ceol ar fhidil,
Beol-ghuth binneas ciuin ceart,
Fóirne ar mire mór le meisce,
Is cóip le sult ag súgradh.

Ever and aye in my hero's house
Is a bright and care-free company;
And in peace and comfort the priests of Christ
Sit at the table's edge;
Salmon from the pool, and sheep and fowl,
The freshest flesh of beeves.
Heady spirits and ales that come
Over the ridge of the sea;
Drinking, gambling, violins,
The sweetness of gentle song in tune,
A crowd uproariously drunk,
And a band eager for merriment.

Of the four poems quoted from, two describe purely Gaelic houses, the other two, Planter houses in Gaelic districts; and it would seem that there was no other striking difference between the way of living in both classes of houses, except that the great stories of the Gael were naturally welcomed in the one and thought alien in the other. The structure of life in such districts as West Cork was still so firm and self-contained that the change of ownership in a big house, like Castle Tochar, from Gael to Planter, did not immediately make much difference in what its ancient walls looked upon, day in, day out: it was only the flowing by of long years, each with its own particular assault, that succeeded little by little in depriving Gaeldom of its vigour, in stopping up its numerous ways of manifesting openly what its ancient spirit brooded upon.

IV

We may reckon such descriptions as true, for Irish poets were not given to dressing up: they wrote for an entirely local audience, their own neighbours, who were, of course, as familiar as themselves with the life depicted, an audience, moreover, not slow of wit or sparing of sarcasm. The other writers on whom we have depended wrote in English, and we could not, therefore, expect to find them dwelling on that side of life which was all-in-all to the Gaelic poets—the singing, the harping, the story-telling, the reciting of the deeds of Clanna Baoiscne and Goll mac Morna. Allowing for this, we receive the one impression from both sets of writers. Moreover, not only do the poets confirm for us what those other writers relate of the activities in kitchen, hall and hunting-field, but, going further, they carry us into the very mind of the dwellers in them, giving us a deeper sense of the whole, as has ever been the privilege of poets. And how soon we become aware that what the writers in English omitted concerned the mind and the soul—the hidden world!

Of that hidden life, that Gaelic spirit, Young came to hear and, as shrewd as ever, noted carefully, even if he did not follow up, the surprise it awoke in him:

At Clonells, near Castlerea, lives O'Connor, the direct descendant of Roderick O'Connor, who was King of Connaught six or seven hundred years ago; there is a monument of him in Roscommon Church, with his sceptre, etc. . . . I was told as a certainty that the family were here long before the coming of the Milesians. Their possessions, formerly so great, are reduced to three or four hundred pounds a year, the family having fared in the revolutions of so many ages much worse than the O'Niels and O'Briens. The common

56

people pay him the greatest respect, and send him presents of cattle, etc., upon various occasions. They consider him as the prince of a people involved in one common ruin. Another great family in Connaught is MacDermot, who calls himself Prince of Coolavin. He lives at Coolavin in Sligo, and though he has not above one hundred pounds a year, will not admit his children to sit down in his presence. This was certainly the case with his father, and some assured me even with the present chief. Lord Kingsborough, Mr Ponsonby, Mr O'Hara, Mr Sandford, etc., came to see him, and his address was curious: " O'Hara, you are welcome! Sandford, I'm glad to see your mother's son " (his mother was an O'Brien) : " as to the rest of ye, come in as ye can."[1]

It was only at second hand that Young came to know of the strange ways of the Gaelic houses; but would it have been any better for him to have gone into them? What could he have brought with him, what report made of the spirit that ruled in them? Little or none; for the Gaels of that day had learned to live a double life: in externals they were on all fours with the Planters round about them, except that they were seldom so rich. To the Planters and their hangers-on, to the troop of officials, they spoke English; they wrote their letters in English; went to law in English; and when they died were laid away beneath English inscriptions. On Art O'Leary's tomb in Kilcrea Abbey we read:

" Lo! Art O'Leary, generous, handsome, brave,
Slain in his youth, lies in this humble grave!"

These lines, and the trite mode of them, Young could well understand, but what could he have made of the keen—some lines of which have already been quoted—Art O'Leary's wife, Eibhlín Dubh Ni Chonaill, cried out to find him murdered in Carriganimma! As little could he have made of the whole Gaelic economy of such houses as those of the O'Connors, the MacDermots, the O'Connells, the O'Callaghans, had he visited them. He would have gone into and come out of them entirely unaware of the Gaelic spirit

---

[1] Arthur Young, *A Tour in Ireland* (1776-1779).

that awoke about their hearths when no alien eyes were present to affright it. Had he gone to Derrynane, the house of Eibhlín Dubh, Art O'Leary's wife, it was only the exterior, official life —life!—that he would have experienced. He would have surveyed the vast flocks and herds (one hundred head of cattle were often bought or sold at a fair), he would have learned of their trading, would have suspected their smuggling, would have heard of their close connection with certain merchants in Cork, would have learned much of the many O'Connells who were serving abroad under foreign kings; but of the hidden life of Derrynane, as it, even still, breathes warm on us in every line of Eibhlín Dubh's keen (Young might have spoken with her), he would have learned little or nothing. He could have, it is probable, spent a fairly long time in the house without suspecting that the Irish language was anything but a *patois* in which the master spoke to his herdsmen and shepherds. He would never have dreamed that that language was the gateway to a complete and unique civilisation, to a world in itself; a world into which retired the souls of the O'Connells whenever they were deeply moved, yearning for the companionship of their own myriad dead, it may be, or because they felt they could not utter their deeper thoughts in any other mode than that which their fathers had wrought for them.

When the O'Connells were writing business letters, or indeed putting their hands to any official document whatever, they signed themselves Connell, omitting the distinctively Gaelic O. But when any one of them succeeded in making his way on the Continent and found himself at last of some importance in the world, little by little he came to sign himself O'Connell again; that is, he resumed the Gael. Of the Connells, Young could have made some report; of the O'Connells, none.

The keen made over her dead husband by Eibhlín Dubh represents the secret life, the Gaelic spirit, of such a house as Derrynane. Behind its mode lies a thousand years of Irish literature. The other side of the life of that family is represented by a large collection of contemporary letters.[1] Whether concerned with business or family affairs, they are all dry, hard, precise, formal; and scarcely once give a hint of the secret world that was all the time so close to their writers' thoughts. The Last Colonel himself, as we find him in them, was a very Wellington for preciseness and frigid common-sense; and we might think that he had never heard of that immemorial world that is the background of the famous keen; yet of his closing years, when his passion for getting on had finally ebbed, we find this written:

Miss Eveline MacCarthy tells me she remembers her venerable grand-uncle, Count O'Connell, in his old age in Paris, reciting and expounding to her long passages in Irish verse.[2]

He had lived on the Continent ever since his boyhood. He had witnessed the scenes that led up to the French Revolution, had suffered under it, had survived it, lingering on into the nineteenth century: during all those long years of army life, of routine, of campaigning in many lands, of battles, of revolution and disaster, the memory of the Gaelic surround-ings of his boyhood among the Kerry mountains lay concealed and suppressed within him; and so far as we are concerned might have lain concealed for ever only for his good fortune in finding a biographer who was nothing better than a free-lance in history. Mrs Morgan John O'Connell, who wrote the book, could not tell the story of that hidden life which came flooding so freely to the old man's lips as the daily business of living grew less and less; she did not know Irish, she had only the vaguest knowledge of either the vastness or the worth of the Gaelic civilisation; nevertheless she saw that it was there, living, and what is more to her credit, said frankly that it was that that ought to be the chief interest of our historians. In such a sentence as: " What it seems to me

---

[1] Cf. *The Last Colonel of the Irish Brigade* for many of these letters.

[2] *Last Colonel of the Irish Brigade.*

Irish people ought to study is the real inner life of the old native Irish Catholics," we find an insight far deeper than Lecky's. He, too, saw that that " real inner life " existed. He wrote: " Ejected proprietors whose names might be traced in the Annals of the Four Masters or around the sculptured crosses of Clonmacnoise might be found in abject poverty hanging around the land which had lately been their own, shrinking from servile labour as from an intolerable pollution and still receiving a secret homage from their old tenants."[1] But he seems never to have wondered if that secret life might not be worthy of study: he never gave it any; nor did he encourage others to do so. He turned him to the little annals of the Parliament in Dublin.

This treasure that so resembled a slumbering fire in the breast of that old soldier, was not peculiar to him alone of all the Wild Geese.[2] Many thousands of them were fundamentally as Gaelic as he; and when one recollects how picturesque and taking the story of their lives is, even as told, one wonders what it might have been if their historians had been learned in, as well as in living sympathy with, the Gaelic spirit that, though suppressed and hidden, had made those soldiers of fortune what they were. Their sense of an immemorial past, the peculiar culture in which they had been trained—all that is omitted, just as, and for the same reasons, it has been, until quite recently, omitted in the " history " of their fatherland. Behind every Gael of those Wild Geese lay the Hidden Ireland; and behind such of them as sought commissions in foreign armies lay very often such houses as Derrynane, a thing we do not realise. Behind them, rolling backward into the primeval clouds, lay that vast hinterland into which swept their eager thoughts whenever the depths of their souls were stirred; into which, in an uncertain way, we ourselves make

---

[1] Lecky, *History*.

[2] Cf. *Duanaire Finn*, edited by Professor MacNeill, for an interesting account of Captain Somhairle MacDonnell—an earlier soldier of fortune—who, while serving in the Netherlands, set Irish scribes to make him copies of Irish manuscripts preserved by Irish Franciscans in Louvain.

entrance when we begin to speak with the Irish poets of their time. The scenes that these describe, and the great stories to which they so familiarly refer, the sagas of the Gaels rather than those of the Greeks, were the pasture grounds wherein the Wild Geese were nurtured. It was not what Young, for all his shrewdness, would have noted, had he gone into their Irish homes, had made these Wild Geese the men they were; it was what he would have scanted.

V

Those big houses, when Gaelic, shared a common culture with the lowly peasant's hut; but they also shared the culture of the Planters. Before he sailed, in his teens, for France, young Daniel O'Connell, not the Liberator, but the Last Colonel, had studied French and Latin, to fit him for his chosen career; and this was the usual practice with all those whose ambitions were the same colour as his. Such studies re-acted, of course, on the intellectual level of the household. The culture common to both Gaelic and Planter houses compares favourably with that of families of equal rank in England. Indeed it may be that the cult of the classics among the Gaels was more alive; it was certainly in closer touch with the Continent.

To fix the notes of the culture of such houses as Derrynane, it may, however, serve us better to recall definite statements and incidents. As for contact with the Continent, we find in Mrs Morgan John O'Connell's book quite conclusive evidence in this passage: " I find by letters that eighteen young and old kinsmen were serving France, Spain, Austria, at one time "— eighteen of one rather undistinguished house! Now, it was the custom for all those Wild Geese to make flying secret visits to their homes; and though the whole eighteen kinsmen of Derrynane were not all of high rank, nor all given to intellectual trafficking, it is impossible to think that such a house was not, through those exiles, informed of European life, culture, and affairs in a more intimate sense than the Planter

61

houses in Ireland or the houses of the nobility and squirearchy in England, where only one or two, father or son or both, would or might have made the Grand Tour in their nonage. Let us, moreover, remember that France, Spain and Austria did not share only one culture; each had its own national language and rich national life; such houses, then, as Derrynane cannot but have been in touch, and not infrequently, with the cultures of those three peoples. This we may feel confident of from the one bald statement quoted; and our confidence is again confirmed if we turn to the poets. In their verses, whenever politics is touched upon, it is sure to be the politics of the European courts, hardly ever the politics of London, and stranger still, never the politics of Dublin! Our historians of that century fill their pages with the strange doings of the politicians in Dublin; there only, it would seem, was history being wrought out; yet the names of the memorable figures that played their parts with such little reserve either of eloquence or gesture, in that city, are never even mentioned by the contemporary Irish poets of Munster.

To these, Paris was nearer than Dublin, and Vienna than London. Aodhagán Ó Rathaille, who probably never went outside Cork and Kerry, reckons up the consequences of the death of the King of Spain (1700); and Seán Clárach Mac Domhnaill, who, though he does seem to have once visited London, passed nearly all his years in a small town in County Cork, troubles himself now with the death of the Regent of France (1723) and then with the war of the Austrian Succession. Brian Merriman, who never wandered far from his native county, Clare, wrote his well-known poem, *Cúirt an Mheadhon Oidhche*, in 1779-80; and the Rousseau-like turn of thought in it is held by some, though perhaps not on sufficient evidence, to be due to his contact with Continental officers in the big houses he was wont to visit. Many other such scraps of evidence could be gathered from the poets of that time; for most of them were familiar with those houses which, like Derrynane, had each its eighteen kinsmen, or more or less, passing to and from the Continent.

Those poets' alertness to what was towards on the Continent rather than in England reflected, of course, the interests of the big houses: but these interests were not alien to those of the community at large; to the people, so many of whose sons were ranging Europe hither and thither, "from Dunkirk to Belgrade," those poets were news-bringers and interpreters; so that Irish Ireland as a whole kept an ear open for the whispers from European courts. The common people were surely concerned in an incident that took place in Galway in 1747. All through the eighteenth century that city was very recalcitrant; and its Governor at this time, Colonel Stratford Eyre, was never tired of complaining it to Dublin Castle: "writing on the 23rd October, he says that at that moment the whole of Galway was illuminated, and that there were candles even in the windows of the convents. Colonel Eyre does not mention the cause of these rejoicings, that being, of course, well known to those to whom he was writing, but we have no difficulty in divining it. Bergen-op-zoon, the strongest fortress in Dutch Brabant, believed to be impregnable, and well-furnished with victuals and munitions of war, was carried by assault by the French on Sept. 16th, 1747. The outlying forts of Frederick Henry, Lillo and St Croix still held out, and the task of reducing them was entrusted to Lally and his Irish brigade. Frederick Henry was· stormed on the 2nd October, and the two remaining forts surrendered on the 8th. No doubt it was the news of this triumph (a triumph over England's allies) which had reached Galway a fortnight later, and the windowpanes of the town were ablaze that night to celebrate the gallant feat of arms which the exiled Irishmen in the service of a foreign king had accomplished."[1]

One can hardly doubt that Lally's fame and name that night were spoken of and toasted in hut as well as in mansion, in tavern as well as in cloister. The mention of the convents reminds us that the Gaels were not entirely dependent on the Wild Geese for contact with Europe: there were also the

---

[1] J. M. Callwell, *Old Irish Life*.

friars. In 1747, when Colonel Eyre was thus indicting the convent as being no better than other houses, very few cloisters indeed were left, but nowhere else was the condition of Europe better understood. From and to Louvain, Salamanca, and Rome, to name, perhaps, the three most important ecclesiastical centres, as far as we were concerned, in Europe, friars were incessantly making their way to and from the most hidden places in Ireland; a trafficking that did not ever cease, no matter how severely the Penal Laws punished it. Those travelling friars, disguised as laymen, commonly acted as teachers in those big houses; and thus other connections with the Continent were established in addition to those created by the trafficking of the soldiers. In perhaps every well-known elegy written by the poets of the time, the lamented deceased is praised insomuch as his house and board were open to those spiritual voyagers; while if the elegy is actually written on a dead priest we are sure to find some reference to his Continental training.

Contact with Europe, then, was one of the notes that distinguished the culture of the Catholic Gaels from that of the Planters. Another was the unity of mind between the Big House and the cabin. The Gaels in the big houses were one with the cottiers in race, language, religion and, to some extent, culture. Those O'Connells, O'Connors, O'Callaghans, O'Donoghues—all the Gaels—were one, it may be maintained, with the very landscape itself. In the poems and stories written hundreds of years, perhaps a thousand years, before, the places mentioned were not fictitious: in those same stories were to be found the names of those ancient families as well, so that to run off the family names connected with one of those houses was to call to vision certain districts—hills, rivers and plains; while contrariwise, to recollect the place-names in certain regions was to remember the ancient tribes and their memorable deeds. How different it was with the Planters round about them. For them, all that Gaelic background of myth, literature and history had no existence. They differed from the people in race, language, religion, culture; while the

64

landscape they looked upon was indeed but rocks and stones and trees.

Perhaps the unity that existed between Big House and cabin in the Gaelic districts was a phenomenon not known anywhere else in Europe, inasmuch as feudalism in Ireland had never been quite the same as feudalism abroad. The first rough vigour of the feudal spirit was spent before it had spread into the farther places in Ireland. Feudalism was, moreover, right from the start, cut across by the Brehon laws—that law system so precise, so well-worn and firmly established; it is, then, very probably, correct to say that the division of the whole nation into high and low was very different in Ireland from what it was elsewhere: there was surely less of a gap. Where else had feudalism to contend with a national law-system so strong and homogeneous? If nowhere else, it does not seem profitable to write of Ireland in any age in the same terms as one does of a completely feudalised country; and one thinks that it is the less profitable according as age or district is the more Gaelic. Definite instances of quarrelling between landowner and labourer—both Gaels—as well as definite complaints in the poems of the covetousness, and even tyranny, of the landlords, may, of course, be come upon, but no matter how stressed, these instances do not contradict the general truth that the Irish side was far more homogeneous than the Planter side of Ireland's life. The Gaels, moreover, were, in Young's phrase, a people involved in one common ruin. In the Irish-speaking districts life was, perhaps, more homogeneous than even in the rural community of squirearchy and tenantry in England. There little or no common culture flowed to and fro, up and down, in hall and cottage; nor were there any traditions of triumphs and disasters shared in common in an immemorial fight, to unify rich and poor in mood and temper. It was for the big houses that Aodhagán Ó Rathaille chiefly wrote, the bulk of his work consisting of elegies written on such of their owners as died in his time. For all that, the greater portion of his days must have been passed in the company of poor men; and we are sure that he died in poverty. Brian Merriman, never a rich man, visited these houses, and perhaps was set to teach the children in some of them. Ó Cearbhalláin knew them only too well, passing from one to another, singing his own songs and playing his own planxties and reels. Eoghan Ruadh Ó Súilleabháin worked for them, not only as *spailpín*, but as schoolmaster, as also did Donnchadh Ruadh and many another. Seán Ó Tuama received their masters at the door of his inn and speeded them on the road when the time was come. Seán Clárach Mac Domhnaill proposed to them a scheme for the translation of Homer into Irish. Seán na Ráithíneach, and many another earlier and later than his time, copied manuscripts for them. It was purely their Gaelic culture that gave these poets entrance to the big houses; no other passport had they; yet that culture was obtained by them in humble cottages and taken by them to the big houses rather than contrariwise. It was a culture alien neither to poor Gael nor to rich Gael; but every passing year, of course, saw it become more and more peculiarly the appanage of the poor.

One is right, therefore, in saying that there was a common culture flowing up and down between hut and Big House in Irish Ireland; and that this phenomenon can be met with in no other country in Europe, since the conditions that had brought it about among us were not known in any country abroad.

VI

We must, to finish, conceive of those Gaelic houses first as very much resembling the Planter houses that surrounded them—each a landmark, the centre of a little world; built of local stone after local traditions; self-supporting, seating a hundred at its tables of a daytime, marshalling its followers by the hundred; patriarchal in its conception of human society, patriarchal in the vastness of its flocks and herds. But then we must, at the same time, conceive of those Gaelic houses as possessed of certain notes of their own—freer contact with Europe, a culture over and above that which they shared with their neighbours, and a sense of historic continuity, a closeness to the land, to the very pulse of it, that those Planter houses could not even dream of.

CHAPTER III

THE BARDIC SCHOOLS

I

What a strange ending Eibhlín Dubh found for the keen she made above her murdered husband:

Stadaidh anois d'bhúr ngol,
A mhná na súl bhfliuch mbog,
Go bhfaghaidh Art Ua Laoghaire deoch
Roimh é dhul isteach 'sa sgoil,
Ní h-ag foghlaim léighinn ná port
Ach ag iomchar cré agus cloch.

Cease now your wailing,
Women of the soft wet eyes,
Till Art O'Leary drain his cup
Before entering the school,
Not for music or learning,
But to bear up clay and stone.

The note of this whole poem is headlong impulse. Scarcely once does the keening abate in swiftness, in wildness, or in grip, if one may use this word of so intimate an out-pouring of grief. While one reads it, it is impossible to think of the matter as having been gathered, sifted, arranged; yet had Eibhlín Dubh searched a whole year long for the one ending that should be more Gaelic than any other, that should more surely than any other pierce the hearts both of O'Leary's kinsfolk in Iveleary and her own kinsfolk in Iveragh, she could not have bettered this ending that we know. The poem is living with the breath and stir of that still Gaelic-speaking corner of Ireland. Its rocks, its little towns, its holy places, its houses, its people, are all swept into the headlong rush of the verse—to be suddenly put an end to with the word "school," with an image that is at once intimate, aloof, and Gaelic beyond our kenning.

When the poem was written—Art O'Leary was shot by

Government troops in 1773—the people of Iveleary needed no instruction as to what sort of school was referred to in those lines: they knew it for a bardic school; furthermore, they were aware why that word " school " had risen to the lips of the keening woman; they knew it was because of the sense of darkness, silence, mystery, aloofness that overwhelmed her to think of the bed in which Art O'Leary was to sleep for evermore.

II

In common with almost every other institution of the Gael, the bardic school as a factor in the life of the nation, has not been so much misunderstood or underestimated as entirely omitted by those who have, previous to our own day, thought themselves fitted to write Irish history. They did not, it is only fair to say, wilfully make such omissions: they could not, however, avoid making them when they employed, in telling the story of Ireland, the same formulæ that had simplified their own labours, or the similar labours of others, in dealing with the chronicles of other peoples. They saw only what they had come to see. How big a thing they failed to notice when this system of the bardic schools escaped them, and how untrustworthy, and indeed misleading, their story is as a consequence, will be understood from these words:

If we turn to Ireland . . . . we find a country where for some 1,500 years, as far back as historic knowledge can reach, one national force has overshadowed and dominated all others. It has been the power of a great literary tradition. Political power was not centralized, and no single man was in a position to determine what the people should think, believe, or do. But in the learned tradition of the race there was a determined order. In their intellectual and spiritual inheritance was the very essence of national life, the substance of its existence, the warrant of its value, the assurance of its continuity.[1]

Who, having risen from the books of the historians—the books on which we were all reared up—will not cry out on

---

[1] Alice Stopford Green, *Irish National Tradition*.

meeting these words for the first time: Can it be true? Can it be true that for all their painstaking conning of haphazard memoirs and crafty State-papers, those writers of history never once happened on the one national force that overshadowed and dominated all others? Can it be believed that not having struck against it, they never missed it, never felt somehow that their stories did not adhere, one to another; did not account, one for the other? One shrinks from saying that the essence of national life, consisting, as it always does, of an intellectual and spiritual inheritance, is stuff for the artist, rather than for the historian, to come upon, to handle, to purge, to shape, so that his duller co-mates may be made a little more wise—one shrinks from saying this, yet the artist's large and even loose way of discourse is in the end often less astray, one thinks, than that patient, anxious chronicling of events that has no feeling for the undercurrents that sweep them along, hurtling, clashing, or sundering.

Elsewhere in that same pamphlet Mrs. Green states: " Irish civilisation was thus from the beginning marked by intellectual passion."[1] Now, the bardic schools were the seat of that passion. In them was the flame nursed, fed, distributed— " síolta teine " (" seeds of fire "). To realise, then, in any fitting way, that national force which overshadowed and dominated all others, one must make some study of this unique factor in Gaelic civilisation: unless we do so, we shall fail not only to understand Irish history as a whole, but we shall fail in our present purpose, namely, to fathom the life of those " pariahs " of the eighteenth century who, so unlike us, had no difficulty in apprehending the power and depth of that image with which Eibhlín Dubh brought her keening to a close.

---

[1] " At this period [9th cent.], whatever may have been their literary attainments, they were more remarkable for a bold independence of mind, a curiosity, activity, and vigour of thought, which contrasted strongly with the genius of Bede and Raban." Newman, *The Benedictine Centuries*. (It did not strike him to ask how these Irishmen had come by this intellectual dexterity.)

It is not probable that we shall ever discover the origins of the bardic schools. "At what time they were founded we don't know, for the bardic order existed in prehistoric times, and their position in society is well established in the earliest tradition."[1] They were ancient when St Patrick came amongst us. In the pagan days poet and druid were perhaps one; and even after those schools had become Christian some vestiges of the old cult still survived in them; but this, of course, could naturally be said of life in general, for pagan ways of thinking, pagan traditions and customs, lingered on through whole centuries. When the schools did at last become Christian, they did not become monastic; and they are not to be confused with the famous monkish schools, the ruins of which are still to be seen in so many of our valleys. The Bardic Schools were lay, officered by laymen; and existed side by side with the great schools of the clerics. Whether there was any connection between the two types of school, monastic and bardic, does not seem to have been given the study it deserves. Did such great establishments as Bangor, Clonfert and Clonmacnoise lay claim, at any time, to include the local bardic schools within their orbits, or did they dominate them while not enclosing them? Or did the bardic schools, maintaining their ancient traditions, think of themselves as set over against the monastic schools, deeming them as only of yesterday? It is easy to say that either type had its own province, the one secular, the other religious; but when we consider that two such neighbouring schools would share in the same patronage, that the professors of both would meet in this patron's assemblies, in his council chamber, for instance, where bishops and chief poets helped him, and that the courses of both schools would freely overlap, it is not so easy to think of them as quite disparate entities, each working within a sphere of its own. Did one type dominate the other?

[1] Professor Bergin, "Bardic Poetry" in *Ivernian Journal,* April-June, 1913; V., 19.

The mere existence of those schools, whether or not the Church schools tutored them, shows how different was the life of Ireland from that of Europe; it gives point, too, to the assertion that a literary tradition dominated the other national forces, for that literary tradition would have been in the keeping of those schools. This being so, rivalry, if such there was, between the two types of school, monastic and bardic, must have had its effects, direct or indirect, on the life of the nation. The question is vast, difficult, and fascinating; and one trusts that someone fitted to do so will take it in hands.

Whatever may have been the relative positions of the monkish schools and those of the bards, the latter, all authorities agree, were the university system of the nation— granting degrees, or what corresponded to such, and bestowing privileges on both professors and students simply because they were professors and students.[1]

In Europe of the Dark and Middle Ages the universities were frankly Church institutions, with Churchmen ruling in their professoriates; whatever influence those universities wielded in European life and thought was, therefore, a Church influence, which means practically that whatever influence the higher learning exerted in Continental thought was a Church influence, for except in those universities where else was there any repository of that learning? In Ireland, on the other hand, the bardic schools, which obviously exerted great influence in the nation's life, were a repository of learning, and were, at the same time, frankly a lay institution. The great monastic schools had, too, of course, much of the university spirit in

---

[1] However that may be, there grew up in several of these cities schools for the study of law. That at Bologna was made famous by the greatest of these early teachers, Irnerius (1067-1138), in the same manner that Abelard raised Paris to distinction, and large numbers of students collected here. Thus Bologna became a centre for study, *and as these students and teachers were given privileges,* it became the first organised university. Monroe, *A Text Book in the History of Education.*

them, and did also exert great influence on the life of the country; this influence, however, one may roughly equate with that wielded by the Church universities of the Continent. But one searches Europe in vain for the equivalent of our bardic school system. In this regard, then, European civilisation was less varied than Irish civilisation. That factor, which Europe lacked, a secular, intellectual centre, who shall fathom its various promptings and achievements on its native soil? What part, great or little, exciting or assuaging, did it play in the local wrestlings of Church and State, if there were such? And in how much is it responsible for that non-European tang which one feels everywhere both in Irish life and in Irish letters in all the centuries down to the nineteenth?

IV

Professor Bergin tells us that he has never come on a description of a bardic school in Irish—naturally, for, of course, the institution was too familiar to all to need any; especially was it familiar to those for whom the poets and chroniclers wrote, the patrician class. Of references to the schools, there is, however, and just as naturally, no end. In English there is an account in the *Memoirs of the Marquis of Clanricarde* (published 1722), which Professor Bergin believes to be trustworthy:

Concerning the poetical Seminary or School, from which I was carried away to clear other things that fell in my way, it was open only to such as were descended of Poets and reputed within their Tribes. And so was it with all the Schools of that kind in the Nation, being equal to the Number of Families that followed the said calling. But some more or less frequented for the difference of Professors, Conveniency, with other Reasons, and seldom any come but from remote parts, to be at a distance from Relations and other Acquaintances that might interrupt his Study. The Qualifications first requir'd were reading well, writing the Mother-tongue, and a strong Memory. It was likewise necessary the Place should be in the solitary Recess of a Garden or within a Sept or Enclosure far out of the reach of any Noise, which an Intercourse of People might otherwise occasion. The Structure was a snug, low Hut, and beds in it at con-

73

venient Distances, each within a small Apartment without much Furniture of any kind, save only a Table, some Seats, and a Conveniency for Cloaths to hang upon. No Windows to let in the Day, nor any Light at all us'd but that of Candles, and these brought in at a proper Season only. The Students upon thorough Examination being first divided into Classes, wherein a regard was had to every one's Age, Genius, and the Schooling had before, if any at all, or otherwise. The Professors (one or more as there was occasion) gave a Subject suitable to the Capacity of each class, determining the number of Rhimes, and clearing what was to be chiefly observed therein as to Syllables, Quartans, Concord, Correspondence, Termination and Union, each of which were restrain'd by peculiar Rules. The said Subject (either one or more as aforesaid) having been given over Night, they work'd it apart each by himself upon his own Bed, the whole next day in the Dark, till at a certain Hour in the Night, Lights being brought in, they committed it to writing. Being afterwards dress'd and come together into a large Room, where the Masters waited, each Scholar gave in his Performance, which being corrected or approv'd of (according as it requir'd) either the same or fresh subjects were given against the next day. This Part being over, the Students went to their Meal, Which was then serv'd up; and so, after some time spent in Conversation and other Diversions, each retired to his Rest, to be ready for the Business of the next Morning. Every *Saturday* and on the Eves of Festival Days they broke up and dispers'd themselves among the Gentlemen and rich Farmers of the Country, by whom they were very well entertain'd and much made of, till they thought fit to take their leaves, in order to re-assume their Study. Nor was the People satisfied with affording this Hospitality alone; they sent in by turns every Week from far and near Liquors and all manner of Provision towards the Subsistence of the Academy, so that the chief Poet was at little or no Charges, but, on the contrary, got very well by it, besides the Presents made him by the Students upon their first coming, which was always at Michaelmas, and from thence till the 25th of March, during the cold season of the Year only, did that close Study last. At that time the Scholars broke up and repair'd each to his own Country, with an Attestation of his Behaviour and Capacity from the chief Professor to those that had sent him.

The reason of laying the Study aforesaid in the Dark was doubtless to avoid the Distraction which Light and the variety of Objects represented thereby commonly occasions. This being prevented, the Faculties of the Soul occupied themselves solely upon the Subject in hand, and the Theme given; so that it was soon brought to some Perfection according to the Notions or Capacities of the Students. Yet the course was long and tedious, as we find, and it was six or seven Years before a Mastery or the last Degree was conferred, which you'll the less admire upon considering the great Difficulty of the Art, the many kinds of their Poems, the Exactness and Nicety to be observ'd in each, which was necessary to render their Numbers soft, and the Harmony agreeable and pleasing to the Ear.

74

As every Professor, or chief Poet, depended on some Prince or great Lord, that had endowed his Tribe, he was under strict ties to him and Family, as to record in good Metre his Marriages, Births, Deaths, Acquisitions made in war and Peace, Exploits, and other remarkable things relating to the Same. He was likewise bound to offer an Elegy on the Decease of the said Lord, his consort, or any of their children, and a Marriage Song when there should be Occasion. But as to any Epick, or Heroick Verse to be made for any other Lord or Stranger, it was requir'd that at least a Paroemion or Metre therein, should be upon the Patron, or the Name in general. . .

The last Part to be done, which was the *Action* and *Pronunciation* of the Poem in Presence of the Maecenas, or the Principal Person it related to, was perform'd with a great deal of Ceremony in a Consort of Vocal and Instrumental Musick. The poet himself said nothing, but directed and took care that everybody else did his Part right. The Bards having first had the Composition from him, got it well by Heart, and now pronounc'd it orderly, keeping even pace with a Harp, touch'd upon that Occasion; no other musical Instrument being allowed for the said Purpose than this alone, as being Masculin, much sweeter and fuller than any other.

In Gaelic Scotland those schools continued to exist into the eighteenth century; and Professor - Bergin quotes from Martin's *Description of the Western Islands of Scotland:*

I must not omit to relate their way of Study, which is very singular. They shut their Doors and Windows for a Day's time, and lie on their backs with a Stone upon their Belly, and Plads about their Heads, and their Eyes being cover'd they pump their Brains for Rhetorical Encomium or Panegyrick; and indeed they furnish such a Stile from this Dark Cell as is understood by very few; and if they purchase a couple of Horses as the reward of their Meditation, they think they have done a great Matter. The Poet or Bard had a Title to the Bridegroom's upper Garb—that is, the Plad and Bonnet—but now he is satisfy'd with what the Bridegroom pleases to give him on such occasions.

Both these descriptions are from without. In Ireland the schools had died before they were written, and in Scotland were dying. Presently we shall find how one who had himself lain in those " beds of booths," in those dark cells, could rise up in spirit to bless them; and Tadhg Óg Ó Huiginn gives us to understand that in his brother's school the students were sorry to hear the cuckoo's first song, for the break-up of the session was then near.

A lucht do bhí 'na bhaile,
lér mhian ceard is comhnaidhe,
do bhí adhbhar fár fhuath libh
labhradh na gcuach do chluinsin.

"O ye who were in his house
and sought art and residence,
well might it be hateful to you
to hear the utterance of the
cuckoo." [1]

The composing in the dark, Professor Bergin thinks, was a survival of some rite or ceremony of pagan origin. No doubt he is correct, yet when we consider the severity of the mental discipline practised in those schools, the care taken to choose a solitary recess, the custom of separating students from their own kindred, we do not find the shutting out of the garish daylight contrary to the spirit of the whole system.

The building was only an ordinary house or hut—the central figure, the chief *file,* the head *ollamh,* was indeed the school: where he went, the school went, sometimes on circuit from king to king. *Filí* and not *bards* it was that both conducted and used those schools, the bards, as compared with the *filí,* being a lower order, *untrained* poets—singers of songs, reciters of verse, strolling jongleurs. The word *bard,* however, in modern times, has come to include all varieties of poets, and it will, therefore, serve our turn now.

The bards never have had any representative in England. "They correspond in a way to the University men, but their fixed place in society was higher than any that his attainments alone have ever been able to secure for the University man in England. They were, indeed, until the fall of the old Irish order, an intellectual aristocracy, with all the privileges and, no doubt, many of the prejudices of a caste. They held their position by virtue of their birth and the practice of their art." [2]

But other writers find the closest analogy to them and their profession in the bar. [3] The bar is not, however, a hereditary

---

[1] *The Bardic Poems of Tadhg Dall Ó Huiginn,* I, edited by E. Knott: Irish Texts Society. (In *Studies,* March, 1924, Professor Bergin gives a fine translation of the whole of this moving and beautiful poem.)

[2] See the introduction by Professor Robin Flower to Professor T. F. O'Rahilly's "Dánta Grádha."

[3] Cf. *Bardic Poems of Tadhg Dall Ó Huiginn,* I.

craft; the bardic profession was; yet since new names are found frequently coming in among the familiar ones—the O'Huiginns and the O'Dalys—in the literary annals, the profession, it is evident, had some means of recruiting its strength with fresh blood. Brilliance in the schools may have had the power of winning to a coveted position, or royal prerogatives may have exerted themselves: it is certain, anyway, that an open door there was somewhere, but whether a back or a front door, and what magic phrase opened it, we do not at present know.

The training in the schools was long and arduous; and having gone through it, the student had little else of his craft to learn. " He was, in fact, a professor of literature and a man of letters, highly trained in the use of a polished literary medium, belonging to a hereditary caste in an aristocratic society, holding an official position therein by virtue of his training, his learning, his knowledge of the history and tradition of his country and his clan. He discharged, as O'Donovan pointed out years ago, the functions of the modern journalist.[1] He was not a song writer. He was often a public official, a chronicler, a political essayist, a keen and satirical observer of his fellow-countrymen. . . . . He might be a poet, too, if in addition to his training he was gifted with the indefinable power, the true magic, of poetry. But whether he was a poet in this higher sense or not, he always composed in verse."[2]

Only those who have read some of the works of those poets, and tried to place them in the national polity, will adequately appreciate the careful wording of this passage. It clarifies our conception of them; it corrects our equating of them with the poets of other times and countries—strayed revellers, without a place in sun or moon; and, finally, it hints that we should seek out from among that literary association those who were poets, judging these on their merits, if poetry be our quest,

---

[1] O'Donovan's words are: " They discharged the functions and wielded the influence of the modern newspaper and periodical press."

[2] Bergin, " Bardic Poetry," *op. cit.*

and judging the others as we will—as chroniclers, perhaps, but not as poets. Our idea of the whole matter is still further clarified to remember that down to the middle of the seventeenth century, prose was not thought of as an art-form: a copyist would transcribe a poem word for word, but was content to record merely the matter of a piece of prose.

Those poets seized and maintained their pride of place not as individuals, but as a body. They were numerous in all centuries down to the seventeenth. Before the Danes came into Ireland they had become so powerful that " They were three times banished by the kings of Ireland; but the province of Ulster defended them against the vengeance of the other Irish."[1]

St Colmcille, as we have all read, pleaded for them at Drumceat; and though at this crisis, and time and again in the following centuries, laws were framed to regulate them, what between their numbers, their wealth, their power of satire, their indispensability as chroniclers, and, it is hinted, their use of the hunger-strike, they seemed to have lived always a little on the thither side of the law. Why they were so numerous is not difficult to understand. " The island was divided up into the domains of a large number of feudal lords, each of whom—at any rate, in the North, West and South— would have his family bard."[2] And Dr Hyde, translating his own Irish, says: " There was neither prince nor great noble in Ireland who had not visits from poets bringing poems or abhráns in their praise, for which they used to receive a large price. Theobald Butler, Lord of Cahir, and his wife, Mary Cusack, had the full of a book of poems in their praise. This Butler died in 1596. In the same way the O'Byrnes had the full of a book of poems written upon them, which is called ' The Book of the O'Byrnes.' O'Conor Donn has a volume in praise of the clann Samhradhain, or MacGoverns, and there is a book in Copenhagen, in Denmark, written in praise of the

[1] Douglas Hyde, *Irish Poetry.*
[2] E. C. Quiggin, *Prolegomena to the Study of the Later Irish Bards.*

Maguires, and it is pretty certain that there was no great family in Ireland but possessed a book of the same kind."[1]

They stood strongly upon their rights. "O'Hosey, or O'Hussey, poet of the Maguires, on being appointed ollave, or poet-in-chief, reminded his patron in his laureate ode that the ollave ranked in all ways as an equal with a king and a bishop. 'To him is due the warmth of loving-kindness, the primest of all largesse, the initiative in counsel; the seat closest to the prince and a share of his bed, with payment, whether " in wood " or " in sanctuary." ' "[2] And with this we may compare: "On his father's death in 1432, Eoghan O'Neill, says the annalist, ' went to Tulach Óg, and was there inaugurated king on the stone of the kings by the will of God and men, of bishops and chief poets.' "[3] And another bard, John O'Cluan, apologising for having struck his lord, Aed O'Connor, writes thus: "Thine 'tis in payment of my blow to lop the right hand from me, O gentle noble countenance; thy due 'tis to have a lay of its value, or else the very hand, O Gairide's griffin. Not kine, not horses, not artificers' gold are promised thee, O ruddy one benign of face! Neither hand shalt thou have, no, nor foot; but a poem in lieu of that which I have done."[4]

Such voices out of the far centuries prompt us to think that in Ireland, if nowhere else, the homely, slighted shepherd's trade held its head rather high! They throve, as one might expect: "It has been computed that in the petty princedom of Tyrconnell or Donegal, the real estate allocated to the maintenance of the *literati* amounted in value to £2,000 a year of our present currency; and we find Daire Mac Brodin, poet to the Fourth Earl of Thomond (about 1570-1650), residing still on his own patrimonial estate in the Castle of Dunogan, Barony of Ibrican, in the west of County Clare."[5]

---

[1] Douglas Hyde, *Irish Poetry.*
[2] Eleanor Hull, *A Text Book of Irish Literature.*
[3] Eoin MacNeill, *Phases of Irish History.*
[4] E. C. Quiggin, *Prolegomena to the Study of the Later Irish Bards.*
[5] Eleanor Hull, *op. cit.*

Neither record will surprise us if we recollect that sometimes a poet received as much as a hundred marks (£600) for a poem or abhrán; and Tadhg Óg Ó Huiginn, who lived in the fifteenth century, says that he never received less than twenty cows for a poem from Tadhg Mac Cathal O'Connor-Sligo.[1]

V

The studies of the students in the bardic schools were chiefly: history, law, language, literature. The history was that of Ireland, the law was that of Ireland, namely, the Brehon Law system; the language was that of Ireland, the literature that of Ireland—and through the medium of the native language were all subjects taught. These schools, then, considered as a university, differed widely from the European type, where the main study was given over on the one hand to a law system—the Roman Law—that was the relic of a dead empire, and on the other, to the literatures of languages that were no longer living. To the same degree as the Continental university cultivated the dead and the alien, the Irish university cultivated the living and the native; and if both lagged far behind the ideal type of university, there is as much to be said for the Irish conception as for the foreign. In the Irish schools, the present-day tendency to use the home-language as the medium of instruction was anticipated by more than a thousand years. National literatures on the Continent had to struggle against the university; whereas there Dante might easily never have written his poems in his mother-tongue, nor indeed Villon his, the Irish language was the very apple of their eye to the bardic schools. That language they took, and ruling out dialect and the passing turn of speech, refined it and set it apart as a special dialect, a language for literature, which became known from

---

[1] Eleanor Hull, *op. cit.*

80

end to end of Ireland. It was known also in Scotland. It remained unchanged for centuries. With all that it came to contain of law, prayer, history and literature, it served at the one time as seed-bed and harvest of the mind of the Gaelic nation.

It was, as stated, the foundation-stone of all the studies in those schools: it was not, however, from very early times, the only language studied in them. Zimmer's theory that there was, as a result of the barbarian invasions, a flight of Gallic scholars to Ireland in the fifth century, is now fairly well understood, if not agreed upon: Professor Kuno Meyer appeared to accept it, while Professor MacNeill rather discredits it;[1] yet, recollecting the studies in those bardic schools, one at least wishes it to be true. To think of these scholars—Christians for the most part—as introducing a new strain into the scholarship of our fathers; to conceive of them as preparing in those schools a path for St Patrick and his disciples, so explaining the bloodless conversion; to see them as opening up these schools to the riches of the Greek and Latin tongues, so establishing the tradition out of which fourteen hundred years later the peasant Donnchadh Ruadh was to write in Latin his memorable epitaph on Tadhg Gaedhlach, another peasant—to derive from that hurried descent on our shores of exiled scholarship certain of the most salient characteristics of those schools in the after centuries—to think thus, is, it must be feared, only that rounding off of a beautiful tale for which the creative instinct in us craves. But when one remembers the traffic of Irish missionaries with Europe in the early centuries, such a theory is not needed to explain the interest of the bardic schools in Greek and Latin—the languages of European scholarship, as their own was of Irish scholarship. Wherever the impulse came from, their professors soon became acquainted with them, and the tradition lived on from century to century, with memorable results, as will afterwards be noted. All down the centuries the chiefs were educated in

---

[1] Eoin MacNeill, *Phases of Irish History.*

81

those schools, and, said Stanihurst, " The Irish speak Latin like a vulgar language, learned in their common schools of leechcraft and law."[1] While, turning to a later writer, we find: " The more one studies the works of these bards, the more one is impressed with the range of their attainments. They were not in holy orders, and yet they must have been better versed in Latin than most of the clergy. . . . . In any case, it was no mean achievement on the part of men like Tadhg Ó Huiginn to show such acquaintance with the voluminous Latin religious literature of the day in addition to the huge store of native learning exemplified in their other works."[2]

VI

Protected by law as well as custom, the academic spirit naturally made its home in these schools. If one pick up at random any set of verses produced in them, one has to hand an example on which to argue either for or against that spirit. Too plainly, almost, that chance set of verses will show the inbreeding from which these poets' flock of ideas came to suffer, a disease most incident to academies. Everywhere in their poems one finds a refinement which, while it never becomes lackadaisical or effeminate, does certainly only too clearly make us aware of their contempt for the crudeness that so often accompanies the note of the daring and novel. That rigid turn of mind which kept their literary medium in a strait-jacket for whole centuries, afraid not so much of growth as the dangers that go with it, kept the doors of the inventive faculties severely sentried, and for the self-same reason. The movement of their minds is swift, precise, and often piercing, but one wishes for livelier contrasts, for richer colour, for readier emotions. There was, however, gain as

---

[1] " Description of Ireland " (1587), quoted by Professor Curtis in *Studies*, June, 1919.

[2] E. C. Quiggin, *Prolegomena to the Study of the Later Irish Bards*.

well as loss. " From their study of good models and their association with the best teachers, the poets derived one characteristic which is common to the whole bardic order, and that is a sustained dignity of style. Their respect for their position, their hereditary pride, and their excessive devotion to traditional precedents, gave them at least a rooted dislike of vulgarity." To which it is hardly necessary to add what the same authority writes elsewhere: " There are several poems in praise of the harp, but the literary classes appear to have looked down upon the singer, whom they classed with the *geócach*, or buffoon. Tom Moore's picture of the bard singing and playing in the intervals of draining bumpers would have shocked the real bard as something very vulgar indeed."[1]

The great bulk of the work left us by them consists of encomiastic verse—panegyrics of their patrons. Of all they wrote, this species of verse was, of course, most likely to be preserved, for each great house had its *duanaire*, or collection of poems, written in its honour. Into these panegyrics the poets wove a great amount of genealogical matter, which to us nowadays is wearisome: our standards are different, our whole world is different; yet one never knows when a beautiful stanza may not suddenly be come upon. From the view of history, the value of such verse, and the amount of it remaining to us is vast, is at present inestimable. Their religious poetry is more attractive than this encomiastic verse: here are freshness and genuine inspiration; qualities that also are found in the stray non-official poems and snatches of poems that the dreadful centuries have spared to us.

It is likely that these poets were more academic than those of any other country ever were—not excepting even the Pléiade of French literature. " Sons of learning " they really were, and as such they were never weary of speaking of the science of verse. It was their dearest study: their metres became more and more intricate, and their verse, what between this intricacy and the special dialect they used, more

[1] Bergin, " Bardic Poetry," *op. cit.*

and more a study rather for the schools themselves than an outlet for a people's emotion. A profession that was hereditary, a rich, strongly-organised caste, an over-elaborated catechism of art—one reckons up such characteristics and finds it hard to equate these darlings of the nation with our idea of poets in general: in art who does not fear privilege and organisation?—yet, after all, some very notable works of art were produced in little Italian cities at a time when many of the self-same characteristics adhered to the artists who swarmed in them. If our colleges of bards, like those associations of artists, only occasionally threw up a man of genius—what else could have been expected? But while we come upon the work of the unique Flemish or Italian stone-carver, with all manner of preparations made properly to apprehend his genius, we happen upon the Gaelic poet, not only heavy with ignorance, but ill-bestead, it is likely, by whatever alien standards we lean upon. What remains to be done is first to publish all the verse we have inherited from these bards, such as it is; and secondly, to make more readily accessible the work of those of them who were poets as well as men of letters. Even when this is done, it will still be difficult, not to appraise the work before our eyes, but to appraise the whole endeavour; for we can never be sure that the best work of these schools has not perished. That portion of it which remains has not been preserved to us through the ordinary sifting-process that a national literature undergoes; Opinion—that of the mass of men, that of the critics, that of the "passionate few," who, more than all others, keep the good things of Art before men's eyes—Opinion, blended of these three voices, has had practically nothing to say to what has survived of the poetry of the bards: nothing else than the self-same chance that brings a soldier alive from the battlefield where thousands have fallen, has decided what was to survive of those academicians' work. Much, therefore, has yet to be accomplished before we can dare to speak of them as we do of the schools of poetry that elsewhere arose and disappeared.

Those poems, because of their close-knit structure, their

subtle music, are the despair of translators—"The lyrics of Aonghus Ó Dálaigh and his fellows are as untranslatable as those of Horace":[1] in choosing, then, some specimens of bardic poetry, it may be well to find a few clustering about a common subject, a subject that will have an interest of its own for us as helping on our study: The theme we choose as fulfilling this condition is, besides, one that the old poets themselves would have rejoiced for, namely, the schools themselves. Here is a little poem that one never forgets. We do not know when it was written, probably in the seventeenth century, nor by whom. It has but one quality to recommend it; that, however, the most difficult of all, the most elusive, the least frequently compassed—we call it "charm":

An Scoláire

Aoibhinn beatha an scoláire
 Bhíos ag déanamh léighinn;
 Is follas dibh, a dhaoine,
 Gur dó is aoibhne i nÉirinn.

Pleasant the scholar's life
When his books surround him;
'Tis clear to ye, O people,
No better is in Ireland.

Gan smacht rí air ná ró-fhlatha
 Ag tighearna dá threise,
 Gan cuid cíosa ag caibidil,
 Gan mochóirighe, ná méirse.

O'er him the strongest lord
Rules not as prince or king;
For him no Church's dues,
Nor fines nor early rising.

Mochóirighe ná aodhaireacht
 Ní thabhair uaidh coidhche;
 'S ní mó do bheir d'á aire
 Féar ná faire san oidhche.

Early rising, shepherding,
These he never yields,
And just as little worries him
Tillage or watching in the night.

Maith biseach a sheisrighe
 Ag teacht i dtúis an earraigh;
 Is é is crann dá sheisrigh
 Lán a ghlaice de pheannaibh.

Great the harvest of his plough
Coming in the front of Spring;
And the yoke of his plough-team,
A handful of pens!

Do b'ait leis greas ar tháiplis
 Nó ar chláirsigh go mbinne,
 Nó fós greas eile ar aiteall
 'S a chumann carad uime.

At backgammon, at the harp
So sweet, he'd love a spell;
Or a spell in joyous company,
With his friends around him.

[1] Preface by Professor Bergin to *Aonghus Ó Dálaigh,* by Fr MacKenna.

But the Irish mode of student life was almost at an end when this nameless one chose so to praise it. Here is a poem, written by Mathghamhain Ó hIfearnáin, or Mahon O'Heffernan—early in the seventeenth century, a time of confiscations and plantations, which more clearly mirrors the troubled state of things:

Ceist! cia do cheinneóchadh dán?

[Edited and translated by Professor Bergin.] [1]

Ceist! cia do cheinneóchadh
   dán?
   a chiall is ceirteólas suadh:
an ngéabhadh, nó an áil le haon,
dán saor do-bhéaradh go buan?

Question! who will buy a poem? Its meaning is genuine learning of scholars. Will any take, or does any lack, a noble poem that shall make him immortal?

Gé dán sin go snadhmadh bhfis,
   gach margadh ó chrois go crois
do shiobhail mé an Mhumhain
   leis—
   ní breis é a-nuraidh ná a-nois.

Though this is a poem with close-knit science, I have walked all Munster with it, every market from cross to cross—nothing gained from last year to this time.

D'éirneist gémadh beag an bonn,
   níor chuir fear ná éinbhean
   ann,
níor luaidh aoinfhear créad dá
   chionn,
   níor fhéagh liom Gaoidheal ná
   Gall.

Though a groat were a small earnest, not one man or woman offered it: no man mentioned the reason; neither Gael nor Gall gave heed to me.

Ceard mar so ní sochar dhún,
   gé dochar a dol fa lár:
uaisle dul re déiniomh cíor—
   ga bríogh d'éinfhior dul re
   dán?

Such an art as this is no profit to me, though it is a misfortune that it should fall to the ground: it were more honourable to become a maker of combs—what use is it to anyone to profess poetry?

Ní mhair Corc Chaisil ná Cian,
   nár chaigil a gcrodh ná a
   luagh,
na réidhfhir ag díol na ndámh-
   slán le síol Eibhir mon-uar.

Corc of Cashel lives not, nor Cian, who never spared their cattle, nor the price of them, open-handed men at paying the bardic companies—alas! it is good-bye to the race of Eibhear.

---

[1] *Irish Review,* April 1913.

Geall bronnta níor beanadh dhíobh,
  Cobhthach go teasda agus Tál:
iomdha drong diongbhaim dá luadh,
  uaim anonn dá ndiongnainn dán.

They never lost the palm for generosity, until Cobhthach and Tál died: many a host I leave untold, for whom I might have continued to make poetry.

Mé im luing cheannaigh ar gcaill laist
  d'éis Chlann nGearailt do thuill teist:
ní chluinim—is cás rom loisg:
  fás an toisg fá gcuirim ceist.

I am a merchant ship that has lost its cargo, after the Fitzgeralds who deserved renown. I hear no answer—a case that has tormented me. 'Tis an idle business about which I put a question.

Surely a beautiful lyric. Even in the prose translation, does not one feel the accent of true poetry? Is not one subtly aware that the theme is heightened—how, when, one hardly knows —to that level where the words take on a new garb, a new life, in short, to the lyric plane? And as we read are we not gently conscious of some effort towards an answering reserve and dignity stirring within ourselves? As for its subject, there cannot have been many poets of that time who did not treat some variation of it: it was in all their thoughts: the patrician houses, that had sheltered them from time immemorial, were broken and deserted or in the keeping of aliens; and in consequence the poets, for the first time dispossessed, found themselves forlorn wanderers—" mar ubhall ó thuinn go tuinn " (" as an apple from wave to wave, I am tossed from neighbour to neighbour "), sings Fearfeasa ón Cáinte, in a poem to the famous Florence MacCarthy—himself a prisoner in the Tower. All these poems are gathered up, one may say, in O'Gnive's funeral lamentation of the bardic schools, as it has been called. In this, as on a tombstone, are enumerated the more famous of the poet families whose world was now in ruins—the O'Higginses, the O'Dalys, the MacMelaughlins, the Keoghs, the MacGraths, the O'Coffeys, the Mac-an-wards, the MacConmees.[1]

---

[1] Douglas Hyde, *Irish Poetry.*

87

It may, however, be more profitable for us here to transcribe the verses of some unknown poet—in Irish literature, significant fact, the name of the unknown poets is legion—who, writing about the same time, gives us poignantly to understand how deep and warm remained the recollection of these bardic schools in the hearts of those who had in the young years of their manhood lain in their " beds of booths ":

Aonar Dhamhsa Eidir Dhaoinibh
[Edited and translated by Professor Bergin.] [1]

Aonar dhamhsa eidir dhaoinibh,
atú anocht go neamhfhaoiligh:
am aonarán a ccionn cháigh,
's ionn gan aobharán d'fagháil.

I am alone among men; to-night I am joyless: left desolate after the others, finding no food of gladness.

Ní thuig mé an lucht so ag labhra,
gá dtá ar tteanga mháthardha:
ar n'aos aithnigh ní léir linn,
mh'aithghin féin ó nach faicim.

I do not understand these speakers who speak our mother-tongue: I can find none that I know, for I see no one like myself.

Ionann liom gach longphort lán
is uaigneas d'éis mo chómpán:
mar sin budh daoinighe dhamh,
aoinfhile as tigh dhá tteagmhadh.

Every full encampment is to me the same as a desert after my comrades, yet it would be crowded to me if there were but one poet within.

Teóra ceardcha 'nar chleacht sinn
áineas d'fagháil dom intinn,
nach taighlim na trí ceardcha,
do shní fhaighlinn mh'aigeanta.

The three forges wherein I was wont to find mental delight, that I cannot visit these forges wears away the armoury of my mind.

Teach meabhraighthe ar mac soirbhidh,
rob áit oiris d'ógbhuidhnibh,
grís deargtha agus sí solas,
rob í ar gceardcha céadamhas.

The house of memorising of our gentle lads—it was a trysting-place of youthful companies—embers red and shining, that was our forge at the first.

Teach luighe ar lochta samhla,
uinivers na healadhna,
dánbhoth ór dhoichealgtha sinn,
roicheardcha ar n-ánroth innill.

The house of reclining for such as we, the university of art, poetic cell that kept us from beguilement, this was the great forge of our trained ánruith.

[1] *Irish Review,* Jan., 1913.

Teach breithibh gach gréasa gloin
an treas tech dar ttrí cceard-
    choibh,
ór lia snáth féithleannta fis,
'nar ghnáth éincheardcha an
    oiris.

The house of the critic of each
fine work of art was the third
house of our three forges, which
multiplied the clinging tendrils
of knowledge, wherein the very
forge of science was wont to be.

Trí rómha a ngabhmaois grádha,
trí ceardchadha congmhála
do dhreamuibh dile re dán,
tighe ceanguil na gcompán.

Three sanctuaries wherein we
took rank, three forges that sustained the loving companies of
artists, houses that bound comrades together.

Beannocht leó a los a saoire,
dronga ar nár cheisd cruadh-
    laoighe
an coimhthionál dar chóir searc,
doircheadhán dóibh nír dhoir-
    cheacht.

A blessing on them for their
nobility, men to whom hard
poems were no perplexity: that
gathering worthy of love, dark
verse was to them no darkness.

Ba haithghearr eatorra sin
lá earraigh, aghaidh gheimhrigh:
an lucht téarnó do-ní a-nois
mí don éanló 'na n-éagmhois.

In their midst a spring day or a
winter's night was brief: lacking
them those who have escaped
make a month now of a single
day.

Ionnsa an t-anshaothar orra,
nach fuighid fir fhoghloma
gréas snáthsholas na suadh nglan,
dar dhual fáthfhoras focal.

Hard is their toil when men of
learning find not the bright-
threaded artistry of illustrious
scholars, to whom belonged the
mystic import of words.

Dursan an taobh dhá dtáinig
a mhoille thrá thionáilid;
fatha sgaoilidh na sgoile
Gaoidhil Macha ag moghsoine.

Woe to the quarter whence came
their slackness in meeting together! The cause of the dis-
persion of the school is that the
Gaels of Macha are in bondage.

A noble poem, rising up mightily to verses 9 and 10—one that
must surely have brought tears in the disastrous aftertime to
the eyes of those who had studied in these schools or come
intimately to know of them. Even to-day, in our very different
world, after giving them even such shallow study as we here
have done, one does not listen to this nameless voice unmoved.
Or do I deceive myself? Do I also deceive myself in thinking
that such a poem illuminates our subject, that Clanricarde's
description, even when helped out by such other particulars

89

as we have added, needs just such an enkindling light as this to heighten our curiosity to that warmth of feeling through which alone we may see into the life of things? . . . . One other poem we will give. In a different mood, another poet, Eochaidh Ó Heóghusa, brings us to feel with him and his fellows on finding their occupation gone: I take the liberty of transcribing Professor Bergin's version, translation and notes, except such as are purely linguistic:

On a Change in Literary Fashions

The following poem was written in 1603. Its date is fixed by the reference to the visit to England of Rudhraighe Ó Domhnaill, when he got the title of Earl of Tyrconnell.

The author was the celebrated Eochaidh Ó Heóghusa, sometime poet to the Maguires of Fermanagh. He deals in a good-humoured manner with the effect upon men of letters of the convulsions of society. The downfall of the Gaelic aristocracy had deprived men like him of the educated audience they had been trained to please. Henceforth they might win a precarious living by competing with strolling singers. It was as if a poet laureate had to seek engagements at a music-hall. A contemporary poet treats the same theme with bitter sarcasm: "A vulgar doggerel—'soft' vocables with which it is all-sufficing that they but barely be of even length—concoct such plainly, without excess of involution, and from that [poor literary] form shall thy promotion be the greater."—(O'Grady, Cat., p. 393.) Though Ó Heóghusa defies anyone to fail to understand him, now that he appeals to the groundlings, I confess that two or three lines of this poem are obscure to me.

The text is from MS. 6131-33 in the Bibliothèque Royale, Brussels.

Osborn Bergin.[1]

Ionmholta malairt bhisigh:
  tárraidh sinne 'san amsa
iomlaoid go suarrach sona,
  do-chuaidh a sochar dhamhsa.
	A change for the better is to be commended: I have found at this time an exchange poor but fortunate, which has turned out profitable for me.

Do thréig sinn sreatha caola
  foirceadal bhfaobhrach ffrithir
ar shórt gnáthach grés robhog,
  as mó as a moltar sinde.
	I have abandoned the delicate series of keen and earnest admonitions for a common sort of easy art which brings me more praise.

---

[1] cf. *Studies,* December, 1918.

Le dorchacht na ngrés snoighthe
   do bhínnse ag tuilliodh gráine:
fa hí ughachta mhóráin
   nár   dhíol   róghráidh   ar
   ndáinne.

By the obscurity of carven ornament I used to earn disgust:
many protested that my verse
was unworthy of favour.

Maithim, giodh mór an sonas,
   énbhonn feasda dá thoradh,
má théid énrand gan tuigse
   dom   dhánsa   ó   dhuine   ar
   domhan.

Henceforth, though great is the
luck, I renounce a single groat of
the profit thereof, if one stanza
of my poetry passes the understanding of anyone in the world.

Dán bog ar bhél na slighiodh,
   ós é anois sirthior oraind,
cuirfeadsa dhíom na fiacha
   go   ccead   d'iarla   Chlann
   gConaill.

Free and easy verse on the open
road!—since that is what is asked
of me, I will discharge the debts,
by the leave of the Earl of Tyrconnell.

Mo gheallsa ar bhuga ar mhaoile
   ní   bhérdaois   daoithe   an
   bheatha:
do-chuaidh mé, maith an tuisci,
   le cách fá uisge an cheatha.

The dunces of the world would
not beat me in softness and art-
lessness: I have gone out in the
rain like the rest—a wise course.

Do thréig mé—gá mó sonas?—
   mo shlighthe docra diamhra:
dá ccluine cuid dar ndáinne,
   beanfaidh gáire as an iarla.

I have abandoned—what greater
luck? — my hard mysterious
ways: if he hear some of my
verse it will make the Earl
laugh.

D'eagla mo chora as gárda
   ón mhéid dá ttárras loise,
diúltaimse flath ó gConaill
   do dhol oraind a ccoisde.

Lest I be put out of the protection of those from whom splendour was won (?), I refuse to let
Tyrconnell's prince go upon a
jury to try me.

Is iomdha tré dhán bhfallsa
   lán dom annsacht a mbliadhna:
do thuillfinn tuilleadh ceana
   muna bheith eagla an iarla.

Through bad verse many a one
is full of love for me this year:
I would earn more affection but
for my fear of the Earl.

Mac Aodha, aigneadh fosaidh,
   fear ler robhog ar ccruaidhne,
ní cás dúinn dénamh tapaidh,
   ó tharla a Saxaibh uainne.

Aodh's son, the sober-minded, a
man who found my hard (verse)
very soft, it is easy for me to be
brave now that he is away in
England.

Beag nach brisiodh mo chroidhe
   gach dán roimhe dá gcumainn:
is mór an t-adhbhar sláinte
   an nós sa táinig chugainn.

Every poem I composed hitherto
used almost to break my heart:
this new fashion that has come to
us is a great cause of health.

Dá lochtaighe triath Bearnais
   énrand dá ndealbhthor linde
budh iomdha   ag   cor   'na
   aghaidh—
ionmholta malairt bhisigh.

If the chief of Bearnas find fault
with any quatrain that is made by
me, there will be many opposed
to him: a change for the better
is to be commended.

VII

These four poems are all from the one period: they breathe
of an old and deep-rooted culture, of long ages of slowly-
maturing thought and patiently-mellowing art. One might
deduce from them that not alone were the bardic schools
academic, taking pride in their aloofness, but that over against
them was somewhere a rebellious spirit. Everything about the
schools—their cult of secrecy, of tradition; their power to
assuage, to excite, to wound; their security, the rivalry
between them—all were of a nature to induce satire, either
bitter or humorous. One could hardly credit the whole tale, if
such a rebellious spirit, native to man, had not left us its
testimony. That fine old story, *Imtheacht na Tromdháimhe*,
is part of that testimony. In it we find the bards, their poems,
their literary language, their pride, their whims, all mocked
and brought to nothing in loud laughter. One wonders if the
Gael ever made any other story so racy of himself. It is more
Gaelic than *Deirdre*, for that story, in common with the tale
of Troy, and indeed every other great tragedy ever written,
has for its chapters—Beauty, Desire, Love, Death—moves,
that is to say, in the vast yet simple regions of man's heart, and
not amid the ramifications of his institutions: with these
comedy nurtures itself, later to exhibit itself most surprisingly
and most takingly when, with malicious relish, with a smack-
ing of the lips, it has swallowed down and digested these same
institutions. Comic satire coming fully home only to those who
are acquainted with the mode of life (and letters) that is
laughed at, we savour the rich marrow of this witty tale of
Guaire the Generous only inasmuch as we have made our own

of the institutions of the Gael. Here are Kings and petty Kings. Here are Hermits and Saints. Here is the College of Bards, or rather one College of Bards, processioning from Court to Court, breaking those they feed upon. Here are Harpers, Timpanists, Storytellers, and the obligations of *geasa*. And above all, here is the Gael's dread of satire—that trait which is over all our literature and history. The comic spirit had gulped them all down, had smacked its lips over them, before this tale emerged from its brain, so cruel yet so wise. The story, then, is of the nature of that literature that does not arise among a people until that people has institutionalised its manners and customs. It is a comedy of manners; it is, with the vast difference that constantly surprises us when we try to equate the Gaelic world with the European, it is our *"Les Précieuses Ridicules,"* it is our *"Les Femmes Savantes."* Lustier, as befits an early tale, than these, its action moving across whole countrysides instead of within ladies' chambers, rougher even, it is for all that essentially the same in theme— satire not on culture, not on poetry, but on pedantry, on the mechanics of culture, inasmuch as these threaten to kill culture's real self. "It is a satire upon the satirists, and is severe enough to have produced the traditional 'three blisters of reproach' on the faces of the entire Bardic Assembly."[1] There must have been many such tales; every age must have fashioned its own variation, and every countryside must have had its own favourite among them; and one is glad of it all; for because of it we may know how alive those bardic schools were, how deep their foundations, how beloved of the people, for, as Turgenev, who was never wrong in his reading of the heart, pointed out, we laugh at those we love.

·   ·   ·   ·   ·   ·

VIII

To make an end: The bardic school, snug in a quiet glen, was clustered about a poet, who was bard to a provincial King

---

[1] See *Guaire,* the modernised version of the Tale.

or to a King of one of the hundred States into which the land was divided. To the school students gathered in the autumn, coming from far distances. They brought their local dialect with them, to be weaned from it, in time, and made adept in the literary language that all the scholarship of Ireland was preserved in. The head teacher often accompanied his patron on his visits to the Kings of the other States, and on such journeys the flock of students followed him, meeting other Colleges of Bards in debate and in rivalry. Everywhere they went they found the self-same literary language awaiting them, and they knew that the treasures of that language, the sagas, the later romances, the Ossianic poems, the mass of bardic poems, the genealogies, the official history, would be as familiar to the other students they fell in with as they were to themselves. And since the learned classes sat at the same table as the Kings and nobles, and since those Kings and nobles had themselves, in all probability, gone through the schools, the discussions on literature, on poetry, on history, were not, we may be sure, confined alone to the students and professors. The number of such schools was large, the number of professors large, great their pride of place, ample their privileges, honourably esteemed their work, lavishly rewarded. And the endeavour, undestroyed, hardly interrupted by the wars or the forays, went on and on for hundreds and hundreds of years. If a great literary tradition did not result, so widespread that in course of time it must have touched every active, every unclouded mind in the community—if this did not result, then the whole endeavour was but an expense of spirit in a waste of shame—a thought that is unthinkable.

CHAPTER IV

THE COURT OF POETRY

Now again we are in the eighteenth century. . . . . I raise my eyes, I peer into the shimmering distance. Along the sky-line of the far-off hills, I look for a clump of trees, gapped in the middle. A hundred motley fields of roots, of pasture and corn, lead up to it; and set haphazard among these fields, clutching them together, grouping them, are thriving farmsteads with trees and hay-barns—a homely landscape, its slope, its thoughts, its heart, one would surely think, set always upon this neighbouring city of Cork, its natural centre; centre, too, for many other places, larger and much farther away. Hidden in that far-off clump of trees are the white walls of a tiny hamlet, Whitechurch by name. To the left, as I look, lies Blarney, and near-by runs the road to Dublin. . . . . For me, to gaze thus into that trembling distance, where the little wind-swept hamlet, trees and all, fades into the light of the sky, is to sink softly, and with, perhaps, some gathering wistfulness, into the Gaelic world of the eighteenth century.

I

With the flight of the Earls after the disaster of Kinsale, the main prop of the bardic schools was broken. Nevertheless, those four poems that we have been reading, some of them written long after Kinsale, are bardic poetry composed in true bardic metres, those metres that were the dearest interest of those immemorial schools. These poems, clearly enough, tell

95

us what was happening. However, even for half a century after Kinsale, many big Gaelic houses, as well as many big Old-English houses—houses that were thoroughly Irish in all except name—remained unbroken; and within them and about them, life flowed on in the channels that the Gael for a thousand years had been digging for it. At the same time, they were all slowly becoming less Gaelic. The old lord, the chief, would die; and his heir would be less learned, that is to say, less Gaelic than he. What Keating wrote on the death of Seán Óg Mac Gearailt (Fitzgerald),

"Do sgaoil gach scoil toisc an bháis seo"
("Every school was scattered because of this death"),

was being written by many other poets in many other places. It was not always death, however, that overthrew one or many schools in a countryside; it was often a turning of the patron to English fashions, for " Seán O'Dwyer " had been worsted in the " game." In 1641 came the Rising, and eight years later, arrived Cromwell, and the schools, already dying, were tumbled precipitately down in the welter of slaughter, transportations, and confiscations. Yet, in spite of all, the Gaelic spirit was not killed. Forty years after, at the Restoration, there was a sudden spontaneous renewal of Gaelic energy—Dáibhidh Ó Bruadair's verses, more especially his *Triumph of Tadhg,* witness to it—which makes us aware how Gaelic the country as a whole still was beneath the surface of things. This revival lasted only a few years, the Williamite wars quenching it. Then followed the long agony of the penal days. So that, notwithstanding this brief revival that brightens a few out of the many dark and bitter pages of Ó Bruadair, we may say that ever since the disastrous surrender at Kinsale, the Gael had been " stepping down."

The astonishingly slow rate of this stepping down may be accounted for by three characteristics of the schools. To take them in turn: (1) The bardic school, as we have seen, was grouped about a person: the chief poet was the school, not the sheltered hut or chieftain's hall. Human bodies are frail tenements, yet in every age imperial civilisers have found them more difficult to break than castles of stone. When the stone walls of the castles were blown to fragments, when their lords were fled over the seas, the poets, though greatly put out, of course, remained; and consequently the schools remained. (2) The bardic school, as we have also seen, existed apart from the Church, unlike the Continental university. In two ways, when misfortune swooped upon them, this latter characteristic helped them to live on. The Church in Ireland had long before taken to Continental ideas of what the institutional meant, induced thereto by the advent from abroad of the great religious orders, the Franciscans, the Dominicans and others, who very soon after their arrival began to erect spacious abbeys and monasteries, each a very centralised and elaborate institution, Continental rather than Gaelic in the type of mind it expressed. After some centuries when, at last, its abbeys were destroyed, and its learning flung out upon the roads, the Church found itself shiftless and dismayed. The bardic schools, with their deep-rooted feeling for Latin, if not also for Greek, then found themselves, shattered and changed though they were, gradually called on to fulfil a new purpose: in the penal days they became the unofficial seminaries of the Church. By unpremeditated steps, although still a purely lay institution, they became a helpmate of the Church; and in return, again without premeditation, the Church became a helpmate of theirs. It was a good thing, in the end, for the Church, that its future priests, while they sat learning their Greek and Latin, should become at the same time saturated with the Gaelic learning which still, as always, held first place in the affections of the schools. All the evidence shows that this new function was undertaken. The number of priests who were themselves poets is very striking: Keating, that great soul, is now remembered as poet and historian rather than as priest; Blessed Oliver Plunket, that most sterling of martyrs, at least wrote some verses in the mode of the schools; the poems of Fr Pádraigín Haicéad have been gathered into a book; the songs of Fr Liam Inglis, after two centuries, are found to-day in newly-gathered anthologies of Irish poetry; Fr Eoghan Ó Caoimh (O'Keeffe) is another poet whose light two centuries of neglect have not quenched; while not alone was Fr Nicholas O'Donnell a writer of verses, but he seems to have presided at times over the School, or Court, of Poetry that assembled at Croom, in County Limerick. Many other poet-priests could be named; and then outside these we have the large number of priests whom we know of through the poets they associated with. On hearing of the death of Eoghan Ruadh Ó Súilleabháin—poor drunken wastrel as he was—it was a priest who exclaimed: " I would rather the best priest in the diocese were dead," and we may gather from the saying how much this fellow-feeling, forged in early manhood, must have meant for the poets. Between parish priest, fearful for his flock, and strolling schoolmaster-poet, with his wild ways, there often arose bickering, and sometimes open war, as we know, yet on the whole the priests protected the poets when all other patrons had failed, and did so entirely for the reason that they themselves were learned in the same Gaelic lore. This good thing happened because the bardic schools, broken down though they were, were now the only institutions left where youths could be initiated into the classical languages: needless to say, their fulfilling of this need was of itself sufficient reason for their existence. How curiously it had come about, then, that for the reason that they had never become Church institutions, had never swapped their native for European traditions, those schools in the end were able to assist the Church in its distress!

In one other way the lay character of the schools helped them to live on. In the stress of the penal times a large number of the richer Catholic families, to save their lands, went over to Protestantism. At that time Irish Protestantism, less in touch with England, was not nearly so anti-Irish as it afterwards became; and that many of those families should continue, after their change of religion, still to patronise the schools of poetry in their district caused no surprise; yet naturally it was a thing that could not happen if the schools in the people's imagination were regarded as Church and not lay institutions. In these two ways, then, the fact that the university system among the Gaels, if we may so speak of it, was not connected with the Church, helped this Gaelic institution to survive, in some fashion or another, when all their other institutions had been swept away in many wars.

The third characteristic that helped to prolong the life of the schools was their feeling for poetry rather than prose. We have seen that even at this time, the seventeenth century, the Gaels had not learned to look upon prose as an art-form. Prose, as opposed to poetry, concerns itself with the civic life of man, with the institutions he sets up to carry on the business of life. Had prose assumed among the Gaels of the seventeenth century the place we now think naturally due to it, Lecky's story of Ireland in the next century would come near being the whole truth, instead of being, as it is, superficial and partial. For the Gaels would have ceased to write at all (as Lecky appears to have imagined they did), their civic institutions having ceased to exist, and the ritual of their daily life become impoverished almost to the primitive. But their soul remained, and poetry, the language of the soul, was needed to express it. Indeed it may be that the vast distress in striking it quickened that soul into a new urgency of declaring itself, of uttering its cry. When the men of the world's armies, in the Great War, went down into the agony of the trenches, so flinging off the multiple institutions that had all along regulated, more than they themselves were aware, their daily and even hourly existence, the new thoughts that began to stir and awaken in their souls yearned for a new mode of expression, a way that was not prose, which, they instinctively felt, would not serve their needs—and yearned in vain. It was for the intensity of poetry that their unwonted sensations longed; but it was only of the form of prose—mould for a less glowing metal—that they had command. For two whole centuries our people were, we may say, down in the trenches, suffering so deeply that they oftentimes cried out that God had forsaken them: their souls were therefore quick with such sensations as must find utterance in poetry or none. Fortunately for their needs, it was of verse-form that they had the better command. As long as there was this natural desire for poetry, there was, of course, a place for the schools that taught the craft of it.

The national life, as Mrs Green has shown us, being bound together by a national literature, depending indeed for its existence on that literature, it was natural for such people to think much of schools of literature; only, however, for those characteristics that we have been dwelling upon—(1) the schools being grouped about an individual, not about a particular place; (2) their being independent of the Church; (3) their being academies of poetry and not technological institutes—it seems impossible that they should have continued their work into a new world, a world so much the opposite, it would appear, to that which first threw them up as a visible blossoming of the ecstasy of life. Their part in the dark winter that overtook the nation was to save the Gaelic mind from extinction; and that part they fulfilled. Yet any " wise " man in almost any age would have counselled them to throw off each and every one of those characteristics! But " God's counsel concerning virgin Erin at every time is greater than can be told."

II

As has been said, the bardic schools shut their doors about the middle of the seventeenth century. What happened then? Here and there the poets who had presided over them maintained, as best they could, though, of course, in an informal and irregular way, the real business of the school, the teaching of history and of the craft of poetry. Though broken down, and often lacking any patron whatever, many of those schools must have for long years after followed the old traditions. Young men still sought them out from a distance for the one purpose of winning Gaelic learning: received into them, they were, as before, trained in the old metres; as before, made familiar with the genealogies of the ancient Gaelic families, though the chiefs of those families were now either wandering exiles in European cities, or dispossessed and often poverty-stricken mourners amid their own fields. Every year, however, sapped the strength of the old features. Patronage failed more and more, and in the end the poet-professor had often to learn a new trade, if he were to live. The school then became less and less a school for poetry, and more and more a school for the humanities in general. Noting this, and irked at its happening, the poets contrived to have meetings among themselves, where poetry alone might be discussed and recited. For these meetings they used the word *cúirt* (court), and the idea of judge and judgments is always present whenever we find them referring in their poems to such gatherings. The presiding poet is usually spoken of as Sheriff, and sometimes as High Sheriff; and it was on his summons that the others attended. This High Sheriff, it should be understood, earned his living in the day-time by ploughing in his own or another's fields, by schoolmastering, or by keeping a tavern. The Court assembled sometimes in one of the local Big Houses, the owners thus giving a sort of intermittent patronage to the poets; sometimes in the Sheriff's own house—if they had any —and at other times at a *lios* or some other historic spot in the neighbourhood. As the century went by, the poets becoming poorer and the Big Houses less and less Gaelic, the Court had nowhere to assemble in except the tavern.

Their own nobility having vanished, and the ceremonies of their own Church having become despoiled, through fear and poverty, of its native grandeur of ritual, of colour and music, the only imposing institution with which the people came at all into contact was the law-court: with the law and its forms they then began to associate all ideas of ceremony, judgments and authority. How significant and pathetic is that English phrase that we find towards the end of Cathal Buidhe's[1] poem

---

[1] See *Céad de Cheóltaibh Uladh*, by Enrí Ó Muirgheasa, for an account of this poet—Cathal Buidhe Mac Giolla Gunna.

of repentance! The last assize in Jehosaphet is not to be free from the phraseology of the English courts! On that dread day:

Cuirfidh mé cré an dá'r éag,
agus glacfar é dar ndóigh
Ar a' ndúil is go ndéarfaidhe
'láthair Dé:
He's not found guilty, my Lord!

I will send up the Creed of the
Twelve (apostles), and surely
it will be accepted,
In the desire that it should be
said in God's presence:
He's not found guilty, my Lord!

That other legal quip, the English word " Whereas," became for them a word of power: previously the summoning-together of a bardic school was spoken of as a *gairm-scoile,* a *school-call,* but in the eighteenth century the *gairm-scoile* which brought together a Court of Poetry was consistently enough called a Warrant; and it usually began with this word of power, " Whereas."

The meeting of the Court was generally made to fall in with some local event—a fair, a marriage, a " pattern " or an important funeral—indeed, with any occasion that would bring the people together from their distant countrysides.

Thus summoned, thus assembled, what took place in the Court? Presided over by the most famous poet of the district, who always took great pride in his authority, the poets read—recited, perhaps, is the better word—or sang such verses as they had composed since the previous meeting. Those verses were nearly always written on current events, as was the Gaelic fashion; and however petty or local the event, as a theme it had at least the merit of being fresh in the minds of all present: yet we may surmise that it was not the theme that was discussed so much as the art of the poet. True to the tradition, the dearest study of those men was still the technique of verse; the question of technique is, however, among artists, largely one of precedents; and so at every meeting the great names of the dead were sure to be evoked, now by those on one side, and then by those on the other. A poet of the sixteenth century, Fear Flatha Ó Gnimh, rebukes a brother-poet for the light-hearted way in which he set to his versifying

—"without a dark hut, without hardship"—and brings up against him the practice of the men of old—Donnchadh Mór Ó Dálaigh (13th century), Gilla Brighde Mac Con Midhe (13th century), Aónghus Ruadh Ó Dálaigh (13-14th century), "Sgolb" Ó Dálaigh, Eoghan Mac Graith (15th century), Gofraidh Fionn Ó Dálaigh (14th century) and Tadhg Óg Ó Huiginn (15th century), "whose face (whilst in the making of a lyric) was wont to be washed by its own drops."[1]

The Gael had had to take, in learning, as in everything else, many a step down since Ó Gnimh wrote these words to his friend, yet the spirit in which they were written lived on in the Courts of Poetry. The poets still held by tradition; it was part of their trade to make copies of older manuscripts; they were, moreover, as we know from their own lips, poignantly aware that it was only the best-wrought of their own verses that would survive to posterity—it would seem, then, that matter very similar to this of Ó Gnimh's poem must have been frequently listened to in these haphazard and informal gatherings to which the bardic schools had shrunken. Like Ó Gnimh, the poets of the Courts tested the new by the old, rebuking the rebellious with the actual achievements of the years of established laws. But youth was not always tongue-tied; then, as ever, it knocked at the door, sometimes peremptorily, it is likely; and so life, which is little else than contention, was served. That it was so is certain; and one is glad of it; for as discussion in these assemblies quickened, they surely lost reckoning of the great change that had overtaken their land and race; they became one with a brighter and stronger and fuller past, and were, for the moment at least, less aware of their own straitened fortunes and dismal outlook. Their voices deepened and their hearts warmed. Whatever else they were, they were adepts in their own tongue; they were steeped in literature; they were given to extemporizing, witty, too, so that those Courts of theirs cannot have lacked for spirit: they were workmen discussing their own craft, one

---

[1] See *Studies* (June 1920), for this charming, lightly-handled poem.

of the greatest in the world, discussing it with energy, an energy all the heartier inasmuch as there was nothing else in their lives for their creative thoughts to settle upon. One is glad to be assured of all this, to know that at least of an odd night, they shut away all that lay outside the walls of the tavern—the poverty, the unjust laws, the lawlessness of their rulers, the desperation of an overtried peasantry, the detested bailiffs. One thinks of the life of the spirit renewing itself in the withered faces of the older poets as the music of verse once more laid its spell upon them; and then one pictures, too, the faces of the younger men introduced among them from time to time—their swift eyes, their astonishment at the vast learning opened out to them,—their self-questioning, their shrinking.

Besides this reciting of verse and the discussions that followed, those gatherings enabled the poets to borrow manuscripts from one another as well as to examine such manuscripts as might have been discovered since the last Court was held. They had no publishers, it must be recollected, no laws of copyright, no press, no printers: it was, therefore, in those Courts that many a famous poem was heard for the first time. They thus had their "First nights," some of which must surely have been memorable. It heartens one still to imagine an assembly of them, with their acute sense of literature, listening to Aodhagán Ó Rathaille, say, reciting his brilliant *Gile na Gile* for the first time, or Eoghan Ruadh Ó Súilleabháin one of his astonishing *aisling* poems, or Micheál Coimín his dainty re-telling of the legend of Tír-na-n-Óg. The fine glow that must have overspread the listeners' faces, lighting up their eyes, was ample recompense both to him who had written the verses, and to those others who now, as members of the Court, were privileged to hear them first of all the Gaels—ample recompense for being of the tribe of minstrels and scholars, poor and shiftless men in the eyes of the world; and in the eyes of the authorities, just common felons and preachers of sedition.

From the Court, the fame of the new poem spread out,

104

crossed here a river, and there a mountain range, reached a different parish, another county. Copies were made of it. It was bound up into many a " duanaire," set side by side with poems written, perhaps, hundreds of years before: in the wider aspect it had become a portion of the national treasury of song; in the narrower, it had become a comforting richness in many a lonely heart, a secret jewel that the mighty ones could not wrest from them.

The metres of the songs, as well as the matter in them, shrunk under the hard fortunes that had overtaken the schools. The famous classical metres, needing more training than was now to be had, gradually fell into disuse, though broken poems were to be occasionally written in them down to the close of the century. For metres to take their place the poets now went to the songs of the people: from being despised of the poets, those *amhrán,* or song, metres were now to become their glory. This, however, did not come about without many a protest from such of the remaining bards as still felt themselves able to work in the old metres: in the using of popular song metres they saw only downfall and ignorance. We have already heard one of them making such a cry: " Ionmholta malairt bhisigh " (" A change for the better is to be commended "). A hundred years later, showing how stubbornly the old tradition clung to life, we find Andrew MacCurtin complaining to James MacDonnell of Kilkee that he has had to frame " a left-handed, awkward ditty of a thing, but I have had to do it, to fit myself in with the evil fashion that was never practised in Eirinn before, since it is a thing that I see, that greater is the respect and honour every dry, scant-educated boor, or every clumsy *baogaire* of little learning, who has no clear view of either alliteration or poetry, gets from the noblemen of the country than the courteous, very-educated shanachy or man of song, if he compose a well-made lay or poem."[1] From Dáibhidh Ó Bruadair, a little earlier, in 1692, we hear the self-same accents. Beginning by saying that

---

[1] Douglas Hyde, *Literary History of Ireland.*

105

his heart is broken that correctly-written verse is no more to be found, he goes on to complain that knowledge is now so corrupt in Corc's land (Munster) that nothing but vulgar poetry is understood.

Such protests notwithstanding, the looser *amhrán* (song) metres of the people established themselves in the Courts of Poetry; and all the living verse of the century was to be written in them. But they underwent a change, for the skill that lingered in the Courts began to play upon them, to transform them; and they soon became inwrought with delicate cadences, with finely modulated assonances, with bewildering alliterative music.

Such, then, in brief, was the way of the Courts of Poetry. Only a shadow of the bardic schools, from which they derived, they were for all that as intimately part of their own time as those were of theirs.

In Clanricarde's account of the bardic schools we had a description of them from without, and this we enriched with the music of certain chance poems of the bards themselves. Of the Courts of Poetry, however, we have, unfortunately, no outside and prosaic description on which to base the many passing references we find in the verses of the poets who frequented them.

Acquaintance with the nature of the bardic schools, out of the death of which the Courts grew up, enables us in some measure to supply this want, to interpret these references, as also indeed to make something of those very curious " warrants " which the poets sent to one another when another sitting of the " Court " was at hand. Those " warrants " were often filled with banter, and, if one did not keep in mind that they were not intended for the uninitiated, that indeed they went intimately from friend to friend, sometimes from one boon companion to another, that their modern equivalent would be an invitation card, say, of an artists' club, intimately freakish, one might easily be misled by them into an underestimation of the place those Courts held in the poets' affections.

If those Courts of Poetry did no more, at a time when seventy per cent. of the population of England could not read their own language,[1] they maintained among the common people the idea of the humanities; so that when Eibhlín Dubh, in 1773, more than one hundred years after the downfall of the bardic schools, used the word "scoil" (school) in her keening, everyone knew what she referred to. Those Courts of Poetry and their works, were, of course, just as much the visible blossoming of the ancient literary tradition as were the bardic schools in earlier and happier times. It was that tradition, stubbornly resisting dissolution, that had moulded the form of the bardic schools into such a shape as the new times could not reject as an institution disparate to their spirit. It was that tradition which, still convinced that poetry was essential to noble living, brought about this transition from Bardic School to Court of Poetry, thus perpetuating the craft of poetry, thus assigning still to learning the dignity of the institutional when the very idea of the institutional must have all but vanished from the minds of the hard-pressed people. By so dignifying the idea of poetry, it stifled protest when young and hearty men gave their days to the writing of it or to the copying of manuscripts; at the same time it prevented many a patrician family from turning their backs on Gaelic learning when they had deserted the Gael's faith.

The Courts of Poetry were thus the institutional expression, however threadbare and famished, of what one of the poets of the time, Andrew MacCurtin (fl. 1718-43), put into bardic metre: "Although rich men of herds, merchants, or people who put out money to grow, think that great is the blindness and want of sense to compose a *duan,* or poem, they being well satisfied if only they can speak the Saxon dialect, and are able to have stock of bullocks or sheep, and to put redness (*i.e.,* of cultivation) on hills—nevertheless, it is by me under-

---

[1] Mary Hayden and George Moonan, *A Short History of the Irish People.*

stood that they are very greatly deceived, because their herds and their heavy riches shall go by like a summer fog, but the scientific work (meaning a well-made poem) shall be there to be seen for ever."[1]

A literary tradition that in so bitter a day could throw out such words as these, so earnest with conviction—one can understand how it could not, without a sense of horror, contemplate a future in which there would be no schools of poetry, no " sons of learning." In these words the race, and not an individual, utters itself, for in every succeeding decade of the century, we may find MacCurtin's faith expressed anew, though no more, perhaps, in the difficult metres of the bards. About the time he died, Eoghan Ruadh Ó Súilleabháin was born. He is one of our greatest lyric poets, far greater than at present we conceive—yet in the catalogue of men, Lecky would have found him written down a farm-labourer, a *spailpín*, and would have rested on the description; and indeed it is not otherwise than as a *spailpín* that he writes to his friend Séamas Mac Gearailt (James Fitzgerald) asking him to put a handle in his spade. That request, however, he chooses to put into lyric form, swelling it out with a full breath, with music, with gesture, with headlong and conscious mastery:

Iar gcaitheamh an lae má's tréith nó tuirseach mo chnámha,	At the close of day, should my limbs be tired or sore,
Is go n-abrann an maor nach éachtach m'acfuinn ar ráin,	And the steward gibe that my spade-work is nothing worth,
Labharfad féin go séimh ar eachtra an bháis,	Gently I'll speak of Death's adventurous ways
Nó ar chathaibh na nGréig 'san Trae d'fhúig flatha go tláith.	Or of Grecian battles in Troy, where princes fell!

" Labharfad féin go séimh " (" I myself will gently speak ") —as if he said: " I will put off the *spailpín*, the earth-delver, and assume my own self, the poet"!

---

[1] Douglas Hyde's translation of some verses by Andrew MacCurtin. (*Literary History of Ireland*, 546.) Cf.: " Greece was; Greece, except in the words it spoke, is not," Carlyle, *The Hero as Poet*.

In evolving the Courts of Poetry, in maintaining them, the literary tradition of the Gaels did its utmost to ensure that its legatees should, at least on occasions, assume their higher selves, their fuller humanity, should put off the mere delver of the earth, should raise themselves, should extend themselves to the contemplation of the adventurous ways of Death, or to the vision of the burning towers of Ilium. . . . . It is a story without an equal in the history of literature.

III

That little hamlet, Whitechurch, on the far-off wind-swept hilltop, brings all that story back to the mind of anyone who knows the history of the place; for to its keeping was transferred the bardic school of the MacCarthys of Blarney, when Blarney itself had become a ruin, a dwelling-place for wolves, as Aodhagán Ó Rathaille said; bartered from hand to hand, as Father Connor O'Brien said, both poets of that time. To trace, then, swiftly, the story of the Court of Poetry which lingered in that countryside so far into the century, is to learn what, in the same years, was also happening in other districts.

The shanachies reckoned the MacCarthys the senior clan of the Gaels: it is in very fact among the oldest of European families, if not the very oldest, as has been asserted. Blarney was one of their dwelling-places; the famous castle there was built by one of them, Cormac MacCarthy, in the fifteenth century. The bardic school which from time beyond counting they had supported, would answer to such ideas of those institutions as we have gained from our study of them. As we might then expect, it ceased to exist in the middle of the seventeenth century.

The families of the O'Dalys and the O'Dinneens had furnished poets and historians for centuries to the MacCarthys; and their last official poet seems to have been named Tadhg Ó Duinnín. When the end was come we find him writing:

Mo cheárd ó mheath le malairt dlighe i nÉirinn, Mo chrádh go rach gan stad le bríbhéireacht.

My craft being withered with change of law in Ireland, O grief that I must henceforth take to brewing!

To which a poet of Duhallow, Eoghan Ó Caoimh by name, made answer:

A Thaidhg, ó bhraithim go rachair le bríbhéireacht, Raghad-sa sealad ag bearradh gach cíléara.

O Tadhg, understanding that you are for the brewing, I for a space will go skimming the milk! [1]

If Tadhg Ó Duinnín did not actually take to the brewing, he did actually become a farmer, or perhaps it may be more correct to say, he retired to his farm, for it is not probable that it was only then he came to acquire some property. More curious the after-story of his friend. On the death of wife and child, he turned to religion, and died parish priest of Doneraile in 1726.

Tadhg Ó Duinnín taking to the plough, the Bardic School of Blarney, Dámhscol na Blárnann, was at an end. In the neighbourhood, however, a school of poetry continued to exist: and for some years the routine of studies was doubtless not very different from that formerly practised; but as time went on and the strength of the Gaels declined, one change overtook another, and gradually the bardic school became a Court of Poetry. In the beginning, before this had happened, students still came, perhaps from the very ends of Ireland, for the one purpose of learning the literature and the history of their own land. The trade of poetry was, in the imagination of the people, still as legitimate as any other. In the end, however, the Court of Poetry was frequented only by the poets of the surrounding countryside, and students came no more from other counties.

After Tadhg Ó Duinnín, we find Diarmuid MacCarthy

---

[1] *Dánta Sheáin na Ráithíneach,* edited by Professor T. O'Donoghue.

(Diarmuid Mac Sheáin Bhuidhe Mac Cárrthaigh) in charge of the school—its first unofficial chief poet. About him, then, a few words, as also about his successors in office:

Of his life not much has been made known. We find him writing poems in Blarney in 1665; and there we know he lived in the shadow of the fallen house of the MacCarthys, under whom it is probable he held some position. His brother, also a poet, became a priest and, subsequently, Bishop of Cork.

The Earl of Clancarty (MacCarthy), on the downfall of Limerick, with the thousands of others, sailed for Europe; and his going from it left Blarney a poor place for poets. Diarmuid has no longer a patron; poverty is his lot; and henceforth all his verse is an outcry over what has been, and a supplication that the heroes may yet return and heal the woes of the land. He becomes poorer and poorer. He was known to Dáibhidh Ó Bruadair, but remembering the narrowness of his horizons, as compared with the stirring scenes Ó Bruadair moved in, we easily understand why the range of his work cannot compare with his contemporary's. His one importance is that he kept the Blarney school of poetry alive, steering it into new if humbler ways when the old ways were no longer possible. His knowledge of Irish learning, gained in the bardic school, was deep, but in his poems[1] one does not come on many traces of lyrical inspiration; the verses are even and indeed often prosaic; yet, as one lingers over them, they begin to grow on one, to take on a life of their own— for they are always earnest and well-wrought. They never excite to ecstasy, but, on the other hand, one becomes assured that no touch of bathos or vulgarity will suddenly chill one's interest: in this they are in the Gaelic fashion. The metres are not bardic; inasmuch, however, as they reflect in almost every line the stir of the passing day they carry on the tradition of bardic poetry. The bards, it will be recollected, though

---

[1] *Amhrain Dhiarmada Mac Seáin Bhuidhe Mac Cárrthaigh,* edited by Professor Tadhg Ó Donnchadha (Tórna).

learned to the finger-tips in their own literature, and constantly referring to it in their poems, never actually made literature the subject of a poem, never wrote a poem on "Deirdre" or "Cúchulain" or any such theme: O'Donovan we found speaking of them as the journalists of their day. Like Mr G. B. Shaw, they may be said to have believed all great art to be journalistic. This bardic character keeps life in Diarmuid MacCarthy's verses, though it may not be the imperishable life of great art. His work mostly consists of keens on such of the MacCarthys as had died in his time. In one of these keens we come on a little list of the great bardic families; and it reminds us of our ignorance of the old Gaelic world. If the greatest poets still lived, the keener cries, only at their best could they write fitly, in golden colour, the deeds of Saerbhreatach MacCarthy from his birth to his laying in the coffin:

Ó Dálaigh is gach fáidh dá phóraibh,
Ó Duinnín 's a bhfuil díobh beó againn,
Tadhg Dall is a bhfuil ann dá shórtsan,
Is Maoldomhnaigh rug geall leis i gcómhdaibh.

O'Daly and every poet of his seed,
O'Dinneen and all of them alive,
Tadhg Dall and all that remains of his sort,
And Maoldomhnaigh who bore off the prize for "comhdaibh."

Dámhsçol Mhic an Bháird na gcómhfhocal,
Ó Maolconaire an t-oide, is Ó hEóghusa,
Clann Dáire, na fáidhe ba mhó againn,
Is clann Chraith aga raibh ceart gach eóluis.

The poet-school of the Wards of the synonyms,
O'Maolconaire the teacher, and O'Hussey,
The Clan Daire, the greatest poets we had,
And the MacGraths, who were perfect in every knowledge.

Ó's é Ó an Cháinte amháin atá beó againn
Do dhéanfadh aiste do cheapadh go cóir dhuit,
Ina gcuirfeadh síos i laoithibh, 'sis eól do,
Do ghníomhartha i ngach tír den Eóruip.

Since it is Ó an Cháinte alone that is now living,
Who could fittingly make a poem for you
In which would be written—as he well knows how—
Your deeds in every land of Europe.

In these verses we touch on that Gaelic culture which, all-in-all to these men, is only a dim-descried country, ill-known and far-away, to us, their descendants. Hecuba herself is not more distant from our affections than the Clan Daire, the Wards and the MacGraths.

In other verses of his we are suddenly in the homely countryside with himself, as when, in a passing way, he sketches for us a smith's forge with a swarm of hounds about its open door—hounds and " bards " (that is, mere strolling singers, not *filí*, not poets) and *dailtíní,* that is, " bloods "; or when he speaks of the thousands of prisoners (political, of course), in Spike Island, lacking food, drink, and bedding, and all awaiting transportation to some region unknown.

> Uireasbha bídh is dighe agus leabtha ortha,
> Ag feitheamh le triall go hiath nach feadadar.

One of his poems, *An Fhalartha Ghorm (The Grey Ambler)* is full of pathetic as well as historic interest. Since, however, it aptly illustrates a characteristic of the Courts of Poetry, it may be well to devote a section to it as soon as the chief poets who succeeded MacCarthy in the Court have been mentioned.

Diarmuid MacCarthy we know as a poet, not as anything else. It was far otherwise with his successor. Liam Mac Cairteáin (Liam an Dúna) was born in 1668, received a good education, and, while still young, served through the Williamite wars in one of King James's regiments of horse. When the wars were at an end, he settled down, farmed his lands, and, when the day's work was done, transcribed ancient manuscripts, or wrote his verses. He lived in Whitechurch, a few miles from Blarney, and it is thus that Blarney fades from the literary history of Ireland and Whitechurch comes into it. In this countryside, he was a big figure. In his youth, it was he who led the young men in their athletic contests; and the new generation of young men, watching him as, in his riper years, he ploughed his fields, thought of how he had fought at the Boyne, at Aughrim, at Limerick. They remembered, too, how, when the war was almost over, Sir James Cotter, another memorable local figure, had with a party of Jacobites fallen on a raiding party of Williamites in these homely fields, and how he had lost the fight if Liam an Dúna had not in a few hours raised the men of the place, flung them into the conflict, and saved him from destruction. Mac Cairteáin was evidently a man of some means: and it is a pity that so attractive a personality, so Gaelic in his learning, so pregnant of his time, should not yet have had his poems made available in book-form nor his story told with the fullness it deserves.

He was followed by Liam Ruadh Mac Coitir (William Cotter); and of him little is told, except that he was from Castlelyons, not many miles away. In a keen written on him by Seán na Ráithíneach (John Murphy) he is described as the sun of the poets.

This Seán na Ráithíneach then became chief of the Court. His life is barren of romance. He was born in 1700, and his editor[1] finds it difficult to account for such learning as evidently he possessed; no mention is made of his having gone abroad, and where were the schools at home? But such culture as these poets gathered and set store on was in the air of certain localities; they hardly knew themselves when or how they had come by it; it was theirs in much the same way as art-culture fell into the possession of illiterates in mediæval cities in Italy and elsewhere, illiterates who may not ever have handled books or chisels or brushes. In Seán's case, however, the puzzle is not so perplexing as with others, for he cannot have escaped coming into contact with those shanachies whom Liam an Dúna, himself a man of education and experience, must have attracted to the place while he maintained his Court in it.

Seán na Ráithíneach lived under the shelter of the MacCarthys, as poets had done, perhaps, a thousand years before; their patronage could now, however, mean little except occasional gifts and the shadow of protection. At one period

---

[1] *Dánta Sheáin na Ráithíneach,* edited by Professor Tadhg O'Donoghue.

he served them as clerk, and later as bailiff; but this he soon
threw up, with heartfelt relief. " Since I am a poet, down
through the lack of the nobles, I will run to my garden, take
spade in hand, and to the devil with bailiffing!"—as he wrote:

Ó's duine dhen dáimh sínn tá síos d'easba na dtríath,
Gan tideal i n-árd dhlighe d'fhagháil puinn eatorra riamh,
Rithfead dom' gháirdín, ránn mhínn glacfad mar riaghail,
Is cuirfeadh an bháillidheacht fá thrí i n-ainm an diabhail!

From his poems we gain some ideas of the big houses in the
district—some of them Protestant—where as poet he found
welcome; and at the same time we become aware of his
friendship with the priests of the countryside—some of whom
were poets, and all of whom were filled with the same learning
as himself. His keens tell us of the important people of the
district who had died—people who appear small indeed if we
put them side by side with those whom Diarmuid MacCarthy
had keened fifty years before. In his other poems we realise
incidentally how circumscribed his life had become: we find
him thanking one neighbour for the gift of a wig, and another
for a pair of spectacles; and a wether having been stolen from
him, he thought fit to make a long poem of it, cursing, with
fine vigour, the robber to a high gallows and a windy day:

Siolán is croch árd lá gaoithe amuigh
Is uchlán ar spreasán an ghníomha soin.

He lived quietly, ploughing his fields, writing his poems,
copying manuscripts, suffering in close union with his race.
When he died quietly in 1762, the last master of the Blarney
school of poetry was dead—a school, the annals of which,
could they now be collected, would fill a hundred volumes.
Unnoticed, with him it passed away, into some grave whose
situation is not known.

A simple, God-fearing man, he nevertheless wrote the
following verses on one David Gleeson, a bailiff, who was
stabbed in Cork in 1737—but perhaps it was his people, his
race rather than himself, who struck out these fierce lines, the

bailiff being, as we have noted, the actual scourge on the defenceless backs of the Gaels:

Sin feasta dhon dáimh cúis
  gháire is aitis le mian,
Ó cailleadh an báille bálthach
  malluighthe dian;
Maithim dhon bhás a ndearnaidh
  d'argain riamh,
Ó threascair an stráille Dáth an
  seana-bhum diabhail.

Geallaim go bráth gur féarrde
  Banba Bhriain
An scramaire thrácht don áit
  n-ar ceapadh a thriall,
Go hAcheron lán ag snámh i
  lasair na bpian;
Sin farra n-a mháighistir Dáth i
  n-ainm an diabhail.

Ba mhalluighthe a cheárd ar sráid
  le fada 's le cian,
An spreallaire d'fhág adhnáire
  trasna 'n-a dhiaidh;
An ceangal 's ag crádh na dtáinte
  pearsan gach bliadhain
Thug acharann brághad ar Dháth
  i nglasaibh an diabhail.

Do theangmhaidh do Dháth
  bheith dána falathach fiar;
Nior thaithnigh a cháil ná a
  cheárd le cealla na gcliar;
Nár chaillidh an lámh do sháith
  an t-arm 'n-a chliabh;
'S mo mhallacht 'n-a dheáidh go
  háitreabh dearbhtha an
  diabhail.

Is sultmhar le cloistin, i gCor-
  caigh 's i gceart-lár críoch,
An struilleadh 's an stolladh so
  ar cholainn an Ghlasáin
  bhuidhe;
A himeall na croiche dhá chroch-
  adh go hiomárd bhíonn,
Is tá teine ná corthar dá loscadh
  age Bhulcán tíos.

Now may the poets laugh and
  freely rejoice,
For the flat-footed, hard, ac-
  cursed bailiff is dead;
I pardon Death all the ravage
  he ever made
Since he has tripped up the lout
  David, the old devilish *bum*.

The sluggard being sent to his
  destined place,
Brian's Ireland, I promise, is
  better for ever more;
There in the devil's name goes
  David with his master,
Swimming to crowded Acheron
  in torturing flames.

Long, long accursed was his
  trade in the village,
The wretch who left a track of
  shame behind him;
Year after year binding and per-
  secuting crowds of people—
Leaves David now a captive in
  the bonds of the devil.

It was kind for David to be
  twisted, mean and rough.
Unloved his fame and his trade
  in the cells of the poets;
—May it flourish, the hand that
  plunged the steel in his
  breast;
And my curses follow him to his
  dwelling-place in hell.

Pleasant the news in Cork and
  in the district's centre,
This rending and tearing of
  yellow Gleeson's carcase,
To be hanging maimed from the
  gallows' edge,
And Vulcan with unquenching
  fire torturing him below.

The translation gives no idea of the onward savagery of the original, with its perfection of revengefulness in the last cadence, body and soul a-tortured.

IV

These, then, were the four men who inherited and passed on, as well as they were able, the traditions of the bardic school of the MacCarthys of Blarney—

> Diarmuid Mac Cárrthaigh,
> Liam Mac Cairteáin,
> Liam Mac Coitir,
> Seán Ó Murchadha (Seán na Ráithíneach).

If we now take from those written by the first of them that rather well-known poem to which we have already referred, we shall, by dwelling a little on it, get a better idea of how such a Court of Poetry gathered the poets of a countryside together, made them known to one another, and spurred them on to the writing of verse. That well-known poem is *An Fhalartha Ghorm (The Grey Ambler)*—a poem full both of historic and human interest. . . . . The poet is now an old man (he had indeed only two more years to live), and he is poor; yet neither war nor loss of wealth, he tells us in the poem, had ever beggared him as does the loss of his old grey horse. He can no more make his way over the mountains; he can no longer make the journey to Mass or to funeral. Let his friends bestir themselves or he will satirize them before the Council of Poets. If the country lacks a man to bestow a horse on a poet, woful is it for him who has been nursed in the school of the bards. The death of his ambler has left him lost to joy, to pleasure—he is like a corpse flung in a dyke to a pack of hounds.

Mar thárla marbh dá sracadh san díg ag cuain.

Far across the sea are those who would have rewarded him with horse and saddle . . . . and so once again he has happened on what had become the burden of all his songs—the nobles banished beyond the seas. It is all the plaintive voice of an old man, except the last verse, where his sorrow blazes up into an angry threat:

> Tá an saoghal so anois am chur i dteannta shíor,
> Gan réim, gan rith, is me go fann i n-aois;
> Is baoghal do'n truip muna gcuirid m'amhailse buidheach
> Gur géire me am chois ná ar ramhaireach groidhe.

The poem well illustrates the nature of all the Gaelic poetry of the time: it was written on an actual occurrence; it was written for the poet's own countryside with no thought whatever for anywhere else. It is simple, it is even quaint, yet there is never a lack of style in it. Its importance for us is, however, that it drew all the poets of the place into " contention "; it set them to sharpen both wits and quills. Those other poets were younger than the master, they were native to that new world which he was finding so strange and cold; their way of thinking was not his, and so they found it difficult to take his sorrow to heart. We can excuse them if we find their answering verses so often, with sly satisfaction, nicely poised between jest and earnest—a truly Gaelic characteristic. One of them tells him to stand on his own feet: since you have spent the candle, don't spare the butt-end. (Is mar chaithis an solus ná coigil an mionórdlach.) To this the master replies that to sit awaiting the return of those who had gone over the sea (the Wild Geese) is, for those who had known them, to find the butt-end longer than the whole candle itself. With a delightful touch, as if time had begun to take the edge off his grieving, he finishes by reminding the poet that the Falartha Ghorm had not been eaten by *crows,* as he had written, but " honourably " by *ravens* and *eagles,*—nobler birds.

> A cliabh níor luimeadh 's níor h-iteadh le fionnógaibh,
> Ach fiacha is fiolair ghá giobadh go honórach.

Seán Mac Cormaic now appears in the "contention." He sends the master some twenty lines of verse—designed in every way to please him utterly—all except one or two words, the last word of all more especially. Strongly and sorrowfully and darkly and fittingly, he writes, will each one of your scholars, on whom you bestowed your good heart (dár bhronnais do dheagh-chroidhese), make keening for you, their messenger of sorrow after war and the enemy's might. Yet, he continues, stand firm; the Earl is coming across the seas, and we will soon have tidings of you, not as a horseless poet, but as one mightily caracolling after the ruinous war. And so he makes to finish: your band (of poets) throughout Ireland are grieved, O merry champion so often in their midst, that they for long have failed to see your steed at the tavern door (and then he reproduces the master's line, all except the very last word), she being torn at by ravens and eagles and . . . . crows! (fiacha is fiolair ghá giobadh agus fionnóga), so renewing the thrust the master had already resented. It is skilfully done, this last barbed word falling into its place seemingly without cunning. Now, this poet, Seán Mac Cormaic, who had but one eye, was Registrar of the Court; and answering him, the master calls him "O grey-haired, one-eyed bard," and twits him with the powerlessness of his warrants. Then follows an exchange of verse between Liam an Dúna and the master, in the last of which we find old Diarmuid in a lovely verse speaking of himself as an Oisin-after-the-Fenians:

Ár gcuraidhe tréana léirscrios uainn tar sáil	Our mighty heroes swept from us beyond the sea
I gcoinghíoll tréith d'fhúig éigse suairce is dáimh,	It is that leaves the merry bards in straitened bonds,
Nó i gcoisidheacht mé ní léigfeadh uaisle Fáil	Else Ireland's nobles would not let me foot my road,
'S in Oisín d'éis na Féinne, is truagh mar táim.	An Oisin in the Fenian's wake, full pitiful.

Another poet tells the master that to be depending on the Earl to return is to be in a worse state than the poor wretch that the ravens have for themselves in the glen.

How many poets entered into this "contention" we cannot now say; but we may still read[1] some two hundred lines of verse written all within a few months around the loss of the old grey ambler that had kept the poor old man in touch with his kind at Mass, fair, and funeral. None of the poems is an outstanding lyric; all are, however, pleasant and very readable; and through them one enters into the very heart of that very different world which, lying within a few miles of the city of Cork according to distance, lay a whole civilisation away from it according to thought. The importance of the collection for us is that it lets us understand how those schools gathered the poets to a given theme; how thus they kept the flame alive. At the same time, it gives us the pressure of the passing moment: here are youth and age, here the last breath of a dying aristocratic past, the rougher accent, the self-trust of the democratic future. The master cannot imagine a world without poets, nor poets without patrons. The younger men are otherwise: they had never received gifts of the Earl; they had always found their living in farming or soldiering or teaching in the hedges, or as priests. We see not only youth and age in pleasant conflict; but we see a gate shutting and a gate opening. From that time onward the spirit of the poetry was to be frankly democratic. The poets knew themselves for what they were. Thus *An Fhalartha Ghorm*, the old grey ambler of our poor grey Oisin, has in course of years arrived at an importance she herself never dreamed of: she is become a book-mark in the literary history of the Gael.

Before passing from those verses, it may not be amiss once again to remark on the homogeneity of the Gaelic world to which they give admittance. How self-contained it is, how assured its notes; and its literary tradition, always the immediate jewel of its soul, how it has now become its one and only jewel! Its passion has become its refuge, as Keats said his poetry became to him when the world grew dark about him.

---

[1] See Professor O'Donoghue's finely-edited book, *Amhráin Dhiarmuda Mac Seáin Bhuidhe Mac Cárrthaigh.*

Here surely is a test case. An old man, a poet, not heard of in Cork, a city five or six miles away, suffering from a swollen knee, laments the loss of the ambler that used to bear him from place to place; others of his neighbours reply to his verses, he in turn answering them. What shall we find when, after two hundred years, we dig those verses out of the darkness? A strange self-contained peasant community, where an old man has the gift of style, in the refining of which many centuries of culture obviously have had their way: not one old man, but many young men as well, all with something of the same talent, for one and all take up the endeavour in the selfsame spirit, a theme to be played upon, to be decorated, to be enjoyed. In this strange land, the old grey ambler has no sooner died than the glow of art begins to transform her; and the glow spreads and spreads until a score of hillsides are the richer for it, the scholars are become busy with the copying of new verses into their books of poems, and the common people bright and eager in a questing beyond "nature's needs." It is this indeed, this sharing of the common people in the activities of their literary circles, that sets these peasants apart from their fellows elsewhere. Where else was to be found a peasantry making their own of a mass of poetry, not for its theme so much as for its style, and that a style Attic in its shapeliness, although for content it had but the "moving accidents" of humble men and villages?

While the Courts of Poetry held sway, such "contentions" were always arising. Of each school, or court, several such groups of poems, as this of *An Fhalartha Ghorm,* may be gleaned. Each group will differ in temper from the last, for time never stands still withal. Still greater the difference between such groups as are harvested from different soils. School differed from school, as place from place, and man from man. But, each and all, those collections of poems, so regional in their feeling and matter, are contemporary documents written in good style and with perfect integrity, ulterior motives having no part in their coloration. They are therefore unique as historical memorials of a hidden people.

121

We do not know how many of those Courts of Poetry existed in Ireland in the eighteenth century. They were, of course, far more numerous in Munster than in any other province. In Munster, Gaelic learning was most strongly entrenched; and there most toughly contested the ground against other cultures. It is strange that the self-same thing happened eight centuries before, when the Danish invasion had left Ireland "a quaking sod," to speak the language of the annalists.

The Whitechurch Court of Poetry does not adequately represent in the matter of quality the whole endeavour; indeed, every other Court we have knowledge of seems to have produced better verse; that Court of Poetry has been chosen simply for the reason that its history has been made available to us with some fullness,[1] while none of the others has yet had its history traced from poet to poet.

Perhaps the most famous of those in Munster was the school of Sliabh Luchra, the district lying between Killarney and Rathmore. Here, indeed, was the literary capital of Southern Ireland, and that poet to whom we have so often referred, Eoghan Ruadh Ó Súilleabháin hailed from it. At Rathluirc (Charleville) there was another famous Court, presided over by Seán Clárach Mac Domhnaill (MacDonnell). Not far away, in County Limerick, was Seán Ó Tuama's school, at Croom—Croom of the Merriment, as it was called. In the south, the district to the west of Youghal—the Barony—attracted poets to it from as far off as County Clare. Near-by, at Ballymacoda, lived Piaras Mac Gearailt (Pierce Fitzgerald), who was chief poet of the Court. In County Waterford, between the Comeragh Mountains and Dungarvan, was a land full of Irish scholarship and poetry. In Tipperary lived Liam Dall Ó hIfearnáin (Heffernan); and at Miltown-Malbay,

---

[1] In the two books already quoted from : *Amhráin Dhiarmuda Mac Sean Bhuidhe Mac Cárrthaigh* and *Dánta Sheáin na Ráithineach.*

Micheál Ó Coimín, who re-told the story of Tír-na-n-Óg in the most musical of verses. In the borderlands of Southern Ulster lived many poets whose poems are now being collected and published. Nobber, in County Meath, was a centre for poets. Mr Enrí Ó Muirgheasa tells us that the tradition of a school of poetry still exists in the place; and that when he tried to coax an old man to surrender a manuscript he had, he was answered: " No, I will keep it here to show that there was once learning in Nobber."[1]

There may have been Courts of Poetry in Connacht, though we have not heard of them. Poets existed there, and in the early part of the century, at least, a poet seems to have meant a school.

It is safe to say that there is not one of those schools but will yet have many books written on its history, its chief poets, its characteristics. When the story of them is told, it will be seen that in spite of all the darkness and the pain, there was a network of song laid over the land, a gleaming network, flashing brilliantly now here, now there, even as the spirit listed: acquaintance with the bright and daring or sweet and gentle strains that arose from those lonely and wind-swept and hungry hamlets makes one turn away with something like impatience from the oratory of the Dublin Parliament, impatience that its fame should for so long have hidden from us what is of deeper and more enduring worth.

In some places those Courts seem to have lingered on into the nineteenth century. In an old book[2] we come on this passage:

" The last Iomahbhaid, or Bardic Contention, known to be held in Ireland took place in Dundalk in the year 1827. There were several competitors for bardic honours, but they dropped off one by one and left the prize to be contended for by Arthur O'Murphy of Grotto Castle and James Woods, Esq., M.D."

This Bardic Contention, however, seems to have been an effort

---

[1] *Amhráin Airt Mhic Chubhthaigh,* edited by Enrí Ó Muirgheasa.
[2] " Collectanea Grahamea, or Bardic Remains of Louth," quoted from in Enrí Ó Muirgheasa's *Amhráin Airt Mhic Chubhthaigh.*

to revive a custom that had already died, seems to have had something of the antiquarian spirit in it. The real Courts of Poetry, we may be sure, faded away gently, the poets in one district after another dying out. In some hidden spot, it is likely, some long-established Court did outlive all others, not knowing itself to be the last: on some wintry night, perhaps, its few remaining old gabblers of verse rose up and bade each other good-night, thinking to meet again, thinking a vain thought. The strange thing would be if, in breaking their little gathering that night, it was given them to know that it had fallen to their humble and withered labouring hands to roll up for ever the Druidic scroll of the bards, that in closing the door that night they were leaving the " booths of the poets " to desolation for evermore: had the thought struck them one imagines they could hardly have survived the vast and lonely wailing that must have begun to re-echo in their souls.

.   .   .   .   .   .

Whether we are writing or reading such an account as this of poets and their works, the frail bodies of the men themselves, and the hard and poor ways among which they moved, little by little draw away from us, and then we are no longer alert and warm as when in the one place with living men. It would not be so if it were their own pages we were scanning: for, thanks to that idea of theirs of what was fit matter for song and poem, neither their world nor themselves would then grow dim for us. The very notes they wrote on their manuscripts are poignant with the pulse of time and place. The manuscript might have been a collection of the old-world stories of the Gael, or a treatise on grammar, or the lives of Gaelic saints, or a gathering of Irish poems—whatever it was, the chances are that in finishing it, the scribe added such an Explicit as this that Seán na Ráithíneach left behind him on some poems he had copied: " Eadarluas airneáin agus árdheifir, drochpheann agus an doircheacht as dual d'oidhche seoch lá, noch ionar scríobhas a urmhór so, fa ndeara nach biadh ní bhus sgiamhdha iná mar atá." ("The difficulty of working late, great haste, and a bad pen, as well as the darkness that is natural to night as distinguished from day, in which I wrote most of this, explain why it is not more elegant than it is.")

In other cases he begs forgiveness for faulty work, again blaming his poor gear, his working late in the night, and " the bad light." It is not difficult to see him: the old man in his miserable hut, bent earnestly upon his manuscripts, his only lamp a flickering candle of rushes, while outside the vast and silent night sits brooding on the hills. Not often, before laying aside a completed manuscript, does he forget to ask the reader to pray to God and St Patrick that his soul may be saved. . . . Scholars working on the manuscripts of the Gael in the Royal Academy in Dublin, or in the library at Maynooth, or in the British Museum, or in the far-scattered libraries of the Continent—in Salamanca, or St Gall, or Rome—or in America—might put down such a manuscript as this of the eighteenth century and take up one of the eleventh or twelfth, only to come upon the self-same prayer. Even from this almost insignificant fact we may understand how short a distance Whitechurch had strayed from the Gaelic tradition. Of how different a world was this Cromwellian-Williamite city of Cork, on the comfort and wealth of which the little Gaelic hamlet was for ever hungrily, and, perhaps, angrily, gazing down! The alien-minded city thought much of itself, was very busy with putting money in its purse; yet, now that both are such old stories, what one thinks is that it was Whitechurch rather than the city of Cork that had the seed of life within it. That unnative Cork had no past, and was destined to have no future. Its memory is not fragrant: it left no memorials; but to raise the eyes, as I do now, to that wind-swept hamlet on the far-off hillside, is to feel the heart grow warm and the pulse quicken.

CHAPTER V

THE *AISLING*

It was first the bardic schools of the previous centuries and then the Courts of Poetry, into which they declined, that had fixed the culture both of big house and cabin in the more Irish parts of the country in the eighteenth century: it was, therefore, not unnecessary to dwell a little on those institutions, since we will soon find ourselves in the presence of poets whose work is to be fully understood only in the light of that culture. That, perhaps, is the best word to use; for the literary tradition was still so strong that, in spite of the depressing poverty and hopelessness, it produced, or at least amazingly developed and perfected, a new genre in the literature. This new genre, the *Aisling,* or Vision poem, is the distinctive contribution of the period to the book of Irish literature: all the others were ancient, and had long since reached perfection. Not only was the literary tradition strong enough to do this, but it, at the same time, developed beyond what anyone could have dreamed of, the stressed metres in which those *aisling* poems were written. The theme, as it grew, called for richer and richer music, and this it was given, lavishly, sumptuously, yet without vulgarity.

On its own account, then, the *Aisling* is worth lingering on; for in those *aisling* poems we come on some of the best verse of the period; but it is still more worth lingering on inasmuch as in it we find intimate expression of the hidden life of the people among whom it flourished. Explicitly and implicitly it speaks to us, as with a golden mouth, of the Munster of those days.

Irish Ireland in the eighteenth century is not a hidden land to us merely because the older historians were either too ignorant or too disdainful to record its life: it was a hidden land in very fact. We have seen how the O'Connells wished to avoid mention in Dr Smith's forthcoming account of Kerry. No more than they did the cabin-dwellers seek a place in the sun. A rush-light, and to be let alone, were all they asked. Their fathers, themselves, had suffered so much from the authorities and their laws, that an overlooked existence had now become for them a boon. This overlooked existence is to be felt in almost every poem they made for their own solacing. Those poems tell us that they were a people on whom the gates had closed. Their art-work consists of literature and music only—arts that require little or no gear. What Romain Rolland writes is surely true: " One might even say that the plastic arts in general have need of luxury and leisure, of refined society and of a certain equilibrium in civilisation in order to develop themselves fully. But when material conditions are harder, when life is bitter, starved and harassed with care, when the opportunity of outside development is withheld, then the spirit is forced back upon itself, and its external need of happiness drives it to other outlets: its expression of beauty is changed, and takes a less external character, and it seeks refuge in more intimate arts, such as poetry and music."[1]

The mere fact, then, that the only arts they practised were poetry and music tells us that the gates were shut and the opportunity of outside development denied: and their manner of practising the arts they were confined to confirms this, if confirmation be required. In the glowing *Aisling* we find unwitting expression of the darkness that lay upon their life.

There is now no reckoning the number of *aisling* poems written in that century. I dare to say that if we had the complete works of every Munster poet who lived at any time from

---

[1] Romain Rolland, *Some Musicians of Yesterday.*

the middle of the century to its close, we would find that every one of them wrote at least one such poem. Eoghan Ruadh Ó Súilleabháin specialised in them; indeed, in this poet's district, Sliabh Luachra—roughly the border lands of Cork and Kerry towards Killarney—a young poet seeking admission to the brotherhood brought his *Aisling* in his hand: it was his thesis.

The *aisling* poems were all written in stressed metres—that is, the most literary poems of the time were written in metres that the old bardic schools had despised as unliterary, if one may use such terms. The stressed metres of the untrained poets, of the wandering ballad-singers, had now displaced the syllabic metres of the bards, had become the recognised mode of the Courts of Poetry. As already hinted, these stressed metres attained their greatest development in the *aisling* poems of the latter half of the century.

The word *Aisling* means vision; and the vision the poet always sees is the spirit of Ireland as a majestic and radiant maiden. This really is the essential feature in the *Aisling*. Of course, before the *Aisling* became recognised as a distinct genre, there were vision-poems in the language—many of them—in which the self-same spirit of Ireland appears and utters her distress and her hopes. Keating's poem, " Mo bhrón, mo cheótuirse cléibh is croidhe " (" My sorrow, my gloomy weariness of breast and heart "), is an *aisling*—as the editor of his poems very properly names it;[1] and the same poet's elegy on John Fitzgerald (died 1626) begins with a description of the sudden starting up of the singer, from a sleep that had overtaken him while wandering by the banks of the Slaney, to behold a gentle, bright, and timid maiden weeping silently in her distraction. In this case, however, the vision is not Erin, but Cliodhna—one of the queens of Irish faëry; in everything else this opening anticipates almost every *aisling* poem that was to be written more than a hundred years later. When Piaras Feiritéir, that gallant soldier-poet, was executed in

---

[1] *Dánta Amhráin is Caointe Sheathrúin Céitinn,* edited by Eoin Mac Giolla Eáin, C.I.

128

1653, some nameless singer made an elegy beginning: "Do chonnac aisling ar maidin an lae ghil" ("I saw a vision on the morning of the bright day"). This vision is Erin bewailing the death of the man who had overthrown hundreds. In such poems, especially in those elegies where some such figure as Cliodhna or Erin bewails her dead, it seems to me we find the beginnings of the *Aisling* proper. The use of the word in the new technical sense may date from Aodhagán Ó Rathaille's poem beginning, "Aisling ghéar do dhearcas féin am leabaidh is mé go lagbhríoghach" (circ. 1700).

It was this poet, Aodhagán Ó Rathaille, who first makes the Vision, the *Spéir-bhean* (literally, sky-woman), bewail the exile of the Pretender; it was this poet who, we may say, bound up the *aisling* type of poem with the Jacobite cause. The *Aisling* proper is Jacobite poetry; and a typical example would run somewhat like this: The poet, weak with thinking on the woe that has overtaken the Gael, falls into a deep slumber. In his dreaming a figure of radiant beauty draws near. She is so bright, so stately, the poet imagines her one of the immortals. Is she Deirdre? or Gearnait? or is she Helen? or Venus? He questions her, and learns that she is Erin; and her sorrow, he is told, is for her true mate who is in exile beyond the seas. This true mate is, according to the date of the composition, either the Old or the Young Pretender; and the poem ends with a promise of speedy redemption on the return of the King's son.

Now, nothing could be more unlike an *aisling* poem, written by Eoghan Ruadh Ó Súilleabháin, say, than this meagre outline of the theme. And this we shall, perhaps, better realise, and realise also the true nature of the *aisling* poems, if we compare these poems in general with the Jacobite poetry written in English about the same time.

II

Comparing these Jacobite *aisling* poems with the Jacobite poetry written elsewhere, mostly in Scotland, the differences we notice throw us back on the two worlds in which the poems flourished. The Scottish poems are simple, homely, direct; and if they have life in them to this day, as many of them have, it is because they were written to and about a living man on whom living eyes had rested with affection. Warm affection is the note of them: the warm affection of a simple, homely, rather unbookish people for kings of their own race; and as the years pass, and the Old Pretender gives place to the Young Pretender, this note of warm affection becomes one of warm love. " Bruce's heir," as one song names him, was, after all, a gallant figure, bonnie, chivalrous, daring, beset by a sea of troubles, yet not " dauntoned " by them. Prince Charlie's own person it certainly was that brought so much of Scotland to his colours; and Prince Charlie himself is frankly the inspiration of all that is best in Scottish Jacobite poetry.

The *aisling* poems had no such close inspiration. The Irish Gaels, since the going away of Sarsfield, whom they loved, were a people with no leader. Nothing so surely tells us of the desperateness of their cause than that the name of no political leader of their own is found in their songs from the fall of Limerick to the rise of O'Connell—a wilderness of more than a hundred years. And of this they were not unconscious: " Gan triath ach Dia na Glóire " (" Without leader save the God of Glory ") is a commonplace in their verse. In this despair, the only banner that promised another fight, if not the reversal of their hard doom, was that of the Stuarts. Moreover, Bruce was a name in Irish history as well as in Scottish, and the Gael was the Gael. For all that, the Stuarts were far away. On the Continent Irishmen had intrigued for them—it took an Irishman to find a wife for the Pretender— and of the Seven Men of Moidart who, venturing all, landed with Prince Charlie in Scotland, some books reckon four to have been Irish. Yet still, for the Gaels of Munster, the Stuart cause lacked the warmth of flesh and blood; only surrepti- tiously could the young men of Kerry slip away in their smuggling craft to join the adventure; while the fighting itself, when there was any, was also beyond the sea—in a place, whether Scotland or England, with which the Gaels of Munster had little or no traffic. The whole struggle, then, was cold with distance. The Scots wrote of " My Laddie," of " Jamie the Rover," of " Charlie Stuart," of the " Blackbird "; and in " Cam ye by Athol " we have " King of the Highland hearts, Bonnie Prince Charlie," and King of the Highland hearts in truth he was—" His very name our heart's blood warms." To anyone who lingers on these songs and who, at the same time, recollects how surely genuine affection tends to the use of diminutives, the story of Flora Macdonald is no miracle. Unlike the Scottish, the Irish song-writers took none of these affectionate liberties with the names of the Stuarts. They wrote of " Saesar " (" Cæsar ")—their most frequent " endearment "—of " Charles Rex," of " The Lion "; and they likened him to Angus Óg, to Conall Cearnach, and the other heroes of the myths, names they had never made free with, names that still stood for the heroic rather than the beloved in their imaginations. So that, to come closer in our examination of these songs, if one inclines, not to the splendour of art, but to its intimacy, its warmth of feeling, one turns to the Scottish songs:

> O my King, God save my King,
> Whatever me befall.
> I would not be in Huntley's case
> For honours, lands, and all.

Such a verse conquers one, as does also:

> He gat the skaith, he gat the scorn,
> I lo'e him yet the better.

In the same song we find:

> I yet may stand as I hae stood,
> Wi' him through rout and slaughter,
> And bathe my hands in scroundrel blood,
> As I do now in water.

131

Then there is the whole of "Wae's me for Prince Charlie," with its:

> "Oh! no, no, no!" the wee bird sang,
> "I've flown sin' morning early;
> But sic a day o' wind and rain!
> Oh! wae's me for Prince Charlie!"

If such verses, and, of course, scores of others in these songs, enter in on one, it is always because of the warmth of feeling in them, and the directness of expression.

It is far otherwise with the *aisling* poems. They do not move us; they dazzle us. Or if one is at all moved by them, it is not by or for the Cause they sing. If for a moment, as we read them, we admit thoughts at all extraneous and away from the wonder of the verse itself, it is never a thought of Prince Charlie or his endeavour that visits us, it is rather feelings of surprise, or feelings of anger—anger that such talents should have wasted themselves on such a cause, surprise that songs like these could find an audience in such a desolate land.

What is imperative in these songs is the art of the singer. If one meets, but once only Seán Clárach Mac Dómhnaill's "'Sé mo Laoch!" it abides with one, solely, however, for the music:

Is é mo laoch, mo ghile mear,
Is é mo Shaesar, gile mear,
Ní fhuaras féin an suan ar séan
Ó chuaidh i gcéin, mo ghile mear.

My hero, Living Brightness mine!
My Cæsar, Living Brightness mine!
No sleep I've known since he has flown
Far from his own across the brine!

It is true that this is not the refrain of an *aisling* poem; it is, however, a Jacobite poem, written in the same spirit as the *aisling* poems. In this verse, the sorrow that banishes sleep from the eyes means nothing to us; neither does the hero's woe—or is it that we feel the bright music of the verse is sufficient recompense for both. About all the *aisling* songs we have this feeling. A beautiful thing is being wrought out

132

before our eyes, and it is through the beauty of it we are moved, or not at all. Indeed their own beauty, not Prince Charlie, is their theme; whereas, in the Scottish poems, to leave out the " bonnie bird " is to leave all out. It is curious how little else except warm affection for the Prince himself is in these Scottish songs—the poet has but scant thought for anything else, little for Scotland, not much for the Cause. On the other hand, Ireland is in all the *aisling* poems; and the only lines in them that strike fire from us are those of her sorrows—her princes dead, her strongholds broken, her lands in the possession of churls, her children scattered across the seas:

Is iomdha mac dílis díbeartha uaim,	From me is many a dear son banished,
Is, a Chríost, nach truagh mé i n-easbaidhe.	And lacking them, O Christ, how pitiful am I!

These lines are direct in their utterance—yes, such lines are to be met with in these poems, but they always concern a sorrow far nearer home than the banishment of the Stuarts.

The place that the Stuarts themselves occupy in the Scottish poems is occupied in the Irish poems by Ireland herself. So that, in spite of their theme, we get from them the feeling that their writers were playing with a far-off woe when the Stuarts are in question, but with a living sorrow when Ireland is their vision.

III

Whatever else the *aisling* poems may lack, they do not lack poetry—one kind of it. They are, indeed, poets' poetry: only literary men will ever again quite feel towards them as their first peasant audiences felt. They are " words, words, words," just as *The Faërie Queene*, for all its moral lessons, is words, words, words. And being such, they convince us once for all that not alone were their writers poets, as is many a peasant, but they were also masters of language: they had all

133

bathed in the well of the Muses, to use a common phrase of their own; they had all frequently held converse with the glorious nine whom Seán Ó Tuama an Ghrínn (John O'Twomey of the Merriment) so memorably arrayed for our vision:

Naoi soillse is naoi lóchrainn 'na lámha.	Nine Brightnesses with nine lanterns in their hands.

That they frequented the presence of these Brightnesses, the *aisling* poems they wrote is evidence enough. Poe, on being asked what poetry was, is said to have replied: " A Midsummer Night's Dream!"—and who that really knows what it is, on being put the same overwhelming question, would not wish to take refuge in some such phrase? Perhaps it was the same thought that prompted Goethe to name the incommensurable as the note of lyric poetry. Well, if poetry be a Midsummer Night's Dream, if the stir and flash of wings, the strains of unseen harps, the unknowable, the ineffable, be necessary to it, then the *aisling* poems are poetry. Turn them into prose, and they have no longer an excuse for existing. Neither would Shakespeare's (or any other body's) " Midsummer Night's Dream," nor some of the best of Goethe's own lyrics. In the *aisling* songs, content and manner are one, so intimately one that to separate them is properly to come on neither. This fact has not been recollected; perhaps, indeed, never even understood, by many who in our own days have severely criticised them. People have been judging only the content of these poems, thinking *that,* in their simplicity, to be the heart of them; and sometimes this they have judged only after first making a prose of it, sometimes English prose! As well judge Hamlet's " To be or not to be " in Voltaire's translation!

The *Aisling* is lyric poetry at its most lyrical. It is decoration; it is, in its highest development, work of and for the *atelier*. " Decoration," " *atelier* "—strange words to slip from one in dealing with any feature whatsoever of that land of ill-used serfs. The *ateliers* could have been only those smoke-impregnated cabins; the connoisseurs, who were critically to appraise the decoration, only the barefoot peasants gathered in from the rough weather of the fields—men of " unbreathed memories," one would think, " which never laboured in their minds till now." It is hard to credit it, yet these two citizen words, " decoration," " *atelier,*" better than any other, perhaps, communicate to the outsider the unexpected quality of these poems.

Though not the folk-poetry of the period, they were the popular songs of the period: they passed quickly from mouth to mouth, were hankered after, were stored in the brain, were given down from father to son. In the summer of 1915, in Kerry, about two miles from Dingle, I heard an old illiterate woman break suddenly into one of them, changing, however, not without a twinkle in her eye, a word here, a name there, to make the poem fit in with the fortunes of the Great War in its early phase. In the Munster of the eighteenth century, there can scarcely have been a single peasant's hut which did not shelter beneath its thatch either such an old woman as this, or an old man of like temper—Gaels who would have thousands upon thousands of lines of well-wrought verse laid up within their memories. Illiterates, yet learned in literature, they were critics who appraised the poems as was right, that is, as lyric poetry, and not as anything else. They gave them welcome rather for the art that was in them than for the tidings. One such poem they put against another, testing both, comparing this poet's opening with that other's; or matching this description (always elaborate) of the flowing locks of the *Spéir-bhean* (the Vision) with that other's painting of them, or evaluating this song's close by the aid of the remembered cadences of a hundred others. Which is to say they took in those poets' work with the judgment that follows on easy comprehension. They were academic in their type of mind, those peasants, and were therefore not astonished, as their differently-educated descendants today are, that one poet after another should choose not only to treat the self-same theme, and almost in the self-same manner, but should, moreover, return to it again and again. They were no more astonished at

135

this than were the monks and merchants of some Mediæval city when their painters chose once again to throw the familiar group of Madonna and Child on wall-space or canvas. Those humble-thoughted old Italian burghers were also, at least as far as the art of painting was concerned, academic in outlook; they knew far more about art than they were ever aware; and, in truth, except in this way of pondering many treatments of the self-same theme, how is one ever to win to intimate understanding of what the artist so earnestly aims at?

Sometimes, again, I picture those ill-clad and half-starved peasants as taking in those *aisling* poems, debating them, rejoicing for them, exactly as did the lords and ladies of Romance chivalry take in and rejoice for the *Aubade* poems, the Dawn Songs, of their minstrels—songs that varied in form and treatment only as little as those *aisling* poems of Munster. To call up in vision the lords and ladies of a twelfth-century castle in Provence—their minstrels singing at their footstools —is to behold a living page of some illuminated song-book of those ages, or a passage from some lovely tapestry—all gold and rich tints, brightened into life. But to call up in vision a motley crowd of Munster peasants of the eighteenth century gathered into a smoke-filled cabin to hear some wandering schoolmaster of *spailpín* poet sing the latest *aisling* he had made, is to recollect some tattered, yet vivid, page of Dostoievsky. The enlivening presence of romance is in both visions: in the first it is full-blown and radiant, like a rose; in the second it half-emerges from the surrounding gloom— a hidden gleam, a secret gem, the more precious for its darkling setting.

No sooner had the ragged schoolmaster or field-stained labourer begun his song, than his listeners recollected themselves, thrust out their heads and bent their brows in concentration: one thinks of them as become once more aware of their estate, as thrilled once again with the keen joy of those who fling wide the gates of their barns to a new harvest of golden grain. It may be that it was the young Eoghan Ruadh Ó Súilleabháin himself—that red-headed Kerryman who was to have spent himself at thirty-six—who had arrived from beyond the mountains and was now to sing to them the latest of his famous *aisling* poems:

I gcaol-doire chraobh-chluthmhar néamh-dhuilleach bhíos,
Im aonar gan suim i n-aiteas 'ná i gceól,
Go féith-singil tréith-thuirseach faon-mhisnigh tinn
Gan chaomhnas ó aoin cois abhann ar neóin.

How do they take such a song, a song so entirely words, words, words? . . . . The wood of young oak-trees, branch-sheltered, bright-foliaged; the poet's loneliness, his *sehnsucht,* his dead-ness to song and music; his utter weariness, he is become gentle and sick for it; his lack of companion, as he wanders by the woodland river in the afternoon—it all is no more real than a dimly-lit tapestry. The words live in their sounds, not in their sense; it is the subtle, irresistible witchcraft of their music, and not what they say, that steals away the listeners' brains. Then from this mist of gentle music emerges the *Spéir-bhruinneal* (the Vision) herself—how can one describe what happens? A subtle modulation in the melody, and perhaps no more than that. And just as the dream-seen woodland of the opening, if one chanced to dwell on the features of it, would not disturb the rich flow of the music, nay, would still further enhance it, so now the features of the Fairy Vision, if one dwell on them, do not contradict or even disturb what the swinging, waltz-like rhythm and reiterated vowel-sounds are, through their own intrinsic power, creating within the ear, within the brain. She is beautiful everyway, in every feature, even if these features never combine into the dazzling perfection of consummate vision—one blinding flash. Her hair is golden, pearly, gentle-tressed, and flows in wreathed, trembling layers to the ground. Her eye-brow is like a single hair, a single stroke of the pen: as an arrow, it deprives her minstrel of sense and vigour. In her cheeks the flushing of red berries contends with the whiteness of a gentle lily. Her eyes are death-dealing stars: they have laid a hundred heroes in weakness. Her conversation is nobly-trained, cultured, is keen and gentle. Her teeth are small and

bright, well-set in her kindly and refined mouth that knows
not mockery or hardness. Her throat and brow are as white
as the foam on a wild lake. Her face is like the glowing sun
seen through crystal. Her breasts are sharp-rounded and
inviolate. . . . . The description of her, it will be seen, is a
swift rush of bright phrases: they flash and tinkle and give
place to others equally bright and musical. And all the time
it is the music in the words, and the turns in the phrasing, the
new adjective, the surprise of coupled words, words never
mated before, on which the mind of the audience is fixed.
But the song proceeds: . . . . The Vision is stooped upon her
tablets, writing—writing what those peasants thought alone
worth reading—their old heroic lays, the annals of their
ancient Gaelic kings, recounting the great blows that, a
thousand years before, laid the treacherous churls at Clontarf
of the Heroes in the trembling agony of death. . . . . And they
stretch yet a more covetous ear when, in reply to the poet's
supplication, the Vision tells of the glories of old. Their imaginations light up to hear ring out once again the names of
ancient kings and queens and heroes; Eibhear, and Niall, and
Conn; Banba and Néimheadh and Féidhlim, Milésius and
Ith. The very sounds of them are music; and, besides, here
is their own secret learning, of which the outlanders were so
ignorant! . . . . And if they decline, within the space of a
verse or two, on Cæsar—the new Cæsar—Charles, Son of
Seumas—well, it was that name or no name, his standard or
none, if the past were to live into the future, if the Gael were
to endure. . . . . For Charles, now in exile, the Vision weeps
—that the poet may have cause to raise his people's hearts
with words of bright hope. . . . . Soon will be heard the music
of gentle harps, the poets will have raised their united voices,
and the priests will be praying to the Father of the Virgin.
. . . . And from this the poet's words pass into the form of a
prayer to the Only-Begotten Son, Who, whilst yet young,
trod this earth in humanity, in divinity, to banish the tyrants,
the perverse " sprats " of falsehood—to blow them beyond
the waves without feasting, without wine, without estates,

without the crown. . . . . There! the lines fall, as is ever happening in these poems, into the bitterness of earnestness as soon as the one root-sorrow of all the tribe is reached—the Gael in bondage, his land in the grip of the alien. The bitterness passes, and the song ends in a gentle cadence that tells of the vanishing of the Vision, and the awakening of the poet on the homely earth of his own countryside.

To the question: How used those peasants to take in such a song? one may safely reply: With perfect comprehension. The story, the message, was familiar: it was the given theme. It was to the decoration of this theme, to the vowel-music, to the handling of the language, they gave all their thought. And such music as is in this wonderful song flooded their souls with rapture, moving them, perhaps, to tears, as some perfect movement in Mozart may move one to tears, although it seem itself to have no element in it that is not gladsome and even bright with the sense of triumph over the drab frailty of mortality.

Every phrase and line in the poem called up other lines and phrases that were only a little less memorable, a little less perfect; and in their ears those other strains sounded like that pleasing chime—the recollected songs of earlier poets—that John Keats tells us sounded in his when he sat himself down to write. . . . . If, after it all, they reeled homewards, drunken with poetry, from that one house, into which they had gathered at the tidings that Eoghan Ruadh Ó Súilleabháin had arrived from beyond the hills, was it not well that, at least for a few hours, a little ease had been interposed, that they had, for a space, forgotten that they were but hewers of wood and drawers of water—to their conquerors, as Swift added with illuminating bitterness?

In their reaching out towards poetry there was a twofold impulse. However untowards their fortunes, they were still the residuary legatees of over a thousand years of literary culture; and this drinking in of poetry was an effort to satisfy in the way that had become second-nature with them, the needs of the human spirit. That spirit can never wholly satisfy

139

itself with the actual, let it be what it may: the actual within its grasp, it is soon again a-hungered. It will have more than that. It will have the actual rounded off into one whole: it will have it made comely, as by the laws of design. And when was the actual ever more in need of rounding off, more in need of the grace of comeliness? When was the music of life, become one prolonged discord, ever more claimant for resolution? From the nightmare that existence had become for them, they rose into the clear, perfected, rounded, unified life that is Art. Thus poetry had for them the double gift of the drug: it put pain aside, it raised vision.

IV

Even from this little study of the *aisling* poems, one comes to feel that the Gaelic mind is academic, if not specialist in type. Given a new genre, it will use it as a mould, day in, day out, until by no possible earnestness or skill or happy chance can a casting be taken from it that is not lifeless at its birth, as one may say. We feel it also to be academic inasmuch as a variation in the decoration is as dear to it as a variation in the matrix. Furthermore, it is academic in the multiple veils of art that it throws about the actual deed or occurrence that impels it to one other song. Irish poetry has always sung the local event, the passing day—the bards were journalists, as John O'Donovan pointed out—yet there is no poetry that contains less of what we now call local colour.

Academic, then, in his build of mind, how out-of-joint the whole world must have appeared to the Gael of the eighteenth century! Where or how was there any prospect of relief, of ordered life, of achievement of ideals? He was in a pit of sorrow, and the gates were closed. Yet it is under such circumstances that the academic spirit repays all the self-discipline that induces it in a man or nation. It can be trusted utterly to thresh the corn that has been laid up against the lean years: more than any other spirit, it can fashion and re-fashion, and

140

re-fashion again, the same material: itself, almost, it can use up and deck out as a vision of life. But if, on the one hand, self-discipline has endowed the academic spirit with such faculties, it has, on the other, left it barren of certain gifts that we find freely in the possession of less exalted types of mind: for instance, it is not daring. When it has threshed the harvest within the gates, it waits, and waits, for these self-same gates to swing open again, incapable of seeing that anything else can be done. Yet other harvests have ripened without, and there are ways of getting to them, if only one be adventurous enough, if not even rebellious.

One often wishes that those poets of the *aisling* poems, who in so many cases were adventurous in life, were adventurous also in song. One wishes them more individualistic; yet to wish them so, is to wish them less Irish.

The *Aisling,* in spite of its being a new genre in Irish literature, is little more than a winnowing, a using up of harvests that had been laid in before the gates were shut. It was a new *motif,* but the mind that played upon it and filled it out was old, very, very old. Not only old, but impoverished. If that mind had not become so impoverished, it is curious, yet, perhaps, correct, to think that those poems would be far less original than they are, far more like the Irish poetry of the preceding centuries. Where they differ from it is in showing less power of concentration, less vigour of intellect. Their texture is softer; their raiment far gaudier, but their limbs far less beautiful, and their bearing far less noble.

Perhaps all this is another way of saying that though academic they are less so than the poetry of the bards, who did indeed " sculpte, lime, cisèle," in a way that would delight the inmost heart of any *Parnassien:* and the fact that we can easily trace in a series of those *aisling* poems the varying pressure of the times that produced them may be only another proof of this. The fall of Limerick marked the end of a short period of great Gaelic activity. Unfortunately, it has fallen to the lot of writers who did not know a word of Irish, who never heard even the name of Dáibhidh Ó Bruadair or

Diarmuid Mac Sheáin Bhuidhe Mac Cárrthaigh to make this period familiar to us, and so this Gaelic revival is realised hardly at all. Better than any document recovered from that time, the poetry teaches us what might have happened had Talbot, as well as Catholic, been also Gaelic, so understanding what the soul of Ireland secretly craved for. But the Gaelic vigour of this short period, 1685-1691, collapses, and Ó Bruadair laments. The voice of the lonely years that followed the sailing of Sarsfield's army from Cork in 1691 is to be heard in the first regular *aisling* poems—those of Aodhagán Ó Rathaille (died 1726), the cadences of which are either tragic or gloomy. With the raising of the Stuart banner in Scotland, hope returns; and we feel it in the spirited poems of Seán Clárach Mac Dómhnaill (MacDonnell) (died 1754). The flame dies away, and hope, chilled, becomes a memory, lingering as Prince Charlie himself lingers on the Continent; and this period of abject waiting and hoping against hope we have reflected for us in the wistful and decorative *aisling* poems of Eoghan Ruadh Ó Súilleabháin (died 1784). At last even this small flickering spark is quenched; and the *Aisling* seems, too, to have died, until the Volunteers stir in the extreme north, and Mícheál Ó Longáin, living in the city of Cork, in the extreme south, himself an active and daring Volunteer, trembles to that stirring, and writes an *Aisling* to record it. After the terror of 1798 the *aisling* poem is heard no more; though the genre may still survive, it is used now to comfort some lover's heart, and not the heart of the nation.

Such, then, is the story of the *Aisling,* the distinctive gift of the century to the book of Irish literature. Indeed, what between the explicit and implicit in those poems, it would be hard to find a better illustration of how a people's art " reveals the true feelings of the soul, the secrets of its inner life, and the world of passion that has long accumulated and fermented there before surging to the surface," as Romain Rolland has put it.

CHAPTER VI

THE POETS

I

From our study, first of the Cabin and Big House, then of the Bardic Schools, then of those Courts of Poetry into which these had declined, and lastly of the *Aisling,* the characteristic art-form of the period—from our study thus far we have, perhaps, won to sufficient intimacy with the life and letters of the broken Gaels to be able to place, with some rough understanding, the poets who heartened them or, at least, comforted them in their wretchedness. It is likely, however, that certain misconceptions still remain, for the Gaelic world was dissimilar to all others, and it is from these others that our ideas of poets and poetry have been gathered. These misconceptions it may be well to clear away before fixing on any one of those poets for closer examination.

This study has not often glanced outside the south-west corner of Munster. The reason of this is, of course, that there the Gaelic world was most self-contained and most intact; still possessed in it more of the light of the brain as well as the impulse of the heart. The literary tradition elsewhere— as, for instance, in large areas of Leinster—was prostrate, become little more than a memory; in other places, again, as in Connacht, though the literary tradition was still vigorous, it had lost touch with its own past; there were still poets, but no schools of poetry; such craft and learning as still remained were unorganised, were entirely individual; and the harvest of song reaped there, as a consequence, lacks refinement, is simple, and careless of the rules of art. Their strength is of the heart, there is much of the folk in them; and though some of them are among the best lyrics in modern Irish, the fact that the literature produced in Connacht consists practically of lyrics and nothing else, except for some folk-tales, is enough to show how different the tradition there was from that of Munster, with its many forms of literature.

The only other part of the country that, in its schools of poetry and poetical contentions, resembled Munster, was South Ulster and Leinster. Near Dundalk, a poet named MacAlindon is said to have kept a school of poetry, where as many as eighteen literary men came together for discussions.[1] But as in Connacht, so here, too, in South Ulster, in spite of this literary activity, the break with the past is noticeable. Anonymous singers in Munster wrote a more refined type of lyric than the most famous of the poets of this school.

In studying, then, the Gaelic world of Munster, we have been studying the Irish Ireland of that period at its fullest and richest.

II

Wherever they lived, in County Armagh, Mayo or Cork, the Gaelic poets of the time were peasants. They dressed like peasants, spoke like them, lived among the other peasants (yet not " unguessed at "); they shared their people's life and, indeed, their thoughts. The subject-matter of their verse— the loss of a sheep or old horse, the need of a new handle in a spade—will often surprise us if we do not remember this. Equally so will their lack of sophistication. Their wit, too, and oftentimes their coarseness, are of the fields, not of the town; while their standing by tradition speaks most clearly of all, perhaps, of life among the hills and rivers, the hills that do not renew their forms, the rivers that do not change their course.

But, and this is what we must remember, they never thought

---

[1] See *Abhráin Airt Mhic Chubhthaigh,* edited by Enrí Ó Muirgheasa.

of themselves as peasants. They thought of themselves as poets, as literary men. They were sons of learning. Everywhere in their lines we come on words like clown, churl, boar, clod, boor, bear—but the word is always used of their Cromwellian overlord or his bailiff. The Cromwellian (and Cromwellianism lingered on in Ireland long after it had disappeared from English life) was no poet; poetry he could not understand, nor even the need for it. He had no learning; and, however rich he may have become, was still but an upstart. He lacked breeding. He was not fit to be named in the one breath with the Gaels, on whom he trampled. The Gaels were "children of kings, sons of Milésius," and they knew it. We have been told of an incident that happened in our own days. At a sports meeting in County Cork a rough-looking, poorly-clad onlooker had so annoyed those about him by his loudness and want of consideration, that at last someone cried at him: "Shut up, you fool!" The epithet stung. He flashed up, and, to the amazement of all, answered back: "I am no fool; I know my genealogy!" Not many of the people in the eighteenth century were without knowing their genealogy, and the poets, most of all, were adepts in such lore; moreover, people as well as poets, they all were aware that the Cromwellians did not know their genealogy, were, therefore, only mere upstarts.

Those poets' claim to be, first of all, literary men could not be gainsaid. Their art was the immediate jewel of their souls; and the craft of verse the one subject where they showed no lack of sophistication. Moreover, were they not, at least in Munster, gathered into schools, each with its own traditions and its recognised head? And did not the names of the gods and demi-gods of Greece and Rome chime as sweetly to them as to any other literary circle in Europe? By plough or spade they lived; but it was for their art they lived. By whatever name they went in the catalogue, schoolmasters or ploughmen, to their own people they were poets.

If they were peasants with a difference, so, too, were they literary men with a difference. For instance, not one of them

145

ever saw his own poems in print; neither was there any system of copyright established among them. Their lack of printing-press and book-making does not seem to have vexed them; we do not find them complaining of it: the Gael had been so long at war with the outlander that he had never been quite able to make his own of the printing-press. The literature those poets read in Greek and Latin existed in book-form, but the literature they read in Irish, and to which they daily added, existed only in manuscripts. Of these manuscripts they made new copies, occasionally adding a poem made yesterday to a collection begun by some hand that long since had become a mere pinch of dust. And yet, though they laboured thus to keep good songs from perishing from men's thoughts, and laboured, too, to perfect the form of their own, aware that only the well-wrought song endured, it does not seem to have worried them that their fame should have only so poor a chance of spreading beyond their own parish boundaries. They made their poem, and seem to have left it to chance whether it should ever cross the neighbouring hills or the sundering river estuary: when it did so, they were probably glad, and still happier, it is likely, when some passing shanachy told them how, in a far-off place, he had seen certain verses of theirs written out in good script on enduring parchment. But primarily it was for their own countryside they wrote, and, the once proud literary language having split up into many dialects, the common speech of the people became more and more their medium of song. Remembering, too, their vigour and their integrity as artists, that gift that is shield and spear against the dragons of the earth, it is hard not to think of them as among those immortal ones who, in the words of John Keats,

> " . . . . died content on pleasant sward,
> Leaving great verse unto a little clan."

No copyright, no printing-press, no publisher, they must, then, have been just simple wayside singers of local events: but this, again, would not be an apt description. They were

146

literary men, very conscious of the proud part the gods had assigned them, jealous of the traditions of their craft, knowledgeable of its history: in Munster, at least, they still employed a great many words, purely literary words, intelligible to, but not used by, the common people. They aimed at literature, and often achieved it. It is, therefore, impossible to think of them as just the local singers of hidden countrysides; the clearest proof, however, that this phrase does not apply is the fact that at the same time, actually living side by side with them, were other poets, poets who produced a very different species of verse, to whom it does apply. Those anonymous poets wrote folk-poetry, with, it is true, the influence of the schools showing clearly through it; but the poets of whom we shall presently be speaking did not write folk-poetry. The metres of the folk-songs, though fundamentally the same, are simpler and rougher; the message more frank and passionate; and the themes are those instituted by the beatings of the heart of all mankind. The tale of Troy was nothing to those singers—nor that of Deirdre, nothing beyond hearsay.

If we take the poems of Burns, we can easily divide them into two classes: those the Lowland ploughman wrote for the easing of his own wild heart, and those the would-be literary man wrote in emulation of the *literati* of Edinburgh. His dialect poems, his most precious work, would correspond with the lyrics that certain other ploughmen were making in Ireland, also for the easing of wild hearts. His literary poems would, on the other hand, correspond to the work of the recognised poets, some of whose names we have mentioned as need served. The correspondence would be, however, not quite exact. Is there even one of Burns' literary poems, in this so unlike his songs in dialect, quite successful? Is there perfect artistic integrity in them? Is there no unwarmed material? No hesitancy in the gesture? In a word, is there not always some slight lack of mastery? If this be so, those literary poems cannot be exactly equated with the poems of men like Aodhagán Ó Rathaille or Eoghan Ruadh Ó Súilleabháin, finished craftsmen, perfect masters of language. With these it is always the mastery that one wonders at—the ease, the spontaneity, the undaunted impulse. One never wishes the poems bettered.

Such men, therefore, cannot be thought of as wayside singers who rhymed the local event. They were what they claimed to be, the *literati* of a people. Indeed, one would think that they, perhaps unfortunately, took only too much pains to earn this description. They never did what Burns did—write in two genres. *All* their work is literary, is of the schools. A French critic has written of Poussin: " La force du Poussin est un composé parfait du meilleur de l'art. Elle n'est donc pas individualiste. Elle ne dit pas: Moi, mais: la Tradition." These words describe not only the work of any one of our poets, but all the work of all of them. The word in its mouth is always: Tradition; and it betrays individuality only to those who have learned to perceive the subtler values.

Nowadays, to know that a piece of art-work is academic is to know that it remains unvisited, unloved of the people. The work of the Irish poets was academic, yet—strange fact! —much of it, almost two hundred years after its creation, has been found alive on the lips of fishermen and ditchers! From this fact, as also from the great number of manuscript-copies made of certain poems, we must conclude that the academic nature of the poets' work did not hinder the " pariahs " of the eighteenth century from welcoming it. The only explanation of the phenomenon is found in that great literary tradition that for a thousand years had been moulding the Gaelic conception of life and letters. Inasmuch as their work was thus greedily gathered up by the people; inasmuch, too, as the names of many of them, even to this day, are household words in their native districts, they may be said to have been popular poets; but if by that phrase we mean poets whose first appeal is to a non-literary audience, as is the case with a Kipling or a Service, then the phrase does not describe them; for, as we discovered in our examination of the *aisling* poems, the appeal of their work is primarily to an audience cultured in literature.

Those poets were the children not only of a forgotten land, where the pulse of being was becoming slower and slower, but of an old-fashioned land that, for better or worse, had never thrown off its Mediæval ways of thinking. The characteristics of the culture into which they were born derived from the Middle Ages rather than from the Renaissance. " The Catholic Christian idea of life took firm root in the soil of Gaeldom. It reduced to order and discipline, it endowed with a meaning and a beauty the vague uncomprehending yearnings of the Gaelic soul. Escaping from the perversity of life and the brutality of nature, the Gaels fixed their eyes on the glory of another world. The flesh was an enemy to be mortified. Asceticism became an ideal, and the Gaelic poet rejoiced in preaching that the world was 'but a mist,' that all was vanity and emptiness in this life."[1] And in a note to this passage, the same writer adds: " Much that I have said about Gaelic art and literature is equally true of Mediæval art and literature in general. This is another way of saying that the Renaissance hardly reached the Gaeldom."

This is a pregnant passage, though the statement that the Renaissance hardly reached the Gaeldom needs to be modified. What really happened was this: Whatever of the Renaissance came to Ireland met a culture so ancient, widely-based and well-articulated, that it was received only on sufferance: it had to vail its crest and conform to a new order; it did not become acclimatised, as had happened elsewhere; it was rather assimilated, assimilated so thoroughly that its features can no longer be discerned, though its effects are felt when the subsequent culture of the Gael is compared with the pre-Renaissance. The same thing happened, at least in the plastic arts, in India. The flamboyant vigour of the Renaissance must not dazzle us to the fact that one of its evil effects

---

[1] See Preface to *Cúirt an Mheadhon Oidhche,* edited by Risteárd Ó Foghludha.

was to whiten all the native cultures of Europe to a common value: it introduced into them all common forms and a common factor—the Greek standard of beauty, such as the Renaissance understood it—and never since has any of these native Continental cultures been really itself. In his very interesting introduction to " *Dánta Grádha* " (Love Songs)— a book of stray poems[1] collected chiefly from sixteenth and seventeenth century Irish manuscripts—Mr Robin Flower writes of them: " Their characteristics are fairly clear. The subject is love, and not the direct passion of the folk-singers or the high vision of the great poets, but the learned and fantastic love of European tradition, the *amour courtois*, which was first shaped into art for modern Europe in Provence, and found a home in all the languages of Christendom wherever a refined society and the practice of poetry met together. In Irish, too, it is clearly the poetry of society. . . . . The love-themes, which were now to make their entrance into Irish literature, usually carried with them on their pilgrimages certain lyric methods which became acclimatised in all the languages of Europe. It was not so in Ireland. There the established forms were too strong. . . . . The question of tradition is the gist of the whole matter. There was not in Surrey's day a stable tradition in English verse in poetry of this kind. In Ireland, on the other hand, an old and honoured tradition gave the poets a firm and steady grasp of style."[2]

The Irish literary forms, meeting and vanquishing those early Renaissance forms, may be taken as symbolic of what happened to the New Learning in general on its contact with the old learning of Ireland. For good or ill, then, the native colour, the Gaelic tang, has prevailed in Irish literature all down the centuries to 1847; and just as one may recognise Mediæval sculpture by a certain earnestness that oftentimes looks like fierceness, almost like savagery, so one may always

---

[1] Collected and edited by T. F. O'Rahilly.

[2] See Introduction, by Robin Flower, to *Dánta Grádha,* edited by T. F. O'Rahilly.

know the best poetry in Irish: there, too, is an earnestness, a "dreadful sincerity"[1] that burns away and away the graceful unessential until the subject emerges keen-edged, stark, and, occasionally, terrifying. Less of this note is found in the poetry of the eighteenth than of any other century, for all that poetry is, of course, only the week-ending of a great tale; but still it is there, yes, even in the *aisling* poems themselves, decorative and all as their nature is. In Aodhagán Ó Rathaille one finds many touches that remind one of Villon —in whom there is so little of the Renaissance spirit, so much of the Mediæval; and if these touches are found more frequently in Ó Rathaille than in any other poet of that century, it is so simply because he was himself the best of those poets; but it would not be wise either for us not to remember that he lived at the beginning of the century, previous to those others we shall soon be considering.

This being the nature of the culture of the Gael, it is obvious that it would not be too sensitive to those whispers of great change that the Wild Geese brought home on their secret journeys. Only in a superficial way—in the matter of language study, in the maintaining of a certain simple animation in the reading of the classics—did this trafficking with the Continent affect the native culture.

Those poems we discover dealing with European politics do not really exhibit to us the massed ideas of the Gael becoming impregnated with those of the Continent: some little impregnation there must have been—it is stated that the spread of French ideas among the richer Catholics after 1750 softened their attitude towards religious tests, so that to retain their lands they became less unwilling to take oaths in which they did not believe; in general, however, one finds but little effect resulting from this contact with foreign armies and foreign courts. The influence of the doctrines of Rousseau on Brian Merriman has been overstated, one thinks. Indeed, one may

---

[1] Rachel Annand Taylor, *Some Aspects of the Italian Renaissance.*

say that there is as much of Rabelais as Rousseau in his great poem, "Cúirt an Mheadhon Oidhche" ("The Midnight Court"); and properly to illustrate it, one must needs resurrect Dürer or Cranach, rather than a French engraver of the eighteenth century.

IV

Those poets were not only peasants, living in a narrow world without printing-press or any system of publishing, but were poor, not to say poverty-stricken, men. As each advanced from youth to manhood and from manhood to age, he became poorer and poorer; and as the century advanced from decade to decade, each new poet that comes into our ken is poorer than the last. There is something strikingly pathetic in this sensitiveness of theirs as individuals, as a class, to the declining fortunes of their race. If we begin our list with Ó Rathaille, we know that his youth did not lack comfort, but that he died in extreme destitution. His successor, Seán Clárach Mac Dómhnaill, wrote of the Gael of his time:

Atá mo chóraid gan fuithin	My cattle are shelterless,
'S mo chuingir gan féar, gan fás,	My team, unfed, thrive ill,
Atá anshógh ar mo mhuirear,	In misery my people dwell,
Is a n-uillinn gan éadach slán;	Their elbows through their clothes;
Atá an tóir ar mo mhullach,	
Go minic ó Thighearna an stáit,	A price is on my head
Atá mo bhróga-sa briste,	At the landlord's will;
Is gan pinginn dá bhfiacha im láimh.	My shoes are tattered,
	And no wherewithal to make them good.

And there was no difference between the Gaelic poet and his fellows. After Seán Clárach Mac Dómhnaill there follows a procession of poor wandering schoolmasters, *spailpíns,* pedlars, poor scholars, wastrels; and if, a hundred years on from Ó Rathaille's time, we end the list with the name of Raftery, what are we looking at?—a blind fiddler poking his way from hamlet to hamlet, from door to door,

152

| Ag seinm ceóil do phócaibh follamh, | Playing music to empty pockets, |

as he himself tells us in a matchless lyric. To behold them thus passing by, like a frieze, group following group, figure figure, each one more tatterdemalion than the last, less erect, less a member of a proud confraternity, is to behold the whole Gaelic race of their day passing by, except that the multitude is heightened and intensified into individual expression—is become wild eyes, bitter lips, and flesh that quivers and shrinks and fails.

The poets becoming poorer and poorer as one succeeded the other, and each becoming poorer and poorer as the years overtook him, this was to be expected, for everything Irish in that stricken land was decaying; the language itself was, of course, decaying, declining everywhere almost into a *patois,* and the learning that it enshrined was shrinking, until, in the end, a true peasant's brain could easily comprehend it. At last we can find no difference between the songs written by the unnamed poets of the folk and those written by the true successors of the old *filí,* no difference either in thought or diction. The Irish people will yet honour the name Ó Longáin as that of one who did inestimable service in transcribing and rescuing verse wherever it was to be had; but his own verse is poor and thin; and the same may be said of, perhaps, all the poets of his time: their patriotic songs are no better than the same sort of songs that in Ó Longáin's time the Irish people were beginning to write in English.

The Bardic Schools have now been closed for almost two centuries, the Courts of Poetry meet no more. The Gaelic literary tradition is slowly making an end. A poet here and there arises, and, stirred by a local catastrophe—as Máire Bhuidhe Ní Laoghaire (Mary O'Leary), by the agrarian troubles of 1822 in West Cork, strikes out a song full of fire and vigour—or emulous of the men of old, writes patiently a few verses in a bardic metre; but the literary tradition is no more, for it has lost the power of creating new forms.

153

V

In reading those poets, then, we are to keep in mind, first, that the nature of the poetry depends on the district in which it was written—if in Munster, it is literary in its nature; if in Ulster or Connacht, it has the simple directness of folk-song. Then we must also remember that the poets were simple men, living as peasants in rural surroundings; some of them, probably, never saw a city; not only this, but they were all poor men, very often sore-troubled where and how to find shelter, clothing, food, at the end of a day's tramping. Their native culture is ancient, harking back to pre-Renaissance standards; but there is no inflow of books from outside to impregnate it with new thoughts. Their language is dying: around them is the drip, drip of callous decay: famine overtakes famine, or the people are cleared from the land to make room for bullocks. The rocks in hidden mountain clefts are the only altars left to them; and teaching is a felony.

Not to excuse, but to explain them, are these facts mentioned; for their poetry, though doubtless the poorest chapter in the book of Irish literature, is in itself no poor thing that needs excuse: it is, contrariwise, a rich thing, a marvellous inheritance, bright with music, flushed with colour, deep with human feeling. To see it against the dark world that threw it up, is to be astonished, if not dazzled.

CHAPTER VII

AODHAGÁN Ó RATHAILLE
(EGAN O'RAHILLY)

One of those Courts of Poetry was assembled in the house of a Dáith Ó Iarflatha at Ballyvourney, in County Cork, when a voice was heard from outside. Catching it, Liam Ó Murchadha, poet, leaped to his feet, flung his head high, and chanted out four lines of welcoming verse, making them as he went on, not conscious of any difficulty in doing so, that single voice from the darkness having set his heart leaping and his brain alight:

> Breathnuighim cuisle cheartchumasaigh Aodhagáin ghrínn,
> Ag teacht faoi 'n dtulaigh seo tuílte de chéill fá ghnaoi,

and then, turning to those present:

> Ní thaithigheadh sibh-se ar an mbile 's níor bh'aon d'bhur dtaoibh,
> 'S le deaghchroidhe chumainn do chumaim dó céad d'fháiltidhibh.

Translation makes but poor prose of lines so skilfully woven:

> I recognise the note of a man of true power, the witty Egan,
> Approaching this height, full of wisdom and respect,
> You have not been acquainted with the great man, nor does he belong to your side,
> And with friendliness of heart I bespeak for him an hundred of welcomes.

Two hundred years on from that night of living poetry amidst the mountains of West Cork, those lines were to be gathered from the lips of a peasant. It would, somehow, be different if they were discovered in a manuscript that had

155

itself to be rescued from the stillness of dust and darkness, or in a book that, once spread broadcast, was now scarce procurable at all. It is as if we receive the lines still warm with human breath, as if the welcome had never grown cold: they, therefore, will now serve my needs when I bespeak for that tragic figure, that Dante of Munster, full of wisdom and respect, an hundred of welcomes.

I

We know so little of his wayfaring through life, that the facts may be set out at once: They amount to little more than that he was born in the Sliabh Luachra district about the year 1670, moved hither and thither from thence through Munster —going never farther afield than the city of Cork—seeking just to live, always suffering, and that at last he died in great poverty and desolation of spirit in 1726, not far from his birthplace. He is buried in Muckross Abbey, but his name is not mentioned in the guide-books to Killarney, nor is his tomb pointed out to American, or even to Irish visitors.

It has been written: " England is a nation of individualists in the matter of artistic expression. In other countries, for example, a poet or other artist usually expresses racial characteristics raised to the highest degree, rarefied and intensified. An English artist of any kind generally manifests entirely personal genius."[1]

The Gaelic poet, as our book has already, we hope, made clear, is, perhaps, an extreme example of the European rather than the English tradition. And of those Gaelic poets, if there was one who more clearly than any other gave intensified and rarefied utterance to what was in the heart of his people, it was Aodhagán Ó Rathaille: the movements of his time, then, perhaps even more than the facts of his own life, are necessary to a full appreciation of his verse.

---

[1]Rachel Annand Taylor, *Aspects of the Italian Renaissance.*

Growing up, not far from Killarney, the people's imagination was still hot and bitter with the memories of Cromwell. The boy must often have had pointed out to him that spot on Sheep's Hill, in Killarney, where, only little more than twenty years before, Piaras Feiritéir, that chieftain-poet, that gallant figure, was treacherously hanged, a priest and a bishop hanging with him. Of Feiritéir's poems he would have learned many; he would, moreover, have listened to many an elegy made for him, every one of them as rich in race as his own elegies were afterwards to be. In such manner did it come about that nearly all the Irish poetry of the sixteenth, seventeenth and eighteenth centuries is, looked at broadly, one impassioned outcry against England.

Rather suddenly, when he was fifteen years old, that very period of life when one's whole being is like a thirsty mouth, hot with desire, a wonderful brightness overspread the Gaelic lands. A Catholic, a sort of Gael, was on the throne (afterwards, when he was driven from it, he was received in Kinsale —that place of fatal memories—with Gaelic dances). Tadhg (Theig) and Diarmuid, the Gaels, and not Ráif (Ralph) and Seón (John), the Cromwellians, were henceforth, it was thought, to rule the country, as we find expressed in some verses of Diarmuid Mac Cárrthaigh:

Cá ngabhann Seón, níl cóta dearg air,	Whither faces John, no more red-coated,
Ná " Who is there?" le taobh an gheata aige,	Where's his " Who's there?" as beside the gate
Ag iarraidh slighe dá luighead go sparainneach.	He sought the least excuse to raise a row
Mo chur fé chíos istoidhche i n-acharann?	And have me fined for quarrelling in the night.
Cá ngabhann Ráif sa ghárda mhalluighthe	Where faces Ralph and his accursed guard,
Printísigh dhiablaidhe na cathrach,	Those devilish city apprentices,
Do stiall, gach aontaobh, séipéil bheannuighthe	Who everywhere pillaged consecrated chapels,
Ag díbirt cléire Dé 's a n-argain?	Plundering the priests of God and exiling them.

157

"You Popish rogue" ní leómh-
    thaid labhairt linn,
Ach "Cromwellian dog" is
    focal faire againn.
Nó "Cia súd ann?" go teann
    gan eagla,
"Mise Tadhg," cé tinn an
    t-agallamh.

No more they dare to cry, "You
    Popish rogue";
But "Cromwellian dog" we
    fling at them,
Or "Cia súd ann?" ("Who goes
    there?") sternly and fear-
    lessly,
"I am Tadhg"—to them a gall-
    ing dialogue.

It almost seemed as if the void created in the Gaelic world by the Flight of the Earls (1607)—Hugh O'Neill in command —was at last filled up, and Gaelic culture was once again set up on secure foundations. In that new dawn the young poet grew up, without forethought of what was to come. What came was, of course, sudden and almost entire collapse, the Revolution in England sending the sort of Catholic Gaelic king about his business. But Catholic Gaelic Ireland would cleave to him, would fight for him; and young Ó Rathaille saw the rush to the battle lines, saw Nicholas Brown lead his Kerrymen into the fray. In a few years it was all over, and then his occupation must have been to sit listening to what fugitive broken soldiers had to say of the fight at Athlone, of the holding of the bridge, of Aughrim's "great disaster," of the defence of Limerick, of the marching out, of the flight of the Wild Geese with Sarsfield.

But even after the Battle of the Boyne, Gaelic Ireland did not conceive of itself as utterly routed. "The natives, those of Milesian race, the O'Neills, the MacGuires, the MacMahons, with the Irish bishops and discontented officers, the Sarsfields, Luttrells, and Purcells, desired a separation from England and a continuance of the war"—and even when these same leaders sailed away from Limerick and Cork, their thought, doubtless, was that another day would come, and that mean-while their armies would remain intact.

During his lifetime, then, Munster changed from being a warlike province, able to put an army in the field, to a condi-tion of absolute defencelessness, leaderless not only on the field of battle, but voiceless in the field of politics. When he was young, his side of Ireland, the Gaelic side, would urge the whole of Ireland towards separation: when he was full-grown, it had not even a vote: according to law, it did not even exist!

II

Only little by little he came to realise the long suffering that overtakes a defeated people; only gradually to know that what was happening in his own countryside was also happening in a thousand others. The great family in the place was the Browns—Nicholas Brown, the second Viscount Kenmare, being then the chief. Originally of English stock, they had become long since rooted in the place, and had remained Catholic all through the hurly-burly. The family is still there, and still Catholic. Ó Rathaille now saw their estates vested in the Crown; he heard of their having been let out to John Blennerhassett and George Rogers. He watched the efforts of these men to plant the district with English Protestants; he heard strange accents calling out along the mountain roads. Other lettings, sub-lettings, followed:

" Gríofa is Heidges, gan cheilg im scéalaibh,
I leabaidh an Iarla, is pian 's is céasta!"

" Griffin and Hedges—without deceit is my tale—
In the place of the Earl, it is pain and torture!"

The same fate had overtaken lesser families in that corner of Munster. Everywhere estates were being bartered from hand to hand. Blarney of the MacCarthys was become desolate— "An Bhlárna gan áitreabh ach faolchoin" ("Blarney with no dwellers save wolves"), Ó Rathaille cried out of his breaking heart; and of the same family:

A Dhia tá ar neimh do chluin na scéalta,
A Rí na bhfeart is a Athair naomhtha,
Créad fá'r fhuilngis a ionad ag béaraibh,
A chíos aca, is é sinnil in' éagmuis!

O God, Who art in heaven, Who hearest the tidings,
O King of miracles, and Holy Father,
Why hast Thou suffered his place to be held by bears,
That they should have his rent while he is straitened for want of it!

And so he goes on making a list of the great families that are now scattered from their holdings, either lurking at home in poverty or in exile beyond the seas.

Seeing all this about him, the image that again and again occurs to him is the destruction of the ancient forests of the lands. He saw the " upstarts "—he uses the English word—not quite sure that they were settled for ever in the land, hurriedly cutting the timber and huckstering it off at sixpence a tree.[1] " Is díth-chreach bhur gcoillte ar feochadh!" (" Woe! your woods withering away!") he cries out; and again, with one eye on what was actually happening and the other on its significance:

A mianach ríoghdha, a coill 'sa haolbhach,
Do dóigheadh do briseadh a connadh 's a caolbhach;
A slata fáis go scáinte réabtha,
I gcríochaibh eachtrann scaipithe ó chéile!

Her princely mines, her woods, her lime quarries,
Her trees old and young, have been burnt and broken down;
Her growing rods, scattered and torn,
In foreign countries severed from one another.

Not only did he see all this, but he also saw some of his own people go over to the enemy, changing their religion for the sake of power, battening on the misfortunes of the race and place! One understands his litany of woe:

Tír do doirteadh fá chosaibh na méirleach!
Tír na ngaibhne—is treighid go héag liom!

A land poured out beneath the feet of miscreants!
A land of fetters—it is sickness to me unto death!

Tír bhocht bhuaidheartha, is uaigneach céasta!
Tír gan fear, gan mac, gan chéile!
Tír gan lúth, gan fonn, gan éisteacht!
Tír gan chomhthrom do bhochtaibh le déanamh!

A land poor, afflicted, lonely, and tortured!
A land without a husband, without a son, without a spouse!
A land without vigour, or spirit, or hearing!
A land in which is no justice to be done to the poor!

---

[1] There is an echo of all this in " Barry Lyndon."

Tír gan eaglais chneasta ná cléirigh!	A land without a meek church or clergy!
Tír le mioscais, noch d'itheadar faolchoin!	A land which wolves have spitefully devoured!
Tír do cuireadh go tubaisteach, traochta	A land placed in misfortune and subjection
Fá smacht namhad is amhas is méirleach!	Beneath the tyranny of enemies and mercenaries and robbers!
Tír gan tartha gan tairbhe i nÉirinn!	A land without produce or thing of worth of any kind!
Tír gan turadh gan buinne gan réiltean!	A land without dry weather, without a stream, without a star!
Tír do nochtadh gan fothain gan géaga!	A land stripped naked, without shelter or boughs!
Tír do brisheadh le fuirinn an Bhéarla!	A land broken down by the English-prating band!

In the English, the passage has not the litany-like quality of the Irish, with its repetition, its music, and its strong rhythm; yet one feels that in both Irish and English the general terms are not far aloof from current and local instances; all around him, in very fact, the woods were being felled, the priests hunted, the poor unjustly oppressed, and the natural leaders of the people either in prison or in exile. His muse did not, therefore, lack for elegiac matter: it was only too close at hand; if it were not, however, it is not easy to imagine him as ranging beyond Munster in search of it. Ó Bruadair was alive during Ó Rathaille's youth, and Keating only a score of years dead when he was born; yet both of these, though Munstermen, took all Ireland for their province. Not so Ó Rathaille. The Gaels had lost grip on Ireland as a whole since 1690. The gates had been shut on them; they were divided up, only stray adventurers, poor scholars and such, bringing news from one Gaelic district to another. Such big Gaelic houses as had survived the storm took refuge, each of them, in the obscurity of its own valleys and hills. Ó Rathaille is the first poet native to such conditions. He is the first Munster poet, in the real sense of the word. Yet in feeling he adheres altogether to the all-Ireland poets who went before him, and not to the other Munster poets who were to follow.

161

For he is frankly aristocratic. In one of those broken-down bardic schools he had been educated, more deeply, it seems, in genealogy than in any other lore. It was but poor learning for one who was to face a future where the big families themselves only strugglingly existed. Their day was gone. Yet for the swarming poor, the cottiers, the labourers, Ó Rathaille had no heart. He never dreamed that the future was with them; that if they survived the Gael survived; that if they failed the Gael was at last forgotten. But he is not to be blamed. That swarming mob had not yet become conscious of themselves as the residuary legatees of all the culture of the Gaelic ages. They had not yet thrown up poets or leaders of any kind; many years had to go by before they learned, out of a thousand experiences, that, outlawed and all as they were, they could still by combination resist oppression and exert influence, that they were indeed the historic Irish nation, that they would grow and be heard. Some at least of those tutoring years had gone by before the next great Munster poet, Eoghan Ruadh Ó Súilleabháin, was born: he was, therefore, child of a new world; he was naturally, then, as democratic in feeling as Ó Rathaille was aristocratic.

If, however, the temper of Ó Rathaille's poetry is one with the past, the temper of his own life foretells the future. He becomes poorer and poorer, and dies in poverty. Eoghan Ruadh Ó Súilleabháin was later to die in the dread loneliness of a fever hut. In another fever hut, this time in Ulster, however, Cathal Buidhe Mac Giolla Ghunna was to die equally poor, equally desolate—unless, as legend has it, the Blessed Virgin, Refuge of Sinners, came and sat by him for comfort. Brian Merriman was to die in poverty in the heart of Limerick City; Piaras Mac Gearailt to die poor, not far from Youghal. One cannot, indeed, recall even one of them whose passing was not to be darkened by want and oftentimes by neglect.

We now, in some measure, understand the conditions which moulded him to the scornful, stubborn, aloof spirit that confronts us in his poetry. And, of course, in his poetry is laid up

162

for us the best of him. But tradition, without contradicting the spirit of his verse, yet humanizes that spirit to more intimate brotherhood with us, inasmuch as it tells us of his wit, even of his buffoonery! He goes into a bookshop in Cork—we are to picture him as the peasant in town. His gesture is uncouth, his garb outlandish, his English all brogue. He takes up a large and expensive classical work, and asks the price of it. The shopkeeper glances at the book, at the quaint figure, and indulgently informs him he can have it for nothing if only he can read it. The poet continues looking at the Greek or Latin, holding the book upside down. He contrives somehow to get the shopkeeper to ratify the off-hand promise—which done, he turns the book aright and reads with ease. . . . . Tradition here dramatises for us the whole story of Irish Ireland in the eighteenth century: learning in rags, speaking English with a rough accent. . . . . But tradition also shows him as attending fairs with a súgán (a straw rope) tied tight round his waist, replying foolishly and very seriously to all who come to price his cattle: " My mother told me not to sell them for less than so much "—a specimen of the sort of humour the Gaels loved—humour that ripples lightly along the mind. Other stories of him have also survived, in every one a note of irony, sometimes of bitterness.

III

His poems we may divide into three classes—elegies, satires, and shorter lyrics.

His elegies are the swan-song of the patrician Ireland of his youth. They were, in a way, the last elegies to be written in the Gaelic mode, for the poets who were to follow him were but poor experts in genealogy: " My head is empty of *ogham*," said Eoghan Ruadh Ó Súilleabháin, in one of his elegies, excusing himself; and all the poets of his later day needed as much clemency as he from the genuine children of Ir and Eibhear, who knew that a Gaelic death-song should be built up of racial, rather than of individual, qualities and recollections.

Twelve of his elegies have been preserved to us, every one of them longer, more elaborate and, as some might say, more conventional than another. To be duly relished, they require that we throw ourselves back into the world of the Gael, of which they were so intimate a feature. The silent eye does violence to them; not only, indeed, do they require the warmth and the sound of the speaking voice, but they would surely be the better for choric utterance: so chanted, loud, free, vehemently emotional, one's spirit might fail before them, as before certain movements in Beethoven's symphonies.

When one of Máire Ní Dhuibh's (O'Donoghue's) sons had died, a relative's wife—a Mrs Charles Philip O'Connell, newly settled among the Gaels, ignorant of their immemorial customs—came to the wake, and fell on her knees in silent prayer. Máire Ní Dhuibh herself looked on in chilled astonishment; and at last, failing to contain herself, broke out upon her in violent abuse. Was this her way of making grief? Had she no words of praise or sorrow to cry out above the dead? Then, as if to teach her, she clapped her hands and gave free utterance to her suddenly-raised emotion in a flood of words: "Where are the dark women of the glens, who would keen and clap their hands, and would not say a prayer until the corpse was laid in the grave?"[1]

Now, this incident opens for us a way into the world of those elegies: without some such instruction, we might discover but conventional grieving where rather is a flood of vehement sorrow: at the same time it helps to explain their structure, their headlong drive, their very length. So chanted, we should not find them wearisome; and were we initiate of the old Gaelic world, we should not reckon those never-ending, intricate, genealogical verses, with their hundred names, an impertinence. As it is, however, we can only darkly sit by in silence, wondering at the ceremony. Yet each and every one

---

[1] *The Last Colonel of the Irish Brigade.*

164

of those elegies is full of the sense of style, and oftentimes rises into passages of fresh and lyrical beauty; while never, on the other hand, does the grief slow down into the mawkish, the sweetly pretty or the pious sentimental. For that to happen, there was too old a civilisation behind them.

If we take his elegy on Diarmuid Ó Laoghaire of Killeen, near Killarney, we find it built on the following plan:—

1. The terror caused by his death . .	(about 12 lines)
2. The man himself	(,, 20 ,,)
3. Genealogical matter	(,, 50 ,,)
4. His prowess in sport and learning .	(,, 8 ,,)
5. The places known to him bewail him .	(,, 10 ,,)
6. The Fairy Women of the Gael bewail him.	(,, 13 ,,)
7. The rivers and mountains of Munster weep for him	(,, 20 ,,)
8. The gifts bestowed on him at birth .	(,, 20 ,,)
9. His hospital house is desolate . .	(,, 20 ,,)
10. His people are now defenceless; his wife's desolation	(,, 16 ,,)
11. The women will weep him. All Munster will do so. I myself till death will weep him	(,, 8 ,,)
12. The *envoi*	(,, 80 ,,)

It is a long poem, yet, after a lapse of two hundred years, the greater part of it has been found living in the mouths of peasants! It seems a miraculous thing; let it be taken as evidence that the whole story of that period is not mythical. Section 9 may be found quoted in Chapter II. But perhaps some verses from his elegy on Domhnall Ó Ceallacháin will better illustrate the genealogical element in these poems:

Son of Ceallachan, the manly, the high-spirited, the vivacious,
Son of Conchubhar, a noble who was bold and brave,
Son of Donogh, son of Tadhg, the staying strength of the learned,
Son of Conchubhar Laighneach, who did not show weakness.

Son of Donogh, the noble, the haven of the poverty-stricken,
Son of Cinneide, the Fair, the chieftain of a province,
Son of Macraith, who was esteemed in his youth,
Son of Maolseachlainn, who despoiled Eoghanacht.

Son of Lochlann, who never yielded in contests,
Son of Macraith, who was skilled in fighting,
Son of Mathghamhain, the Fair, sage and hero,
Son of Murchadh, son of Aodh, of the battle-brands.

165

So the run of names continues for eighty more lines! The pedigree is carried back to son of Enos, son of Seth, son of Adam the wise, who conceived great evil. And then it concludes:

> There is no link to record from Adam to Domhnall
> But high kings who ruled the world,
> Kings of countries, kings of provinces,
> Generous chieftains, lords, and heroes.

Is it not all a strange, a Pindaric world, a land of ancient rituals and immemorial traditions? Unsatisfying to our modern appetites, perhaps; yet no one who has ever experienced the cumulative effect of a litany will content himself with estimating merely the value of the words, as the eye gathers them in. He will grant them the speaking voice, the interest in ancestry that was part of Gaelic breeding; he will grant them, too, the memory of the dead man, the death chamber in the mind's eye, the rigid body—and these given, it is only the unimaginative who will remain unquickened as to what must have been the effect of such headlong evocation of the illimitable past, its violences, its heroisms, its hundred names, its dynasties, shadowy, .vast, well-nigh immortal. Moreover, there is still to be added the effect of the strong, simple rhythm, the swiftness, the flood of sound, rich, dark and sonorous. So taken in, one of those keens cleanses the mind, causes the heart to shrink and shrink, that afterwards it may greedily expand, avid of higher experiences.

To illustrate another element of those keens, we may take these lines:

I gCaonraighe n-a dhíleas caomh-cheart,
Cíobán áluinn ag fáscadh déara;
Una, Aoife, Clíodhna, is Déirdre;
'S i Sídh Beidhbhe Meadhbh ag géarghol.

At Kerry in his own fair land,
Is beautiful Cioban pressing forth tears;
Una, Aoife, Cliodhna, and Deirdre;
And in Sidh Beidhbh Meadhbh bitterly weeping.

Cioban, Aoife, Cliodhna, Meadhbh and Deirdre are, of course, the brightest queens in the Irish sagas—each the heart, as one may say, of a great tale which would be familiar from child-hood even to the common people. Sometimes not only will these natives of the isle come to weep above the dead, but their kindred from far-off Greece and Rome will proffer assistance. These latter, perhaps, we could wish away; and yet as great a poet as Milton, under similar circumstances, remembers them:

> Where were ye, nymphs, when the remorseless deep
> Closed o'er the head of your loved Lycidas?

—as, of course, also did Shelley:

> Where was lorn Urania when Adonais died?

Instead of these bright presences, conjured from secret rath and dun, from grove and shrine, it may be the rivers of Munster, or even its little towns, that help to raise the dirge:

> Do ghoil an Laoi trí mhí go ceólmhar;
> Do ghoil an tSionainn an Life 's an Chróinseach;
> An Mang, 's an Fhleasc, Ceann Mara is Tóime;
> An Fhéil, 's an Ghnaoi, 's an Bhrighdeach mhór thoir.

> For three months the Lee wept musically;
> The Shannon, the Life, and the Croinseach wept;
> The Mang, the Fleasc, Ceann Mara, and Toime;
> The Feil, the Gnaoi and the great Bride in the east.

The keener had as much right to name them as had Milton to mention floods farther afield:

> O fountain Arethuse and thou honoured flood,
> Smooth-sliding Mincius, crowned with vocal reeds.

. . . . . .

When we parcel out the keen thus into its different elements, we find in them but the trappings and the suits of woe. All these elements, however, the strong, headlong rhythm bears onward, one overtaking the other before we are aware. The modern reader, for all that, will find his treasure-trove in and among these conventions: it may be a description of the desolate house, a sudden evocation of wholesome days of

167

sport on the hillsides, a touch of personal feeling, a freshness of imagery:

Súil ba mhire 'ná druide na gcoilltibh;
Súil an tseabhaic gan ainimhe laoi ghil.

An eye that was quicker than the starling's in the woods;
A hawk's eye that blanches not in the bright day.

A gcrann bagair, a ngeata, 's a ri-phort;
Fál a mbeathadh 's a mbailte 's a maoine;

Their threatening staff, their gate, their chief stronghold,
The protecting wall of their crops, of their homes, of their treasure,

A scáth roimh anfhaithe mara agus taoide;
'S a mbuachaill fartha san macha thu ist oidhche.

Their defence against storm of sea and tide,
Their watchman in the cattle-field at night wert thou.

Sometimes a little vignette is flashed upon us:

Luin na seilge ag sceinnim le fórlucht,
Is cearca feádha go fánach glórach,
Conairt an ríogh 's a shaoithe tóirseach,
D'éis a reatha i n-aghaidh sleasaibh na gceochnoc.

The birds of the chase starting up with great force,
With pheasants dispersed and wildly screaming;
The prince's hounds and his men fatigued
From their pursuit up the slopes of the misty mountains.

Sometimes it is a note of homeliness that remains in our memory:

Tobar lachta na n-anbhfann tréith-lag
Bó na mbocht, 's a ndorus aonair.

A well of milk for the weak and prostrate,
Cow of the poor, their only door.

And always there is the solemn music, sometimes overwhelming:

Crádh ar an mbás, is gránna gníomhartha—
Argthóir d'fhág ar lár na daoine—
Do rug le fána bláth na tíre,
A gceann gan cháim, 's a n-árus díona.

168

So far we have written of these elegies as pure poetry, self-contained, its beauty its own justification. Their extra value is, of course, the insight they give us, first into the Gaelic civilisation, and then into the life of those distant days. They are local documents, but they are also national records. The attitude of mind in them is as valuable as the pictures they give us of the big house, of the hunting, the gambling, the watchman in the cattle-field at night, the dependence of the swarming poor on the few rich that controlled the country-side. Not only are they a surer guide to the history of the place and period than the official statements, but they are a swifter guide, while, at the same time, they bring us deeper into the heart of things. To examine even a few of them is to find ourselves gifted not so much to understand the historian's page as to judge it through realising it, even to the forgetting of it sometimes as a thing very often specious and shallow.

IV

His satires are not remarkable: perhaps the most pregnant thing to be said of them here is that they illustrate that pre-Renaissance note which runs through all Irish literature from the tenth to the nineteenth century. The Renaissance, as already mentioned, whitened every well-known national culture in Europe to something of a common tone. The watered-down Hellenism of the Renaissance, like an oil-painter's dull medium, deprived each of these national cultures of something of the homeliness, the raciness, the intensity, that previously were in them. It is not to our purpose to inquire what the New Learning gave back in the way of compensation to them. What we have to recollect is that that common flavour for which the Renaissance is responsible was once an alien note in European literature—" a strange, a rich, a savage food "—this, however, is not easy for us to realise, for long since it has become the most characteristic quality in modern culture. It is the original national note that we now find strange and rich and savage. The homeliness of the miracle plays in English, the sharpness in Villon and Dante, the buffoon-grossness of Rabelais, the fierceness of Mediæval sculpture—how difficult for us to realise that these are the notes of national Christian art! Yet so it is; and the study of the Gaelic literature of any century will verify the statement. Even in the beginning of the nineteenth century there were lines of verse written in Irish that Villon might have written, and whole passages of homely grossness that Rabelais would have relished—and, in both cases, written by people who had never heard of either of these writers. In the satires, naturally, we come on the Rabelaisian note—not so pronounced in Ó Rathaille as in many another, but still there, as in his description of a fellow-poet, Domhnall na Tuile, who had written in similar terms of himself. Some stanzas are not quotable, but here is the characteristic note of it:

> Soraire sramach, sopaire salach,
> Rothaire reatha an bréagaire;
> Crotaire tana, slogaire smeartha,
> Shloigeas gach treas 'n a chraosgoile.

The translation gives no idea whatever of the grip in these lines:

> A fellow full of vermin, of running eyes, a dirty gaunt wad,
> A fugitive vagabond is the liar,
> A slender hunchback, a greasy swallower,
> Who swallows every rubbish into his greedy maw.

Or we may take another verse:

> Ar dheilbh an mhongcaoi, i n-eitim, nuair imthigheas
> D'fheirg n-a rith tri thaobh bhalla;
> Nó mar fhrangcach ag rith tré chlabhstrach,
> Is tóir n-a deabhaidh ag tréanchataibh.

> He looks like a monkey, frightened, when it goes
> In anger running against the side of a wall;
> Or like a rat running through a cellar,
> Hotly pursued by strong cats.

This certainly is not the note of Dryden, Pope or Byron; it is even very different; yet in the Irish it is expressed with as good

170

a " slap " as anything any of them ever said of a brother bard
or politician. This pre-Renaissance note is the quality of Irish
poetry that most disturbs, and even repels, the new arrival in
its domains. So might the fierceness of Mediæval sculpture
disturb the thoughts of one brought up, say, in the city of
Rome.

Except that his satires, like all others in the language, give
us to feel this pre-Renaissance tang, there is little other
significance in them.

V

It is far otherwise with his lyrics: by them he stands or
falls; on them was his fame first built, on them it rests. His
themes are scanty: one might, indeed, say he had but two;
the first, Ireland and it broken, that is, Ireland as he understood it, the Land of Ir and Eibhear; the second, himself,
broken too; and sometimes those two themes become one, as
we shall see. But in a lyric, the question of theme must ever be
of small moment, the method of treatment being so nearly
everything. A lyric is happy inasmuch as it sings, sings
spontaneously, swiftly, sweetly, brilliantly. So tried, his lyrics
are true and sterling. The poets of that century were, it seems
to me, the first adequately to respond to the music that had
been ripening in the language for hundreds of years. Those
who went before them, living members of a society whose
culture was, perhaps, become too highly organised, knew of
that language as peculiarly a medium of thought, a refined
medium, all too precise, somewhat hard, all too clear. Their
nature was intellectual; and with them a thought to be
expressed finely must first be cleansed of the adventitious.
They oftentimes, therefore, achieved, through this clear-
sightedness, this severity, those selfsame surprisingly vasty,
sometimes overwhelming, effects which we occasionally come
upon in the classical writers of France—in Racine, for
instance. But the colour, the deep sound, the full harmonies

171

that were to their hand in the thousand-years old language, these they seem to have scanted, although no other tongue in Europe, perhaps, so teemed with them. It had had a unique development. While others were evolving as printed rather than spoken languages, Irish was not being printed at all. It therefore escaped the artificial check that printing is to the natural evolution of the sounds of a language. It became more and more *legato,* more and more shedding its sibilants and stopped sounds. Those poets happened on, rather than sought for, this characteristic of their native speech. They must needs discard the old syllabic metres, for these were become impossible to men so haphazardly trained as they had been; even if they were to make use of them, the results must be as nothing compared with what had already been done in them: theirs was but a rude world, narrow, dull and starved, as compared with the courtly realms in which their predecessors had passed their lives. They had, perforce, to use the simpler assonantal metres, the song metres of the people; and the sound-value of the language seems at once to have broken tumultuously upon their ears. None of the whole band of them took more toll of this adventitious element of lyricism than Ó Rathaille, except, perhaps, Eoghan Ruadh Ó Súilleabháin, who was to follow him. One ignorant of the language could hardly credit that such music, such overwhelming music, as is in these two poets could at the same time make good sense. Swinburne very aptly described his own earlier poems as a " revel of rhymes ": Ó Rathaille's lyrics, too, are often a revel of rhymes; but they never suffer from the want of sincerity, and not often from the want of intensity. Swinburne was always rhetorical, frequently eloquent, but never intense: It must, however, be recollected that he found his themes laid up in old parchments:

> O daughters of dreams and of stories
> That life is not wearied of yet,
> Faustine, Fragoletta, Dolores,
> Félise and Yolande and Juliette.

Ó Rathaille's urge to sing was stronger and deeper: not otherwise than " bitter constraint and sad occasion dear." Life pressed upon him, struck him, wounded him, and he cried out. Or, rather, it struck his race; but that was the same thing, for his whole race seems to have been individualised in himself, so entirely at one with its spirit was his spirit. In the same way as Dante was a Florentine poet, filled with the local stir of things, unchronicled as often as chronicled, so Ó Rathaille was a Munster poet, its legends, its troubles, its towns, rivers and fields, its families, its houses, entering into his work in as full a measure as similar knowledge into the Florentine's. In how much such closeness of vision, such nearness to the actual, makes for intensity is too big a question to be discussed here; intensity is, however, as indubitably his characteristic note as it is Dante's. It is never a comfortable note. It does not compromise, and Lady Vere de Vere might very often speak of it as simple bad taste. " Créachta Crích Fódla " (" The Wounds of the Land of Fodla ")—that is, of Ireland—is the title of the first lyric we find in his collected poems,[1] and it might fittingly stand as the description of them all—an ominous title if we recall, on the one hand, his gift of intensity, on the other, the fact that his Land of Fodla was little else than one wound all over. His own " dreadful sincerity," his bitter irony, may be reckoned as portion of that general wound. He looks into the future and, addressing Ireland, says:

Beir feasta aca it mhéirdrigh fé
    gach críonchóisir,
'S gach ladrann caethach d'éis
    do chlí-dheólta.

Henceforth shall thou be an un-willing handmaid to every withered band,
While every foreign churl shall have sucked thy breasts.

That was how it came to him, taught of the homely parochial, to express what the nineteenth-century orators meant when they spoke of Ireland as a corpse on the dissecting table: perhaps the difference is not great, a degree of intensity, a degree of breadth, but none of the latter-day orators have spoken like this:

[1] *The Poems of Egan O'Rahilly*, edited by Patrick S. Dinneen and Tadhg O'Donoghue. Irish Texts Society.

Is dearbh gurab é gach éigean
  íogcórach,
Ganguid is éitheach, claon is
  díoth cómhaill,
Gan ceangal le chéile, ach réa-
  badh rinn-scórnach,
Do tharraing ar Eirinn fraoch an
  Ríogh chomhachtaigh.

In sooth it is every violence of
  injustice on our part,
Deceit and falsehood and
  treachery and non-fulfilment
  of pledges,
Want of union, and, instead, the
  tearing of each other's
  throats,
That have drawn down on Erin
  the rage of the Mighty King.

Remembering the inept use that is made of such " confessions,"
one hesitates to quote such lines; yet Ó Rathaille is the greater
for having so spoken, and his people the greater for having
thrown him up so to admonish them; both they and he sharing
in the tribute, if now there be any, given to passionate
sincerity. Throats were cut, literally as well as figuratively,
pledges denied, deceit practised—yet not to such an extent as
undermined the morality of plain speaking. The bitterness of
defeat, which cries out in these lines, is in all his verses, and
only that frequently their perfect music wings us beyond the
poignancy of all earthly grief, we could scarce bear to dwell
on them.

Yet the most famous of them all is at the same time the
most decorative; to think of it, however, as nothing else than
decoration is not possible: its pulse is just a little too earnest
for that, a little too disturbing. It best gives the sense of him
as lyrist, all wings and music, but not as man, all sincerity
and onward force, ironic and bitter. It is one of the first *aisling*
poems ever written, if not the very first, giving the note to all
that were to follow; and now when all these are garnered for
our scrutiny we still see it for the best. " Gile na gile do
chonnarc ar slighe i n-uaigneas," runs the first line of it—
" The brightness of brightness I saw in a lonely path "—and
that phrase, " brightness of brightness," is the poem's description. It is all sparkle, charm and life. It resembles some perfect
movement of a Mozart sonata, compact of brilliancy, spontaneity and poise. It is flawless, as secure in its magic when
heard for the thousandth time as for the first time. Mangan,
translating it, makes a slow-paced, dull-voiced attempt to

174

reproduce its rhythm and melody, but every single phrase of the original surpasses in music, ease, and swiftness the corresponding phrase in the English. How different is "flashing dark-blue eye" from "guirm-ruisc rinn-uaine"! And the commonplace "Descended to the earth and swept the dewy flowers" from the swift and brilliant "Bhaineas an ruithneadh den chruinne le rinn-scuabaibh"! And the insufferable "She seemed like some fair daughter of the Celestial Powers" from "Do geineadh ar gheineamhain di-se 'san tír uachtraigh." Phrase after phrase right through has suffered a dull change, has become coarsened and inept. Yet it is this translation that must serve:

Gile na gile do chonnarc ar slighe
  i n-uaigneas;
Criostal an chriostail a guirm-
  ruisc rinn-uaine;
Binneas an bhinnis a friotal nár
  chríon-ghruamdha;
Deirge is finne do fionnadh n-a
  gríos-ghruadhnaibh.

The Brightest of the Bright met
  me on my path so lonely;
The Crystal of all Crystals was
  her flashing dark-blue eye;
Melodious more than music was
  her spoken language only;
And glorious were her cheeks of
  a brilliant crimson dye.

Caise na caise i ngach ruibe dá
  buidhe-chuachaibh,
Bhaineas an ruithneadh den
  chruinne le rinn-scuabaibh;
Iorradh ga ghlaine 'ná gloine ar
  a bruinn bhuacaigh,
Do geineadh ar gheineamhain
  di-se 'san tír uachtraigh.

With ringlets above ringlets her
  hair in many a cluster
Descended to the earth, and
  swept the dewy flowers;
Her bosom shone as bright as a
  mirror in its lustre;
She seemed like some fair
  daughter of the Celestial
  Powers.

Fios fiosach dham d'innis, is ise
  go fíor-uaigneach;
Fios filleadh dhon duine dhon
  ionad ba rígh-dhualgas;
Fios milleadh na druinge chuir
  eisean ar rinn-ruagairt;
'S fios eile ná cuirfead im laoidh-
  thibh le fíor-uamhan.

She chanted me a chant, a
  beautiful and grand hymn,
Of him who should be shortly
  Eire's reigning King—
She prophesied the fall of the
  wretches who had banned
  him;
And somewhat else she told me
  which I dare not sing.

Leimhe na leimhe dham druidim
  n-a cruinn-tuairim!
Im chime ag an gcime do snaidhmeadh go fíor-chruaidh mé;

Trembling with many fears I
  called on Holy Mary,
As I drew nigh this Fair, to
  shield me from all harm,

175

Ar ghoirm Mhic Mhuire dhom
    fhurtacht, do bhíodhg uaim-
    se;
Is d'imthigh an bhruinneal n-a
    luisne go bruighin Luachra.

When, wonderful to tell! she
    fled far to the Fairy
Green mansion of Sliabh Luachra
    in terror and alarm.

Rithim le mire im rithibh go
    croidhe-luaimneach.
Tré imeallaibh curraigh, tré
    mhongaibh, tré shlím-ruaidh-
    tigh;
Don tinne-bhrogh tigim, ní
    thuigim cia an tslighe fuaras,
Go hionad na n-ionad do cumadh
    le draoidheacht dhruadha.

O'er mountain, moor, and marsh,
    by greenwood, lough, and
    hollow,
I tracked her distant footsteps
    with a throbbing heart;
Through many an hour and day
    did I follow on and follow,
Till I reached the magic palace
    reared of old by Druid art.

Brisid fá scige go scigeamhail
    buidhean ghruagach
Is fuireann do bhruinnealaibh
    sioscaithe dlaoi-chuachach;
I ngeimhealaibh geimheal mé
    cuirid gan puinn suaimhnis;
'S mo bhruinneal ar bruinnibh ag
    bruinnire bruinn-stuacach.

There a wild and wizard band
    with mocking, fiendish
    laughter
Pointed out me her I sought,
    who sat low beside a clown;
And I felt as though I never
    could dream of Pleasure
    after,
When I saw the maid so fallen
    whose charms deserved a
    crown.

D'inniseas di-se san bhfriotal do
    bhfíor uaim-se,
Nár chuibhe dhi snaidhmeadh le
    slibire slím-bhuaidheartha,
'S an duine ba ghile ar shliocht
    chinidh Scuit trí huaire,
Ag feitheamh ar ise bheith aige
    mar chaoin-nuachar.

Then with burning speech and
    soul, I looked at her and
    told her
That to wed a churl like that
    was for her the shame of
    shames,
When a bridegroom such as I
    was longing to enfold her
To a bosom that her beauty had
    enkindled into flames.

Ar chloistin mo ghotha dhi goil-
    eann go fíor-uaibhreach,
Is sileadh ag an bhfliche go life
    as a gríos-ghruadhnaibh,
Cuireann liom giolla dom choi-
    mirc ón mbruighin uaithi;
'S í gile na gile do chonnarc ar
    slighe i n-uaigneas.

But answer made she none; she
    wept with bitter weeping,
Her tears ran down in rivers, but
    nothing could she say;
She gave me then a guide for my
    safe and better keeping,
The Brightest of the Bright,
    whom I met upon my way.

Mo threighid! mo thubaist! mo
thurrainn mo bhrón! mo
dhíth!
An soillseach muirneach mio-
chair-gheal beol-tais caoin
Ag adharcach fuireann-dubh mio-
caiseach cóirneach buidhe;
'S gan leigheas n-a goire go
bhfillid na leoghain tar
tuinn.

Oh, my misery, my woe, my sorrow and my anguish,
My bitter source of dolour is evermore that she,
The loveliest of the Lovely,
should thus be left to lan-
guish
Amid a ruffian horde till the
Heroes cross the sea.

This single lyric, its attitude, its mode, justifies one in speaking with bitterness, even with scorn, of those who have dared
to tell the story of the Ireland of that period not only without
thought or feeling for, but with disdainful ignorance of, the
deep-rooted, widespread culture which could throw out so
manifestly superb a blossom. Its own perfection is not its only
significance: " If we may judge by the number of copies of
this poem extant in the MSS. of the eighteenth century, it
must have been very highly prized by the Irish public "[1]—
the " Irish public " that is, the " pariahs " of the mud cabins
in the bogs and the shielings on the mountainsides!

In this poem we may easily lose the poignancy of the
message in the sweetness of the song; but this is not often
Ó Rathaille's way. On the death of Tadhg Cronin's three
children he writes with Mediæval directness:

Trí téada ba bhinn, trí créachta
san tír,
Trí naomh-leinbh naomhtha,
thug géar-shearc do Chríost;
A dtrí mbéal, a dtrí gcroidhe, a
dtrí saor-chorp fá líg,
A dtrí n-éadan ba ghléigeal ag
daolaibh, is díth !

Three melodious strings, three
chasms in the earth,
Three sainted, holy children who
fondly loved Christ,
Their three mouths, their three
hearts, their three noble
bodies beneath a stone,
Their three fair, bright foreheads
the prey of chafers, it is ruin!

Here is his characteristic note—that note of pre-Renaissance
intensity which, dying out centuries before in the great tongues
of Europe, had lived on in Irish. One, however, accepts it as

---

[1] *The Poems of Egan O'Rahilly.*

personal to Ó Rathaille. His period, his language, his own
soul, are one whenever he sounds it, and more and more frequent it was to break from him as life more and more pressed
sore upon his spirit that yet would not be mad. How terrible
it is in that unforgettable poem which still, like a living voice,
remembers the most desolate of all his desolate nights! Poverty
has driven him in his declining years into the land of Duibh-
nigh. He has laid himself down to sleep, but he cannot sleep
for the loud wind that has raised the sea. Tonn Tóime, one
of the four great waves of Ireland, is thundering beneath him
on the rock-bound coast. And to pit against this discomfort,
induced from outside, as one might say, he has nothing of
internal peace, well-being, or hope:

Is fada liom oidhche fhír-fhliuch
  gan suan, gan srann,
Gan ceathra, gan maoin, caoirigh, ná buaibh na mbeann;
Anfhaithe ar tuinn taoibh liom
  do bhuadhir mo cheann,
Is nár chleachtas im naoidhin
  síogaigh ná ruacain abhann.

This truly wet night seems long
  to me, without sleep, without
  snore,
Without cattle or wealth or sheep
  or horned cows;
The storm on the wave beside
  me has troubled my head,
And I was unused in my child-
  hood to dogfish and periwinkles.

In that wild land, living on poor and unaccustomed foods,
dogfish and periwinkles, it would not be necessary for him
to remain if the MacCarthy Mór, or the MacCarthy from
the Lee, or the MacCarthy who was prince of Kanturk, still
lived and ruled each in his dominions. But foreign hosts have
ravished their dwellings—those warriors who were never
known to be niggardly, who inherited the land from Cashel
to the wave of Cliodhna and across to Thomond. . . . .
Gradually his thoughts fall away from his own dereliction to
that which has overtaken the princes under whom his fathers
had served, as he tells us, even before the death of Christ.
But the strong wave beneath breaks in upon his meditation
—only to find him, won from the plane of personal anguish
to the vast plane of a people's sorrow, now equal to it, it
would seem, in force, in loudness, in gesture:

A thonn so thíos is aoirde céim go h-árd,	Thou wave below, of highest re- pute, loud voiced,
Meabhair mo chinn claoidhte ót bhéiceach tá;	The senses of my head are over- powered with thy bellowing;
Cabhair dá dtigheadh arís go hÉirinn bháin,	Were help to come again to fair Erin,
Do ghlam nach binn do dhing- finn féin it bhrághaid.	I would thrust thy discordant clamour down thy throat.

What a gesture! And note how he achieves it only when he has flung his own personal torment into the massed sorrows of his race. In this lyric we seem to find our poet in his entirety—his poverty, his oneness with his race, his oneness with the fortunes of his province; and his gesture remembers the Gael to have been once on the necks of the Cromwellians. Yet even more characteristic is the poem he wrote on his death-bed. He is come to the end of all. Always poor, his lands, cattle, house, have been finally swept from him. More- over, the desolation of his last illness is upon him; yet, how does he begin this lyrical message to a friend?—

Cabhair ní ghoirfead go gcuirtear me i gcruinn-chomhrainn.

That is:

For help I will not cry until I'm put in a narrow coffin.

It seems we are hearing a voice that out-Lears Lear's! And the whole poem rings equally true: What use to cry for help? Those—the MacCarthys—who could and would have helped, they themselves are struck with decay:

Do thonnchrith m'inchinn, d'im- thigh mo phríomhdhóthchas,	My brain trembles as a wave, my chief hope is gone;
Poll im ionathar, biorrannaibh trím dhrólainn,	My entrails are pierced, veno- mous darts penetrate my heart;
Ar bhfonn, ar bhfoithin, ar monga, 's ar míonchomhgair,	Our lands, our shelter, our woods, our fair neighbour- hood
I ngeall le pinginn ag fuirinn ó chrích Dhóbher.	In pledge for a penny to a band from the land of Dover!

179

Again he has lost the sense of his own troubles in those of his race. Soon follows a note of characteristic irony: " I am a man under injustice," he says,

Fonn ní thigeann im ghoire is me ag caoi ar bhóithribh,
Ach foghar na muice nach gointear le saigheadóireacht.

No tune comes nigh me as I weep along the roads
But the squeal of the hog that dart-throwing cannot wound.

The hog that, unlike himself, is not to be wounded by darts is the Torc waterfall in Killarney, the word *Torc* meaning *Hog*. In the last verse he makes his farewell to life and song, and surely a more dignified farewell was never taken:

Stadfad-sa feasta, is gar dam éag gan maill,
Ó treascradh dreagain Leamhan, Léin, is Laoi;
Rachad-sa a haithle searc na laoch don chíll,
Na flatha fá raibh mo shean roimh éag do Chríost.

I will cease now, death is nigh unto me without delay;
Since the warriors of the Laune, of Lein, and of the Lee have been laid low,
I will follow the beloved among heroes to the grave,
Those princes under whom were my ancestors before the death of Christ.

It is not on record that he ever wrote another line. How great the whole thing is! It is as if going to meet the Shades, he had already clothed himself in their own severity and dignity. In poetry he has relieved the strain of a too-wrought-up heart; and now advances into eternity as into a place prepared for him. . . . . As we have associated his *Gile na Gile* with some perfect movement of Mozart's, so surely we may link this high strain with the music of him who said: " He who understands my music aright is lifted above the sorrows of the world."

VI

When one has gone some distance away from his pages, everything of his that comes back on one is strong, mournful and aloof. The elegies recur to us as great litanies of racial sorrow: we are conscious of loud, dark voices chanting vehemently the praises of the dead, raising "the twelve *ologóns*":

> Seabhac Mumhan, curadh laochais,
> Seabhac Gleanna, mac na féile,
> Seabhac Sionann, Oscar éachtach,
> Seabhac Muimhneach Inse Féidhlim.
>
> Phœnix croidhegheal, mín a ghéaga;
> Phœnix míre, gaois ba thréitheach;
> Phœnix Lithe agus Life, mo mhéala!
> Phœnix beodha, cródha, caoimhnirt.
>
> Péarla Bhaile na Martra méithe;
> Péarla Chluana, suaindreach gnégheal;
> Péarla Shiuire, is clú bhfear nEirinn;
> Péarla Luimnigh, is fuinnebhreach Féile.

The first epithet in every line—Hawk! Hawk! Hawk! Hawk! —Phœnix! Phœnix! Phœnix! Phœnix!—Pearl! Pearl! Pearl! Pearl!—sounding like a strong, firm chord. At other times it is detached phrases of happy music that return:

> Do bhís-se ceannsa d'fhann nó ró-lag,
> Do bhís-se teann le teann gan ró-cheart.

Or fresh and happy imagery:

D'fheoigh an fíonúir caoin, fionn, páirteach,
D'fheoigh géag phailime ó Pharrthas áluinn.

Withered is the gentle, fair, affectionate vine,
Withered the palm-bough from beauteous Paradise.

Or:

Aon dos tearmuinn d'éigsibh Chuinn.

The only bush of refuge for Erin's poets.

Sometimes, again, comes back a saying full of the high wisdom of simplicity:

Ná sáruigh naoidhe le dlighe de fhriotal gan áird;
Dar láimh mo choim tá nídh nár thuigis le fagháil.

Do not injure anyone in law, for the sake of a dishonourable word,
I pledge my heart that thou will obtain a thing thou knewest not of.

181

A saying worthy of Whitman. At other times it is a strain of music dazzlingly wrought:

Aisling meabhuil d'aicill mh'anam, seal gan tapa seang tím tréith:
Frasa carb trasna mara ag teacht andeas go teann faoi réim.

Or a flood of words rich with all the large effects that troop with majesty:

Is mar sin thug Dia cumais dúinne,
Tar éis bheith i gcumhangrach go mór,
Tighearna, agus árdfhlaith is prionnsa,
Sciath nirt, is úrchlogadh óir.

In like manner has a mighty God given to us,
After we had been in sore straits,
A lord, a high chieftain, a prince,
A shield of strength, a bright helmet of gold!

Words perfectly orchestrated. But, above all, what comes back to us is the man himself—utterly tragic both in soul and features, perplexed, exposed in every cell of his being to the darts of an inexpressible world, yet vigorously unyielding. His ear is scornful of the earth-whisper of coming change. His thoughts were all with the past, as befitted one who was writing the elegy of the Gaelic race. In his youth a poet would still sing a song for a patron and find rich reward for his labour: in his old age even the Browns themselves—the Kenmare family—could not follow the songs made for them. They had turned to the English scheme of things; and after the '15, the English scheme of life was already becoming bitterly anti-Gaelic. While Ó Rathaille, gathering his singing robes about him, haughtily unyielding, was preparing to take refuge among the MacCarthys in the fields of eternity, his younger poet-contemporaries, born into a new world, were finding an audience, if not patronage, in the taverns to which the stage coaches brought life and movement. The Gaels were become democrats.

.   .   .   .   .   .

" I entreat every prudent reader to excuse me on account of my haste, seeing that it is not I who am at fault, but hastiness of hand and the great trouble of heart and mind by which I am oppressed." . . . . So wrote Eoghan Ruadh Ó Súilleabháin as apology for any mistakes he might have made in transcribing one of Ó Rathaille's poems. There was no Gaelic poet of that century, whether he was forging out a new song of his own or merely transcribing the verses of another, that might not have written the self-same words. They were all oppressed by great trouble of mind and heart. To quote Montaigne: "Anaximenes, writing to Pythagoras, saith: 'With what sense can I amuse myself in the secrets of the stars, having continually death or bondage before mine eyes?' For at that time," explains the essayist, "the kings of Persia were making preparations to war against his country." In the case of our poets, the Persian was no longer merely at the gate; he had broken in, conquered, and was now dividing the spoils. It was, indeed, no time for contemplating the beauty of the stars. The charms of natural things, so intimately a part of the consciousness of the ancient Gaelic singers, were hidden from them as in a mist of sorrow. This mist of sorrow the others sometimes dissipated in passionate excesses; not so Ó Rathaille. It became the stuff of his brain. Yet it made no weakling of him: on his death-bed he could still cry out: "Cabhair ní ghoirfead go gcuirtear me i gcruinn-chomhrainn" ("For help I will not cry until I'm put in a narrow coffin").

To walk with him in spirit, hearing his accents, is to be purified as by terror and pity: leaving his presence, we move quietly as those move who have been witnessing tragedy.

CHAPTER VIII

EOGHAN RUADH Ó SÚILLEABHÁIN
(OWEN ROE O'SULLIVAN)

Aodhagán Ó Rathaille, that spirit so quick with all the proud and lonely sorrows of the Ireland of his time, had been buried only a little more than twenty years when, almost in the same spot of outland—one mile away, to be exact— another poet was born who also may be said to have been quick with Ireland's sorrows, no longer proud and lonely sorrows, however, but reckless and wild. Ó Rathaille is a tragic figure, mournful, proud; Eoghan Ruadh's life was even more tragic, but then he was a wastrel with a loud laugh.

That piece of outland, in which both were born, was truly Irish in its fortunes, and its story is full of meaning. It stretches eastward from Killarney to Rathmore, the Abhainn Ui Chriadh (the Quagmire River) running through it south-wards to join the Flesk. On the north-east lies the mountain mass known as Sliabh Luachra; and the school of poets, of which Eoghan Ruadh is the greatest, is known as the Sliabh Luachra school. When the Geraldines were crushed, the piece of outland was swept and harried and left desolate—houseless and unpeopled. In time some few of the O'Sullivans came northwards from Kenmare and set up new homesteads in it, undoing with patient labouring the work of the despoiler; and from these O'Sullivans sprang the boy Eoghan Ruadh.

In another way, too, the piece of land helps us to realise history. Let us look at it: All to the west of the little river belonged then to the MacCarthy Mór; all to the east was part of the Kenmare estate. That estate was in the grip of middlemen, those " deputies of deputies of deputies "; but the MacCarthys' tenants do not seem to have been rack-rented at all: it was probably one of those half-forgotten spots where many immemorial customs supplied the place of law; and, as compared with the rack-rented eastern river-bank, was a land flowing with milk and honey. Milk and honey may, indeed, have been actually the most plentiful of foods in it; and if it were so it was only fitting, for nowhere else in Ireland were so many sweet singers gathered together: the south-west corner of Munster was the Attica of Irish Ireland and Sliabh Luachra its Hymettus.

We are told there was a " classical school " in it—but what we are to understand by the phrase is that the Irish tradition had somehow never been quite extinguished there; that one or more bardic schools had flourished in the district of old; that a broken-down bardic school or Court of Poetry still assembled there; that the study of Irish poetry was the chief business of that school; that among the students would be found certain " poor scholars " who had travelled thither on foot, some of them hundreds of miles, from those places where such schools had ceased to exist; that of those students some would later enter Continental universities and become priests, while others would obtain Commissions in the armies of France, Austria or Spain.

"On Sunday evenings throughout the summer season a 'patron,' or dancing festival, was held at Faha, and in the plain beneath, a vigorous hurling match was carried on. . . . . The whole district on both sides of the river was permeated with the spirit of learning and the spirit of song. The O'Rahillys, the O'Scannells, the O'Sullivans and other families included men of conspicuous ability and no mean poetical talents. Between the people on either side of the river a rivalry, reminding one of the supposed derivation of that word, sprang up in hurling and in poetry. The people grew critical; each new poem or song was subjected to a severe examination, and if approved, was inserted in a book specially

185

kept for the purpose, called ' Bolg an tSoláthair.'[1] In the winter evenings the neighbours assembled to see what new piece was added to the *bolg*, and thus a constant stimulus to poetic effort was maintained. Native music, too, was fostered with native song, and an Irish piper was an institution at Faha which the surrounding rent-crushed villages could not afford. The academy at Faha prepared students for the more advanced seminary at Killarney, where candidates were educated for Holy Orders, and was not a mere grinding establishment, but fostered poetry and music and supplied a strong stimulus to the efforts of genius. The course comprised, besides Irish, English, Latin and Greek. In Greek, Homer seems to have been a favourite, and in Latin, Virgil and Cæsar and Ovid."[2]

" The more advanced seminary at Killarney "—yes, for the penal laws against religion were being relaxed; and the Church was just beginning to re-organise itself as an institution with a body as well as a spirit. From day to day, the passing of priests to and from the Continent was quickening; and parishes were beginning to set up regular services in buildings set apart for the purpose. But though the penal laws were becoming less rigorous the condition of the people was worsening rather than improving; they were growing poorer and poorer. The peasants, almost all Catholics, were increasing rapidly, while the whole political and social economy of the country was still working towards their extinction, a tug-of-war that led to widespread brutality and wretchedness. The Church had begun to grow active, and only in time, for the long period of social disorganisation had undoubtedly sapped some of the moral stamina of the people: in ever-growing numbers the richer Catholics were openly turning Protestant to save their estates; and the example both of these and the hard-drinking and boisterous squirearchy was influencing the

---

[1] " Bolg an tSoláthair " (" The Wallet of the Provider ").

[2] *Amhráin Eoghain Ruaidh Uí Shúilleabháin,* leis an Athair Pádraig Ua Duinnín.

mind of the labourers: Jack would have his fling as well as his master. The Church had not yet, however, had time to chasten, except in the least degree, the almost melodramatic spirit of violence that was abroad, common to both high and low, so that the peasants still took to the cudgel as readily as the squires to the pistol. All this we note as we turn the pages of Arthur Young, who went through the country just when Eoghan Ruadh was in the prime of life; and all this we should keep in mind if we would understand the tragic wayfaring of this child of song.

I

Meentogues, where he was born, was a place of poor land, of small holdings, of struggling people. Across the river was Faha, where the school was. Over the threshold of this school, a sooty cabin, it is likely, no boy of the place ever stepped who more quickly won the attention of the poet-teacher, for Eoghan came of a household where poetry was still, in the Gaelic mode, accounted as riches and as a stay against misfortune. He quickly learned to read in tattered and dirty manuscripts those great Gaelic stories and poems, the outlines of which he had already become acquainted with at home. So, too, in Latin and Greek he made his own of the world-famous stories that he would have heard already spoken of among his people and their visitors: ever afterwards the bright figures of those stories were to haunt his imagination. In English he must have learned to read with ease, to judge by the occasional poems he wrote in it.

The " poor scholars " caused him but little surprise, for these were now an old institution in the place. To such a school they were accustomed to come without books, without money, without a way of supporting themselves; and Eoghan's people, not the poorest in that countryside, would very likely have had, in the traditional way, one or more of them as guests upon their hearthstone. But he might have wondered at the differences between their language and his own; certain poets, that he would have little or no difficulty in understanding, must have, in many cases, needed much study from them; and beginning with this fact, he might have learned that his native parish was not typical of all Ireland. It took him a longer time, probably, to realise that he himself was not typical of even the boys of Sliabh Luachra.

One morning, we are told, he was late for school, and that he made his excuse in verse:

Ar dhrúcht na maidne is mé ag taisteal go ró-mhoch.	In the dew of the morning while journeying early.

And the story is credible, since no day would pass over those fields about his house without impromptu verses having been made, the labourers flinging them out almost as readily as the schoolmasters. But it is not right to think of him as a studious boy. If it is true that he was intended for the priesthood, it is only fitting to imagine him as restrained and docile; but remembering what he became while still in his young manhood, and the name he left behind him, to do so is impossible. One pictures him as good-looking, with hair as golden as red—not, indeed, far different from the colour of his sun-tanned brow and cheeks—as narrow-headed, high-crowned, lithe, tall, sinewy; as carrying himself well, daring, and not easily put down; as full of life, witty, and given to laughing; yet one must also recollect that he could be very still over a book and very patient in copying a manuscript.

When he was eighteen he opened a school on his own account at Gneeveguilla, a place two miles to the north of Meentogues. A contemporary of his, out of bitter experience, had called schoolmastering an empty trade, yet all his life through, whenever his fortunes were hopeless, on this empty trade Eoghan was to fall back. This first school of his did not last long—" an incident occurred, nothing to his credit, which led to the break-up of his establishment."[1] Such incidents, it

---

[1] *Amhráin Eoghain Ruaidh Uí Shúilleabháin,* leis an Athair Pádraig Ua Duinnín.

may be as well to say it, were afterwards to occur frequently; and because of them, and the want of self-control they denote, we may be certain that from this time, when he had to fly Gneeveguilla, with a threatening priest behind him, he scarcely ever afterwards knew what peace was, however much he laughed or sung. He returned to his home.

The boy-schoolmaster then became a *spailpín,* a wandering farm labourer. It may not have been necessary for him to start off on such unprofitable wayfaring, but the life of itself had much in it to appeal to one of his gifts and years. It was when the turf had been brought in from the bogs and had been built into stacks, that the *spailpíní* of Kerry tied up a few oaten cakes in their handcloths, shouldered their spades, and set off for the rich lands of Limerick, of North-East and East Cork. Their wives would then lock up their cabins, and, with their children swarming about them, set off to beg along the roads until their men returned at Christmas-time. Year after year this break-up and re-union of the family took place; and one imagines those *spailpíní* as railing at their lot, and yet finding it not easy finally to give it up, as is the way with sailors and wanderers of every description; the charms of the change of skies, the change of companions, the free-dom, renewing themselves in the memory the moment the home-life sinks again into dullness. But, of course, it was only rarely that the *spailpín* had any choice in the matter, no other way of living being left him: when the rich Catholic was hemmed in on every side, the poverty-stricken peasant must have had about as much freedom as a slave in choosing how he should live.

One can imagine, too, how eagerly a band of these labourers, and it was in squads that they traversed the countryside, would entice a young man of Eoghan's character to accompany them; for since the beginning of the world wit and song have not failed to shorten a lengthy road. Whatever the reason was, before he was twenty years old he shouldered his spade and set off to mow the meadows and to dig the potatoes in the County Limerick. One thinks of him as setting out with high heart and quick nostril: the roads were crowded with life; and taverns were frequent, the coaches swinging up to them in noise and dust and bustle; and in every tavern there would be new stories of highwaymen, of duelling, of kidnappings, of elopements and forced marriages, for it was the heyday of that melodramatic tragi-comedy that meant life for the Anglo-Irishman. For Eoghan, moreover, there would be a Court of Poetry here and there, hidden away in quiet villages, to be discovered; and in any countryside a poet, or a group of them, with their manuscripts and their traditions, might be come upon. Yes, at least on his first round, for he was never to cease making them, what between his youth, the novelty of the roads, and the freedom, his heart must have been high and his eyes alert at this setting out for the unknown.

There remain three poems of his, with which we will afterwards deal, that keep still fresh for us, in spite of the century and a half that has since gone by, those autumn wanderings on the roads of Munster of the young Kerryman in his knee-breeches and peaked cap. They make us certain of everything: of his wit, his daring, his way with the lasses: certain, too, that the memory of him that even to-day still lingers on these roads is not far astray when it recalls him as a playboy, a Mercutio, albeit a rustic one, with the same turn for fanciful and even dainty wit joined to the same fatal recklessness of spirit.

II

A little before Christmas he returned to his homeland by the little river; and it so happened that the stage was set, as if for his coming. The unmarried and the married men of the place had met in the hurling field, and the ancients had won the bout. To perpetuate the triumph, songs had been written; and these songs did not go unanswered; so that presently the hurling contest was thought of as but the cause of the greater effort in song that, before Eoghan's arrival, had, like a fever,

190

overtaken every poet from Knocknagree to Ballyvourney. As is usual, the younger generation were being scoffed at for their having dared to knock at the door. In their extremity, it had become necessary for them to induce an aged poet, Tadhg Críonna Ó Scannail (Old Theig O'Scannell), by dosing him with whiskey, to take their side, and write them verses satirising the feebleness and the ineptness of old men (the poor poet needed but to behold himself!). These verses, however, Matthew Hegarty of Glenflesk had roundly replied to, calling the writer of them a senseless renegade to deny his friends for the sake of drink; so that the married men still maintained their pride of place. The battle stood thus when Eoghan Ruadh returned from his first round on the roads of Munster.

In a poem he had previously written on his having to mind his own illegitimate child while its mother was out, he promised it, to quiet it, with a hundred other dainty and impossible gifts, the staff of Pan: to read now the poem he contributed to the contest, its assurance, its hearty gesture, its boastfulness, is to see him entering the fray armed, indeed, with that selfsame staff, wherever he, not yet twenty years of age, had come by it. He took the part of youth, and without misgiving he might well have done so, for he was never to reach middle age, not to mention old age; and his song sung, there was an end to the struggle. Indeed, there are nooks in Munster to this very day where, if an old man, forgetting his impotence, raises his voice against the young, he will find himself answered in one or another couplet from that head-long poem that the young labourer then flung disdainfully from his lips, as if to show what youth could do when it had gone afield and mixed with many men.

III

For the next ten years he wandered annually, either as *spailpín* or schoolmaster, over the roads of the South. Sometimes, it is likely that instead of returning to Sliabh Luachra

191

when the crops were all gathered in and no further work was required in the farms, he would remain where he was, open a school, and carry it on until the coming of summer again. We know for certain that at one time he did keep school at Donoghmore, which is not more than ten miles from Cork—a countryside that was then and for long afterwards well known for Irish scholarship and poetry. In other places, of which we have now no record, he must have done the same; but again he made his way back to Meentogues, never, however, to settle down or make himself a home. His wanderings have not yet been traced on any map; perhaps they never will; and our only way of filling up this period of ten years is to think of him as travelling the autumn roads with his spade on his shoulder, or as seated in a hut or by a farmer's hearth, a group of young men about him, all of them deep in the story of Ulysses, another wanderer, while the red glow of the turves lights the pages for them and the winter's winds sweep past outside.

So went the years; but how passed the slowly trailing days of them?—those days with their tally of pain, insult, longing, sickness, fierceness, weakness; with their fits of wild love-making, drunkenness; with their dull slavery of teaching, of turf-cutting, of potato-digging, of grass-mowing; with their discovery of kindred spirits, of young poets, of Courts of Poetry; with their patient labouring upon almost indicipher-able manuscripts; with their ecstasies of new songs dreamed or fashioned or sung in a triumphant voice—how those slow-trailing days passed for him, dark or bright or wild or slow or fast, we shall never be able to imagine, except dimly and, therefore, wistfully. " Tidings of him are to be found in every county of Munster. There is no town nor stronghold nor fort from the Siuir to Beara that he did not walk there; and in them there remained the memory of him so long as even a remnant of the Irish language remained in the mouths of the people. Here he was a teacher; there a labourer. In this town he drank and took his pleasure. At fair and market he was often seen with a crowd about him, for whom he made sport or poured out verses, or retaliated on someone who had tried to put him down. Usually he was among the poets, making sport for them, answering and counter-answering them, satirising or making a laughing-stock of someone who appeared too officious. Often, again, he went on foot from house to house, spending a night here, another there, letting on to be a poor, simple man that had had no rearing or schooling, putting foolish questions to the woman of the house, and failing to understand her replies, speaking out clearly at last his own opinion, and praising or dispraising the family in good verses. Sometimes, again, he made bold on some priest, in the form of a poor tramp who did not know the Commandments; only to break out, when the priest had done his best to teach him them, in impromptu verses, satirising the priesthood. He was fine company for the labourer. Neither conversation nor song nor story failed him from morning till night."[1]

Except in some such general terms, we cannot speak of the ten years from 1770 to 1780—that is, from his twenty-second to his thirty-second year. It is probable that it was during these years he made the greater number of his poems, verses of pure poetry, of poet's poetry; but it is certain that it was during them he established the tradition of himself that the winds of a century and a half have not yet quite swept from the roads of Munster. In point of character, he was sinking lower and lower; and at last it became necessary for him to take refuge in the army, although every better impulse of his nature must have rebelled against the act. He was at the time schoolmaster to the children of the Nagle family, whose place was near Fermoy, and how, from being one of their farm labourers, he had come to be in this position lingers still as a legend in the Irish-speaking parts of Munster. I have had it told to myself that one day in their farmyard he heard a woman, another farm-hand, complain that she had need to write a letter to the master of the house, and had failed to find anyone able to do

---

[1] I translate from *Beatha Eoghain Ruaidh Uí Shúilleabháin,* leis an Athair Pádraig Ua Duinnín.

so. "I can do that for you," Eoghan said, and, though mis-doubting, she consented that he should. Pen and paper were brought him, and he sat down and wrote the letter in four languages—in Greek, in Latin, in English, in Irish. "Who wrote this letter?" the master asked the woman in astonishment; and the red-headed young labourer was brought before him; questioned, and thereupon set to teach the children of the house. Other accounts vary slightly from this, but it may be taken as illustrating the legends of him that even yet survive in corners of Munster. Owing to his bad behaviour he had to fly the house, the master pursuing him with a gun. Fermoy was an important military station, and he soon put the walls of the barracks there between himself and his pursuer. From Fermoy he was sent to Cork, and from Cork he sailed almost immediately in a transport for the West Indies—and a new chapter had opened for him.[1]

IV

To say nothing of the alien rabble of the lower decks, the scourings of English prisons, among whom he now found himself, to be thus caged in was a dismal change for one who had had whole counties for his adventurous feet. What manner of men swarmed in a man-of-war at that period, as well as what manner of men ruled over them with ruthless authority, we know from the realistic pages of *Roderick Random*;[2] and Mr John Masefield has in our own days written for his countrymen these terrible words: "Our naval glory was built up by the blood and agony of thousands of barbarously maltreated men. It cannot be too strongly insisted on that sea life in the late eighteenth century, in our navy, was

---

[1] But see the later edition of these poems, where the editor throws doubt on the whole story. It may be yet proved that the poet was pressed for the Navy, as he himself states in one of his poems.
[2] Published 1748.

194

brutalising, cruel, and horrible; a kind of life now happily gone for ever; a kind of life which no man to-day would think good enough for a criminal. There was barbarous discipline, bad pay, bad food, bad hours of work, bad company, bad prospects."[1] And stressing the phrase "bad company," he quotes from the contemporary Edward Thompson: "In a man-of-war you have the collected filths of jails: condemned criminals have the alternative of hanging or entering on board. . . . . There's not a vice committed on shore that is not practised here; the scenes of horror and infamy on board a man-of-war are so many and so great that I think they must rather disgust a good mind than allure it."

Between these lower decks, then, Eoghan Ruadh, the landsman, the wandering minstrel, was now imprisoned, one of those thousands of barbarously maltreated seamen. His one talent was no longer of use: if in his few hours of sleeping, *aisling* poems still brightened in his brain, it was only bitterness to recall them once they had scattered in the hurry-scurry of the seaman's uprousing. In those silent night watches of his across the unfamiliar waters, he no doubt comforted himself with the quiet singing of the songs of Munster, his own and others; and also, doubtless, he would often astonish his illiterate English shipmates with his strange stories of Greece and Rome, with his amazing gift of tongues; he was not, therefore, utterly forlorn both of moments of forgetfulness and moments of triumph. Must we not also recollect, however, that as surely as it was in his nature to give way to wild fits of loud-voiced recklessness, it was also in him to sit tongue-tied, revolving his fate, and finding but little comfort in looking either backwards or forwards. In such moments he saw himself with clear eyes: in one such, the Spirit of Ireland came before him, as radiant as ever, with reproach in her eyes: "Do not insult me, Bright Shape of the Fair Tresses," the tortured poet cried to her; "by the Book in my hand I swear I am not of them; but by the very hair of the head I was snatched away

---

[1] John Masefield, *Sea Life in Nelson's Time.*

195

and sent over the floods, helping him (the English Monarch) that I do not wish to help, in the ships of the bullets on the foaming sea, I that come of the stock of the Gaels of Cashel of the Provincial Kings!"

Ná tarcuisnigh mé, a gheal-scéimh na gcúil-fhionn,
Dar an leabhar so im ghéag, níl braon dá gcrú ionnam,
Ach taistealach théid tar chaise le fraoch,
Do stracadh i gcéin ar úrla,
Ag cabhair don té nár bh-fonn liom,
I mbarcaibh na bpiléar ar chubhar-mhuir,
Is gur scagadh mo thréad as caise d'fhuil Ghaedheal
I gCaiseal na réacsa cúigidh!

To the longing that is so heavy a weight in every exile's heart was added in his case the pain of helping those whom he, the descendant of Provincial Kings, despised. Though it is quite certain that in the rough-and-tumble of the seaman's life, he could, as well as the next, take care of himself—the Munster of his day being no bad training ground in such arts, there was still an implacable round of circumstances leagued against him: he was one of a despised race; he was a peasant; his strange accents were an offence; his messmates, we have seen what they were; and he was a poet. Taking everything into account, among the thousands of maltreated men between the decks of Rodney's ships, perhaps there was not one more miserable than this baffled son of music and dreams.

It was his lot to assist in one of England's most famous sea-fights. "The ship in which he sailed joined the English fleet under Rodney, then vice-admiral of Great Britain, somewhere before the West Indies were reached. On the morning of the twelfth of April in that year, 1782, Rodney, who had lately been blundering, was awakened by Sir Charles Douglas with the intelligence that God had given him the French enemy on the lee bow 'not far from old Fort Royal.' De Grasse, the French admiral, in vain tried to get to the windward. The engagement began at seven o'clock, and at close quarters. As the French line got southward under the lee of Dominica, it was gapped by varying winds. Through one of the gaps

196

Rodney's own vessel, the 'Formidable' passed, the 'Bedford' followed, another leading vessel found also a passage. The ships astern followed. The French fleet were routed, and De Grasse's flagship, the 'Ville de Paris,' surrendered to the 'Barfleur.' Rodney, whose recent manœuvres had ended in failure, was in ecstasies of delight. He had won a victory, perhaps, hitherto unsurpassed in the annals of British naval warfare, and was fully conscious of the importance of his triumph. In an account of the fight, written by himself, we read: 'The battle began at seven in the morning and continued till sunset, nearly eleven hours, and by persons appointed to observe, there never were seven minutes' repose during the engagement, which, I believe, was the severest ever fought at sea, and the most glorious for England. We have taken five and sunk another.' "[1]

On that fight Eoghan Ruadh, almost before the heat of battle had left him, wrote this curious song in English:

Rodney's Glory

Give ear, ye British hearts of gold,
That e'er disdain to be controlled,
Good news to you I will unfold,
   'Tis of brave Rodney's glory,
Who always bore a noble heart,
And from his colours ne'er would start,
But always took his country's part
Against each foe who dared t' oppose
Or blast the bloom of England's Rose,
   So now observe my story.

'Twas in the year of Eighty Two,
The Frenchmen know full well 'tis true,
Brave Rodney did their fleet subdue,
   Not far from old Fort Royal.
Full early by the morning's light,
The proud De Grasse appeared in sight,
And thought brave Rodney to affright,
With colours spread at each mast-head,
Long pendants, too, both white and red,
   A signal for engagement.

[1] *Amhráin Eoghain Ruaidh Uí Shúilleabháin,* leis an Athair Pádraig Ua Duinnín.

Our Admiral then he gave command,
That each should at his station stand,
" Now, for the sake of Old England,
    We'll show them British valour."
Then we the British Flag displayed,
No tortures could our hearts invade,
Both sides began to cannonade,
Their mighty shot we valued not,
We plied our " Irish pills " so hot,
    Which put them in confusion.

This made the Frenchmen to combine,
And draw their shipping in a line,
To sink our fleet was their design,
    But they were far mistaken;
Broadside for broadside we let fly,
Till they in hundreds bleeding lie,
The seas were all of crimson dye,
Full deep we stood in human blood,
Surrounded by a scarlet flood,
    But still we fought courageous.

So loud our cannons that the roar
Re-echoed round the Indian shore,
Both ships and rigging suffered sore,
    We kept such constant firing;
Our guns did roar and smoke did rise,
And clouds of sulphur veiled the skies,
Which filled De Grasse with wild surprise;
Both Rodney's guns and Paddy's sons
Make echo shake where'er they come,
    They fear no French or Spaniards.

From morning's dawn to fall of night,
We did maintain this bloody fight,
Being still regardless of their might,
    We fought like Irish heroes.
Though on the deck did bleeding lie
Many of our men in agony,
We resolved to conquer or die,
To gain the glorious victory,
And would rather suffer to sink or die
    Than offer to surrender.

So well our quarters we maintained,
Five captured ships we have obtained,
And thousands of their men were slain,
    During this hot engagement;
Our British metal flew like hail,

198

Until at length the French turned tail,
Drew in their colours and made sail
In deep distress, as you may guess,
And when they got in readiness
    They sailed down to Fort Royal.

Now may prosperity attend
Brave Rodney and his Irishmen,
And may he never want a friend
    While he shall reign commander;
Success to our Irish officers,
Seamen bold and jolly tars,
Who like darling sons of Mars
Take delight in the fight
And vindicate bold England's right
    And die for Erin's glory.

" The ode was sent to the Admiral in the flush of triumph. He was delighted with the composition, and asked the author to be brought to him. An officer named MacCarthy, a Kerryman, accompanied the poet in his visit to the Admiral. Rodney was gracious, and offered promotion, but Eoghan only wanted to be set free from service. Ere the Admiral could reply to his request, MacCarthy interposed and said: ' Anything but that; we would not part with you for love or money.' Eoghan turned away, saying: ' Imireochaimíd beart éigin eile oraibh ' (' I will play some other trick on you '). MacCarthy, who understood his remark, replied: ' I'll take good care, Sullivan, you will not.' "[1]

The group makes a curious cabin interior: The proud Admiral, new-flushed with victory; the officer, MacCarthy, representing, it is likely, one of those Gaelic families that had changed their religion for the sake of retaining their lands and, generally, winning to worldly honours; and then the drab seaman, the heart-sick exile, the darling of the peasantry of Munster, the self-conscious descendant of the Provincial Kings of Cashel. The song, which, doubtless, the heady seamen in the revel of victory had sent roaring across the waves, lies there on the table beneath the Admiral's eyes. We know it for

[1] *Amhráin Eoghain Ruaidh Uí Shúilleabháin,* leis an Athair Pádraig Ua Duinnín.

a song written in a language which never crossed the poet's lips whenever he spoke what was in his own heart or in the heart of his race; yet Rodney, though it was his privilege to have the living poet there before his eyes, could not have known this: to him the song is complete in itself, a good song, worthy of being paid for somehow or other. One thinks of him as looking from manuscript to poet and from poet to manuscript, not without some sense of wonder; and one further reflects: How much greater wonder if in this rough seaman, awkward as one in a strange place, he could have seen the author of " Do rinneadh aisling bheag aereach " or " I gcaol-doire chraobh-chluthmhar néamh-dhuilleach bhíos," two perfect lyrics, with the refined artistry of the intuitional poet in every line of them! What would his wonder have been could it have been revealed to him that only more than a century later this peasant-sailorman would begin to come into his due; or that one hundred and forty years later a certain warm feeling of envy would arise in at least one narrator of the episode to think that he can never, except in fallacious vision, behold what he, Rodney, then looked upon with his mortal eyes!

V

We do not know how it came about that the poet was transferred from the navy to the army: as a soldier, however, stationed in England, we find him no less unhappy than he had been at sea. Beyond the poems that he wrote at this time, no other information either of his whereabouts or his condition, seems to have been discovered; and in these poems what we are chiefly aware of is his disgust at being mistaken for a rake from London, his bitterness at having had to undergo some term of imprisonment, and in *Ceo draoidheachta i gcoim oidhche (A fog of wizardry in the depths of night)*— as good a poem as he ever wrote—we find him again visited by the Spirit of Ireland, with whom he makes equal sorrow, finishing, however, on the universal hope: " Should our

Stuart come to us from beyond the sea with a fleet from Louis
and from Spain, in the sheer dint of joy I'd be mounted on a
swift, stout, vigorous, nimble steed, driving out the ' ospreys '
at the sword's edge "—and then, with this couplet, he entirely
and triumphantly shakes the trouble from his mind:

> Is ní chlaoidhfinn-se m'intinn 'na dheághaidh sin
> Chum luighe ar sheasamh gárda lem rae.

" And after that, as long as I lived, never more would I dull
my mind with mounting guard "—an unforced expression that
opens up for us the many-sided miseries of a soldier who is
aware that he has any mind to dull.

Aching still to be at home, he blistered his shins with spear-
wort when all other stratagems to get free had failed him.
His companions, it is said, refused to mess with him, so terrible
had the sores become; and doctor after doctor having tried in
vain to cure him, he was at last free to go home.

He seems to have made straight for Kerry. Arrived there,
he sent a letter to Fr Ned Fitzgerald, asking him to publish
from the altar that he was about to open a school at
Knocknagree—a bleak, wind-swept hamlet, only a few miles
from his birthplace. The letter, which was in verse, was written
both in Irish and English, and it is strange that only the
English portion has come down to us in its entirety:

> Reverend Sir—
>> Please to publish from the altar of your holy Mass
>> That I will open school at Knocknagree Cross,
>> Where the tender babes will be well off,
>> For it's there I'll teach them their Criss Cross;
>> Reverend Sir, you will by experience find
>> All my endeavours to please mankind,
>> For it's there I will teach them how to read and write;
>> The Catechism I will explain
>> To each young nymph and noble swain,
>> With all young ladies I'll engage
>> To forward them with speed and care,
>> With book-keeping and mensuration,
>> Euclid's Elements and Navigation,
>> With Trigonometry and sound gauging,
>> And English Grammar with rhyme and reason.

> With the grown-up youths I'll first agree
> To instruct them well in the Rule of Three;
> Such of them as are well able,
> The cube root of me will learn,
> Such as are of a tractable genius,
> With compass and rule I will teach them,
> Bills, bonds and informations,
> Summons, warrants, supersedes,
> Judgment tickets good,
> Leases, receipts in full,
> And releases, short accounts,
> With rhyme and reason,
> And sweet love letters for the ladies.

The school did not last long; it may be that it broke up naturally at the approach of summer, or that the ex-soldier, though not yet thirty-six years of age, had lost the power of working on steadily day after day. In either case, in the early summer of 1784, he paid a visit to Colonel Daniel Cronin, of Park, near Killarney: it was only lately that Cronin had become colonel of a body of yeomanry, and before his honours had had time to dull, the poet thought to present him with a complimentary poem in English. The Colonel either neglected or refused to acknowledge the song in the only way that could now recompense the poet. When we learn that he thereupon blazed up and put all his wits into composing a fierce satire on the Colonel, we somehow indulge the thought that the unfortunate poet had not even yet quite come to the dregs of his self-respect; for the faculty of resentment finally ceases altogether in those whose only plan is to live on the bounty of others. Soon afterwards some of Cronin's servants and himself chanced to meet in an ale-house in Killarney and a quarrel arose between them; blows followed, and the Colonel's coachman is said to have struck the poet a sharp blow on the head with a pair of tongs—the weapon first to hand in the place. The one blow was sufficient: with his head bound, and hot with fever, he made his way back to Knocknagree.

On that wind-swept hilltop, " on the eastern side of the fair field on the northern side of the road opposite the gate of the pound," was a hut for fever patients. It was about two hundred yards distant from the houses—far enough away to prevent contagion, far enough also to be as lonely and desolate to the dying man as the middle of the sea. In this hut he was laid, and some woman of the place went in and out, attending on him. He was putting the fever off him, he was convalescent, when " an act of self-indulgence, it is said, brought on a relapse from which he never rallied."[1]

When his end was not far off, he sat up in bed, asked for pen and paper, and set himself to write his last verses, his poem of repentance, as the Irish fashion was; but he was weaker in limb than brain—the pen slipped from his fingers, to his own sudden enlightenment, it seems, for

Sin é an file go fann
'Nuair thuiteann an peann as a láimh,

Weak indeed is the poet
When the pen falls from his hand,

he whispered, lay back, and in silence died. Eoghan an Bheóil Bhínn—Eoghan of the Sweet Mouth!

" Pen," " poet "—a poet, in his own thought, to the very end, no matter to what misguided uses the rough racket of the world had put him while he lived.

The winds still played with him: though it was mid-summer (1784), a thunderstorm broke upon the uplands as he lay in the midst of the keeners, and had not ceased when the time for burial was come. To reach Muckross Abbey, the Blackwater had to be crossed, but there being no bridge, the floods made this impossible. A temporary grave was, therefore, quickly dug, and the mourners dispersed for the night. On the following day the coffin was shouldered again, and he was carried over the river and laid with his people in the Abbey. This, though it is now generally accepted as the truth, has been always disputed, and even to-day some of the people of that countryside assert that the poet lies at Nohavile, where the first grave was dug.

---

[1] *Amhráin Eoghain Ruaidh Uí Shúilleabháin,* leis an Athair Pádraig Ua Duinnín.

He was dead for almost a century and a half when his poems were collected from various sources by Father Dinneen and, for the first time, published in book-form. Perhaps from time to time some few others may be added to this collection; but there is scarcely a doubt that we have in it practically the entire harvest that remains to us of that vagrant and feverish life. It is certain that many of his songs are lost, and among them some, perhaps, that we should especially value, for the bye-poems of that period, with their intimacy and human interest, were not the sort of poetry that the rather academic, though peasant, scribes thought best worth copying and preserving; yet, taking one thing with another, this book of 121 pages is as large as one could fairly expect. With a passing thought that the poet himself never had the wistful, gentle pleasure of turning its pages, let us first roughly reckon up what it contains, afterwards trying to feel the qualities that made these poems the dear inheritance of a province.

In the book there are nineteen *aisling* (vision) poems. The specimen we have examined in the chapter on the *Aisling* is one of these nineteen, and some authorities would not agree that it is the best of them. The high level of this whole set of *aisling* poems is surprising; and to determine for ourselves that this or that is the best of all is straightway to have the opening lines of some other one begin to sing in our ears. The *Aisling* beginning:

Cois na Siúire maidean drúchta is mé támhach lag faon,	Beside the Suir one dewy morn and I weak, cast down and faint,

is a perfect lyric; as indeed also is:

Do rinneadh aisling bheag aerach gan bhréig trím néal dam	In sleep there came a vision light, fleeting and true

—a poem full of the most beautiful lyric qualities; and who definitively would place

Trím aisling araoir do smuaineas-sa	In my vision last night I fancied

second to any of these mentioned without lingering regret for the tripping and dainty music that hovers above its firm resolve? And so one goes from one to another, the charm in each varying as the mood. What distinguishes one from another is the temper of its mood, that dictating the music, the colour, everything. Yet there are some readers—and even writers!—who find these *aisling* poems " all the same "; and no kind friend whispers them that it may not be unwise for them to keep their colour-blindness, their tone-deafness, to themselves.

Following these nineteen *aisling* poems we have two songs classed as Songs Against the Pirates (that is, the Planters). The first of the two is interesting as being one of those poems, so frequent in the Munster manuscripts, which glance at political disturbances on the Continent, their writers still clinging to the hope that France or Spain, or both together, would yet come to help the Gaels. The second is interesting as a versification of the names of the Cromwellian settlers in the poet's district: here are the concluding stanzas of it:

(" is " = " agus " = " and ")
Gibson, Brown, Townsend, Gill, Tonson, is Gore,
Dickson, Nowls, Boulton is Buttons is Bowen,
Kickson, Southwell, Moulton, Miller is Dore
Glas is gobhann is lom ar a maireann dá bpór.

Southwell, Steelman, Stephens, Stanner is Swain,
Parnell, Fleetwood, Reeves, is Shutman is Lane,
Gach crochaire coimhightheach, ciar-dhubh, ceannan, dá bpréimh,
Treascartha claoidhte sínte i gcaismirt na bpiléar.

Lysight, Leader, Clayton, Compton is Coote,
Ivers, Deamer, Bateman, Bagwell is Brooks,
Ryder, Taylor, Manor, Marrock is Moore,
Is go bhfaiceam-na traochta ag tréin-shliocht Chaisil na búir.

Upton, Evans, Bevins, Basset is Blair,
Burton, Beecher, Wheeler, Farren is Fair,
Turner, Fielding, Reeves, is Wallis is Dean,
Cromwell 's a bhuidhean sain scaoileadh is scaipeadh ar a dtréid.

The list of names in every verse is followed by an imprecation, thus the last line in the third stanza quoted may be translated:

May we see the boors routed by the mighty descendants of Cashel.

The interest in the poem is many-sided: the preserving of the vowel-music of Irish verse in the mere listing of alien names is of itself testimony to his lyrical ear; then, if for Eoghan Ruadh's own day it had the immediate interest of the topical, for our time it has the aloofness of a passionate face on which the coldness of death has fallen: it is one of those invaluable poems which confront the historian with a challenge that cannot be put aside, testing his message or, on the other hand, adding to it the poignancy of flesh and blood. The opening of the poem may be translated: " O keen and correct poet who reads the old authors and quickly solves each hard difficulty, do you relate to us completely and with learning, are the Gaels to be long under the sharp yoke of the pirates (the Cromwellians)?" And the close is:

A Íosa, a Dhia aoibhinn, is a Athair an Uain,	O Jesus, O dear God, and O Father of the Lamb,
Do chídheann sinn a gcuibhreacht 's i gceangal go cruaidh—	Who beholds us hard bound in fetters and bonds—
A Rígh néimhe díonta, freagair mo dhuan,	O mighty King of Heaven, answer my poem,
Scaoil agus díbir an ghraithin seo uainn.	Scatter and banish from us this contemptible breed.

And between opening and close we have the actual names of the local Cromwellians who in those days ruled with such strong and surly power the poet's countryside, and who in our days are vanished from the place; vanished, moreover, with no song sung nor any other work of the spirit left in their wake to save their name from oblivion; they live now only in the passionate verse of the *spailpín* who in a " sconnsa fhliuch," a wet trench, dug out their potatoes for them or, heavy with weariness, ploughed their wide lands for them " ag treabhadh go tréith do dhaoscur Cailbhinists," crying out:

An réidhfidh Críost ar gcás go deo?	Will Christ ever ease our lot for us?

206

The wheel has come full circle. These *spailpíns'* estimation of their masters we must accept, since, as has been said, the Cromwellians have left no perdurable monument that would contradict it.

Reading such verses, one often wonders if those hard-drinking, duelling, gambling buckeens that Arthur Young in those very days questioned so closely ever realised how passionately the peasants who swarmed about their lands felt towards them? or ever dreamt that in a century and a half practically all their houses and lands would have reverted to the Gaels? Again, to the reader who is not ignorant of his literary history, the list of names will remind him of other such lists, for the homeliness, the plebeianism, rather, of the Cromwellian surnames caused great humour among the highly-descended Irish people; they made many rhymes of these names both in English and Irish, as the one in English that begins:

> The Fairs, the Blacks, the Blonds, the Brights,
> The Greens, the Browns, the Greys, the Whites,
> The Parrotts, Eagles, Cocks and Hens,
> The Snipes, Swallows, Pies, Robins, Wrens, etc.[1]

While Dáibhidh Ó Bruadair was making one in Irish:—

> Gúidí Húc is mudar Hammer
> Róibín Súl is fádur Salm
> Geamar Rú is goodman Cabbage
> Mistress Cápon Cáit is Anna
> Ruiséal Rác is Maighistir Geadfar, etc.

almost at the very time that Milton was writing of those Gaelic names that would, to his mind, have made Quintilian stare and gasp—and so we have glanced at both sides of the picture.

Following on these there come a very interesting group of poems dealing with his own life. The first, that addressed to a love-child of his, is full of daintiness and bright music. Then

---

[1] See " Cromwell in Ireland," by Denis Murphy, S.J.

we have three poems which renew for us his life as a *spailpín*. Each is addressed to some smith or other of his acquaintance: a spade is to be made, or a handle fitted in one, or thanks returned for work done. These songs are not alone interesting as bearing directly on his own life, but each is self-centred, sterling poetry, as good to-day as when written; and it is certain that the second of them would be known to the world if Villon had made it. In it are found the lines, already quoted, where he tells his friend James Fitzgerald, smith, that should the steward begin to chide him as not of great account at spadework, he, the poet, will gently begin to relate the adventurous wanderings of Death, or the tale of the Grecian battles at Troy, where the princes fell. The poem grows swifter then, and finishes with a wild gesture: He will not spend a sixpence of his wages, stored away and tied with hemp in the bosom of his shirt, until, returned home, he finds himself in the smith's company. " Then since like myself you are a man that Old Thirst has often tortured—to the tavern at the stage with us, and let the tables be struck until the wines and ales are spread, and no stop to the carousing while even a halfpenny remains!" In the original the lines rush ahead to the perfect climax.

The next poem in this group is a request to a priest to announce that he intends to open a school in the neighbourhood—sixteen lines that remind us how the *spailpín* would pass the winter months when the land was idle. Then we have a " Confession " of a rather conventional type, though some of the verses are striking, now for their quaintness, and then for their frankness. In the Mass, he confesses, he took but little interest, failing in reverence even at the most sacred moments, moments when the fish in the stream stood still, owning to the miracle (of the Consecration). We then find a curious poem beginning: " Here's what I think of a rake's life " (" Sin agaibh mo theastas ar beathaidh gach réice ")— and, indeed, it is little else than a frank account of what he thought of himself when the heat of excitement had passed and thought began to say its bitter word:

An uair tigeann an laige, agus druideann an t-aos liom,
'S mé ar uireasbaidh éadaigh, is caillim mo threoir,
Bíonn pairthis creathach gach maidean im ghéagaibh,
Ní blasta mo bhréithre is níl tathach im ghlór;
Is searbh an aiste liom labhairt ar chéithlinn,
Tigh an tabhairne séanaim mar chaitheas mo stór,
Dearbhaim, admhuighim feasta, 'gus géillim
Gur damanta an chéird í, is go mb'fheárr léigeann dóibh.

When weakness comes and old age draws up to me,
I lack for clothing, I lose my strength,
My limbs in the morning shake and shiver,
My words are savourless, and weak my voice;
Bitter it is to me to speak of a woman,
I shun the tavern where I spent my all,
I swear, I admit henceforth, I yield
That it is a damned business and they are better let alone.

He finishes by counselling the free and manly youth to settle down and marry, to avoid drinking and quarrelling at the fairs. The two remaining songs in the section are also concerned with drinking.

Then we pass to his satires. Of the most famous of them, *An t-Arrachtach Sean (The Aged Monster)*, we have already given some account. Perhaps the next most famous is a poem satirising the priests of his time. He addresses one of them, evidently a poet, praising him at the expense of his brethren; and the burden of his song is twofold: once there was a Church that was friendly to the poets, the priests generous in their houses, feast-giving, humane, charitable; but now there is left to us only the chaff after the sieving—a rabble of dunces: the other burden is that while a rich man may do as he likes, let a poor man but look at a girl and there's " running routing " for him and the curse of clergy and bell. In his next satire he relieves his mind on Kate O'Leary, who had " sequestered " his pair of stockings because he owed her fourpence—a right good poem, flung out, hot and heady and as reckless as it could be. " May I see you with an ugly child in your lap, and neither father nor tidings of father to be had for ever ":

Go bhfeicead-sa gárlach gránna id chlúid agat
Is gan a athair le faghbháil go bráth ná cunntas ann

209

—one of the many curses in it—may be taken as a sample of the whole. All over it we find those touches of time and place that make all his poems, except, possibly, the decorative *aisling* poems, so real and alert. He wishes that she may die without the priest and be waked without keeners—a hard wish in the Munster of that time:

> Gan ola chum báis ná gáir ós cionn do chuirp.

It is not very intellectual, perhaps, but as one reads it one fancies that Villon or Rabelais would have howled it out with vast delight, so full of verse is it, so lacking in all restraint: it is, moreover, an example of that headlong run of overpowering invective, so common in Irish poets, that influenced John M. Synge both in his dramas and poems.[1]

We have only one elegy in the book. It was written on the death of Father Con Horgan, 20th January, 1773; and in every line of it one feels the influence of Ó Rathaille. This verse might be taken from almost any of his famous keens:

> Uaill is gáir is crádh-ghol éagnach,
> Is gruaim is glámh is lán-tocht éighmhe,
> Greadad bas is stracadh céibhe,
> Brón is caoi go cíocrach céasta.

What is said in the lines is not of the same importance as the solemn music in which the message is wrapped up, the dark vowels resounding, one to another—the very note of Ó Rathaille's keens. Here are two other lines which nobody would believe were written by any other poet except him:

> An bocht 's an nocht go docht 'san mhéala
> Tré theascadh an bhile ceann urraidh na cléire.

But here we have two lines with Eoghan's tenderness in them:

> Níl agam ach guidhe le h-intinn éagnaigh
> Chum aingil is naoimh bheith síor dá aodhaireacht.

> What can I do but pray with wistful mind
> That angels and saints may shepherd him for ever.

---

[1] See his curse on his sister—not wholly serious, one believes.

The very thought, however, which these two lines round to a close tells us that the poet was all the time aware of the difference between himself and Ó Rathaille as keeners. Where is the genealogy? The priest that he was lamenting was, the poet tells us, learned in song, practised in the difficult lore of the poets, trained in the genealogy of the race:

> Do chuireadh le slacht 'na gceart gach Gaedheal-treabh
> I mBanda ghluais anuas ó Éibhear.

Literally:

> Who used to put neatly right every Gaelic tribe
> In Banda that descended from Éibhear.

The poet himself felt very unlearned in all this; his head is empty of *ogham,* he tells us. All he can do is to pray the angels and saints to take the dead priest into their shepherding—a prayer possible to the most ignorant of men. But in many another of his poems he is also conscious of this want of the old learning: and the solacing thought that he may have been better without it never broke even once upon his mind.

The next five poems are grouped under the heading Amhráin Molta Ban, Poems in Praise of Women, but, though in each of them there are very beautiful and very tender lines, they are only the conventional love-poetry that was then in fashion.

Then we have a few " Warrants "—humorous verses which are all readable, but of little importance. The first is called " A Warrant against some person who stole his hat," and while conventional in the scheme, the handling is as neat as it could well be: who could think of bettering these lines in point of style?

> Cá tairbhe damh-sa a mhaitheas do chómhaireamh,
> D'éis a ghuidighthe?
> Is gur bh'álainn gleoidhte sásda an t-seod é
> Ag saor-fhlaith chumasach:

>> Níl ainnir ná bé do dhearcadh an té
>> Ar a shuidhfeadh seal
>> Ná tabharfadh searc rún is gean
>> A cléibh 's cumainn dó.

And another verse is curious:

> As I am informed that pilfering roving
> Rakes gan dearmaid,
> Juris quoque contemptores,
> Fé mar mheasaim-se,
> Nightly strollers haunt these borders,
> Déanaidh faire ceart
> To apprehend aon chladhaire faolchon
> Claon-sprot cealgach.

VII

In reading Ó Rathaille we cannot help thinking of him as an " Oisin in the Fenians' Wake ": a new world had come upon the Gael, but to its strangeness he would most willingly shut his eyes. His world was the few scattered big Irish houses still remaining in his countryside rather than the thousands of dismal huts where the swarming peasants gathered themselves at nightfall. Of the Big Houses, of their sorrows, it was that he sung; to and fro amongst them he made his way; when they failed him he died, stepping into the grave, as one may recollect, with the name of the most memorable of them all on his lips—the MacCarthys.

Far otherwise it is with Eoghan Ruadh. He was a stranger to the Big House; he trudged the roads with his spade on his shoulder, truly one with the other labourers in whose gang he was numbered. Yet, while it was for them he sung, he was not a folk-poet, as the term is now understood: he was a literary man singing for a literary audience, though it was in a tavern or in a farmer's kitchen that that audience assembled. Every day, however, both the language and the speakers of it were becoming less literary and more folk, if one may so speak; and of this the poet was very conscious—we have seen how he frequently refers to himself as an unlearned poet, unlearned, that is, in the craft of song, which then, of course, included both history and genealogy.

Though only a little more than twenty years had passed between the death of Ó Rathaille and the birth of Eoghan

Ruadh, there is, due to the decaying of all things Gaelic, a world of difference between the feeling in the verses of the one and the other; the difference, therefore, is not so much the measure of the disparity between two poets as between two periods.

Knowing Eoghan Ruadh, then, as the wandering labourer who sung his own songs in the wayside tavern, we feel ourselves, while we read them, warm as with the very breath of the peasants who crowded about him while he did so. For them he wrote; and always, it is evident, in hot haste, fitting the song to the day that was passing over. Those peasants, then, what manner of learning they set store on, how they felt towards their masters, their sense of race, of religion—all this we cannot help apprehending while we read him, their poet. But of himself we are also poignantly made aware; of himself at his almost every new fling at fortune. His opening of the school, while still a boy, at Gneeveguilla and what happened there; his travelling the roads; his taking the part of youth in the famous contest; his venturing over the sea; his home-sickness in exile; his return; his love of the great stories of Greece; his love of learning—all this is, even to-day, fresh and vivid in his songs. In them also his revelry, as well as the repentance that followed it; no phase of his stormy life remains unsung, while his last moment of consciousness is enshrined for us in a memorable couplet. Indeed, so marked is the personal note in the greater part of his work that one can understand how those who will not, or cannot, content themselves with sheer artistry, find the decorative *aisling* poems uninteresting and pale.

Yet, close-linked as are his songs with the real things of his days, there never was a mind more essentially poetic; that is, a mind on which no vision shone that was not fledged with music.

There is always music, and most frequently it is the very heart of the poem, not a running accompaniment. " Is that Eoghan an Mhéirin?" we are told a priest once cried from the altar, only to be answered: " No, it is Eoghan an Bhéil Bhínn "

—Eoghan of the Sweet Mouth; and when the people put this name upon him they did so with the sure instinct that had come of a thousand years of literary traditions. In one of his *aisling* poems the Spirit of Ireland recalls the great past when her lot was chieftainship and feasting " *le seascaireacht ceoil* " ("with the comfort of music")—the comfort of music!— the one phrase to denote the excelling charm in his own verse, the exact phrase to describe what it was he gave his down-trodden and hungry people, endearing himself to them in spite of his recklessness and his wilfulness.

The critics of our own day who have tried to reverse the judgment of his contemporaries forget all this, or, rather, while they begin by paying tribute to his gift of music, do not seem to have anything pregnant to remark of his work until they have first put that music aside—as if, that put aside, anything of great importance remained to be said! Surely the critic's task is to give a fuller sense of the masterpiece he deals with (just as a poet's task is to deepen our sense of life); and the fuller sense of this man's poetry is the proper realisa-tion of the music that is in it—the realisation of it, not only as the hidden vital force from which the song took being, but as the bloom, the charm of perfection, in one word, the achievement which, when he had sung his song, left the poet himself full of ease and sighing for content, as a woman who has been delivered.

There might be some sense in this impatience with the orchestration of these poems if the rich medley, whether by its self-willed frenzy or loudness or unmanageability, had made foolish or niggard or weakling the musician who attempted it. But this did not ever happen: in not even one song, one verse, does he go astray in the whirlwind he has raised about him, or forget his destination. No other lines were ever more spontaneous, free-running, unburdened, triumphant, carrying their message up to the very gate intended, laying it there on the threshold of our consciousness, clean and beautiful: if we do not glow to receive it, it is because we have given our hearts away, if ever we had any.

214

Thinking of him, so gifted, "born with thy face and throat, Lyric Apollo!"; thinking of the *Aisling,* a form created as if in expectation of such a singer, one wonders how much of him is due to the *aisling* songs his young fancy dwelt upon as in his boyhood he roamed the slopes of Sliabh Luachra. It was these *aisling* songs made him what he was; in turn he left other *aisling* poems to those who should come after him—not for their good: the form had reached perfection in him; and there is a weariness and a hint of coldness in all of them that were to be made after his time. But in his own, what brilliancy! What perfect understanding of what lyric poetry should be— the music arising from the perfect blending of the word, as a word, heavy with its own especial treasures—music, colour, associations—the blending of this word with the thing it repre- sents, that also heavy with its own enrichments, haphazard or integral:

> Mar a raibh cantain na n-éan ar ghéagaibh crainn ghlais,
> Lachain is éisc ag scéitheadh ón dtaoide,
> An eala go glé ag téacht ar tuinn ann,
> 'S an péarla i n-íochtar trath as cómhair.

These four lines I recall to justify the common peasants' appreciation of Eoghan Ruadh as their best singer. Are they not perfect as lyric verse—spontaneous, swift-running, light, unburdened, a shower of sweet sounds—the perfect blending of the word and the thing? The choiring birds on the green tree-branches, the sea-birds and fish swarming from the tide, the swan brightly taking the wave's crest, and—perfect artist! —he reserves to the close the touch that will add radiance to all the others—the pearl in the water's depth, *sometimes visible*—this is how they translate into English prose, the lightness, the music, the swiftness, the brilliancy destroyed.

He brought something of that fresh radiance to all that his young eyes rested on. The old names in those Greek stories he loved, it is seldom that he invokes them without some life- giving word in his mouth. Hebe is " an réilteann óg " (" the young star "). Helen is " ríobh chailce an choimheascair thug ár na Trae " (" the lime-white lady of the conflict who

215

brought destruction to Troy "). Elsewhere she is "an bhrígh-deach Hélen" (" the bride Helen "). Not since the days of the Pléiade, if even then, did the bright-robed Grecians play their various parts so entirely unburdened of text-book scholarship. The Irish poets of that time read those classic tales as good, bright stories: they seem, happy folk, to have had the blessed privilege of reading them as the far-off creators of them intended—greedily rather than critically; with the glory that was Greece they made free, finding entrance to it through their own sagas, where there are grotesque figures as well as lovers and queens; of the warriors and, indeed, deities of Greece they expected the same homeliness, none welcoming their gracious presence as did Eoghan Ruadh.

They crowd pell-mell upon his vision; and the living word that thereupon leaps quickly from his mouth lets us know the heart-ease he has always found in their coming. So, too, when that more frequent visitor of his sad hours—the Spirit of Ireland—brings speech to his lips, there is sure to be some unexpected word that, piercing our imagination, makes us at once, and whether or not we will it, initiate of what is towards. Only a truly poetic mind is so seized upon by its own visions as to be unaware of what the next word will be until it falls upon the air; and it is strange that the more entirely the mind is in the grip of the vision, the more precise and hard-edged will be those sudden and unpremeditated words that describe what is happening in the happy trance. Saluting, once, that great Spirit of Ireland, Eoghan Ruadh, without ado, tells us he bowed to the grass *with his (three) cornered hat in his hand:*

Is tapa d'umhluigheas lem hata cúinneach im lámh go féar.

This swift daring is to be seen almost in all his songs: is it the " invention " that Keats thought of as the quality most neces-sary of all to a poet? It, anyway, achieves; for whenever that assured timbre rings in a poet's accents, one accepts his state-ment as the living truth, no matter what the dimensions, the colours, the topsy-turvy or the impossibility may be.

216

To his climax he sweeps on; and it is always effective. Take any one of the *aisling* poems: imagine it recited or sung in a voice equal in earnestness to the artistry in the song, and one cannot help hearing the applause at the end, more especially when the close of the poem is loud and triumphant:

'S dá bhfeichinn-se, mar shamh-
    luighim, na samharlaidhe
    treascartha,
Do bhéadh lampaí ar lasadh
    agam le éigean spóirt.

And were I to see, as I dream,
    the churls overwhelmed
Lamps would I set blazing in the
    dint of joy.

But when the song dies gently, or even sadly, it is no less the firm closing of the tale: the song has been sung cleanly to its end. How praise sufficiently the last line of the song in which he requests a smith to make him a new spade? He describes in rapid and dainty verse of great dexterity exactly the sort of spade he wants, and then:

Is mar bharra ar gach nídh bíodh
    sí i mbinneas an chluig!

And, crowning all, let it have in
    it the sweetness of a bell!

Every inch a poet! That is what one exclaims of him; and it includes all.

A mind enamoured of music, bestowing radiance, is rightly described as lyrical; yet this sense of form that was his, this sweeping along to his climax and then ceasing, bespeaks a strength that was capable of something on a higher, if not a lovelier, plane than the lyric. This mastery of form is seen in almost every poem that remains to us; but in *An t-Arrachtach Sean (The Aged Monster)* there is in addition a sense of reality, a grip on the lie of the human land, a certain hardness of vision that surprises one who thinks of it either as written by one who had just reached his twenty-first year or as written by the singer of the decorative *aisling* poems at any age. It is boastful, vigorous, mature, assured—the work, one would take it, of a man who had not sufficient tenderness in him ever to write lyric poems of any worth either as regards lightness or

217

music. Critics have wondered at Brian Merriman's view of life in his *Midnight Court (Cúirt an Mheadhon Oidhche)*; they have praised him for his grip, his substance, and his disregard for the merely lyrical; but even in these qualities is he so far ahead of the young lad who wrote these lines?—

'Nuair d'amharcann ainnir do snaidhmeadh le h-ársach,
Faraire bláthmhar álainn ar each,
Go meanmach acfuinneach abaidh glan ceáfrach,
Lannmhar láidir lan-chumais mear,
Biodhgann a croidhe-sin is líonann le taithneamh dhó,
Tigheann dortadh díleis is caoi-ghol 'na haigneadh,
Adeir, galar gan chasadh go leagaidh mo cháirde
Cheangail go bráth mé le hurrachtach sean!

Here, surely, we find the " modern " note; though not quite so strongly, perhaps, as in " An Cailleach Bearra," which was written in the tenth century!

And how Molièresque is this:

Ar shéadaibh na hÉireann ní | For the jewels of Ireland the
thréighfeadh an seanduine | Ancient would not cease
Aodhaireacht a chéile tré éad leis | Shepherding his wife through
na fearachoin. | jealousy of heroic youths.

That " shepherding " is a good word.

This core of hardness is scarcely ever lacking to the Gaelic poet; track him right down the centuries, and one never finds it missing. It is intellectual in its nature: hard-headed and clear-sighted, witty at its best, prosaic when not eager; and to its universality in the truly Gaelic world is due the fact that one can turn over the pages of the Gaelic book of poetry, century after century, without coming on any set of verses that one could speak of as sentimental: Tennyson's " Queen of the May " would have thrown Eoghan Ruadh or indeed, any of his companions, whether poets or not, into wild fits of laughter. Brian Merriman had so much of that hardness in him that one could not expect delicacy or sensibility to go with it; of his one gift he certainly made the best use; yet, when we keep this whole poem of Eoghan Ruadh's, *An t-Arrachtach*

218

Sean, in mind, we find it hard to account for the rhapsodies that Merriman's *Cúirt an Mheadhon Oidhche* has excited. Great it is, but those who have spoken of it as a thing unique in Gaelic literature must have forgotten, not only this whole poem of Eoghan Ruadh's, but the whole vast volume of Irish proverbial lore, not to say those numerous floating quatrains that Professor Thomas F. O'Rahilly has gathered into his book, " Dán Fhocail."

No, *Cúirt an Mheadhon Oidhche (The Midnight Court)* is not a unique thing in Irish literature; it is, however, a big thing successfully wrought. But we must not attempt to group Eoghan Ruadh and Brian Merriman together either as opposed, one to the other, or as kindred spirits: they were contemporaries (though Brian Merriman lived on for twenty years after Eoghan Ruadh); otherwise they had only very little in common. Brian Merriman's vision was prosaic: the distance between his verse and good idiomatic prose is, or seems to be, measurable; but the distance between even the best prose and almost the weakest of Eoghan Ruadh's work is immeasurable; for it is always in that higher plane where the thirst of music is necessary to full understanding. Brian Merriman may be said to derive from Dáibhidh Ó Bruadair, with a loss of sensibility, of flexibility; and Eoghan Ruadh from Aodhagán Ó Rathaille, with a loss of intensity and high-mindedness.

Eoghan Ruadh's gifts, then, were manifold: there was that intellectuality that so effectually staved off the sentimental; there was that intuitional sense of form which accounts for the perfect articulation of his most winged lyrics; there was that freshness of vision which accounts for his daring epithets; there was, above all, his thirst of music, his lyric throat. Of these great gifts he did not make the most; but how could he have done so, even were his passions less violent and his will-power greater, in the Irish Munster of his day? What was all that land but a death-stricken country, an outland, one might say, far from the stir of life? In such a land, he could have done nothing were it not for those thousands of other Gaelic poets who for a thousand years had been using the Gaelic language and enriching the Gaelic mind.

VIII

" What Pindar is to Greece, what Burns is to Scotland, what Béranger is to France, what nobody in particular, unless it be Mr Kipling, is to England, that and much more is Eoghan Ruadh to Ireland."[1]

Alas! it is by no means so; but were Fr Dinneen to write: " that and much more was Eoghan Ruadh to Gaelic Munster," he would have understated rather than overstated the matter. When I first learned Eoghan's language I went, summer after summer, now to one, now to another, Irish-speaking district in Munster; and, city-born and city-bred, I for some time found it difficult to find matter to chat about with the peasant ancients of those hidden vales: later on, however, I found there were two subjects which never failed to arouse the dying fires, to bring light into the fading eyes, and a flood of speech to the toothless gums: the Great Famine of '47 was one, and Eoghan Ruadh, the wastrel poet, whose voice had been stilled for more than a hundred years, whose poems they had never seen printed, whose life they had never seen written, was the other. One who has been trying to raise an interest in Irish literature among the teachers of Munster tells me: " When I speak of the other poets they pay no heed, but when I mention Eoghan Ruadh, the old men raise their heads." " Among labourers," writes one[2] who, living not far from Eoghan's homeland, has always taken a deep interest in all that concerns the poet—" Among labourers, *A Ghaibhne Chláir Fódla* was very popular. The cultivated Irish speakers favoured *Seó hó, a thoil,* and I've heard a good old singer giving *Mo léan le luadh. An t-Arrachtach Sean* and *Eascaine*

---

[1] *Amhráin Eoghain Ruaidh Uí Shúilleabháin,* leis an Athair Pádraig Ua Duinnín.

[2] Mr John Kiely, of Cullen, Co. Cork.

ar Cháit ní Laoghaire were well known to the last generation. My father used to sing *Mo Chás mo Chaoi mo Cheasna.*
Ag Taisteal na Blárnan and *Cois na Siúire* were very popular."
In the back lanes of the city of Cork I have met old women
who at the mention of his name forgot all the hardship they
had come through since their young days in the country; and
once I remember meeting in a lodging-house with two very old
men who were full both of his life and his poetry and wit;
one helping out the other: when they had gone I was told that
they had just come from Chicago, in the toil of which they
had spent a full half-century of years. "Though quite a
distance from there now, in my mind's eye I can see the spot
where, as I was shown, Eoghan's house stood, that is the
house in which he died, about two hundred yards from the
village of Knocknagree, in the County Cork; the place is
called Park. I was born myself about half a mile from there,
and I well remember the old people years ago tell about
Eoghan a hundred stories illustrative of his peculiar life. Such
discussions relative to Eoghan usually wound up with a
reference to his last days, the penniless and impoverished
condition to which he was reduced, dying of fever in that
little hovel."[1]

·   ·   ·   ·   ·   ·   ·

Such, then, is an account, altogether inadequate, of the life,
the works, the genius and the legend of Eoghan an Bheoil
Bhínn—Eoghan of the Sweet Mouth.

---

[1] See *Beatha Eoghain Ruaidh Uí Shúilleabháin,* leis an Athair
Pádraig Ua Duinnín. The words quoted are from a letter received
by Fr Dinneen from a gentleman in America who wished to erect a
monument to the poet.

CHAPTER IX

BRIAN MERRIMAN

Their different periods account for the difference in style and matter between Ó Rathaille and Eoghan Ruadh Ó Súilleabháin. There is, perhaps, even greater dissimilarity between the work of the latter, Eoghan Ruadh and Brian Merriman; but since these were contemporaries, born within a year of each other, the same explanation does not satisfy us. Seeking another, we find it in the fact that there was a difference in place, Merriman being of the County Clare, Ó Súilleabháin of the County Kerry, with the Shannon, during their formative years, flowing between. That river prevented the one from being like the other as surely as the river of years hindered Eoghan Ruadh from writing a death-song in the way that Ó Rathaille wrote his. That this could be so makes us realise how great a ruination had come upon the Gael. Their "watertight" clan-system was broken up, broken up for good; but, indeed, it was only now that one Gaelic district lost touch with its neighbouring district, each developing its own dialect and its own way of looking at and expressing life! Their ancient literary tradition had been, we recollect, a cement that bound into one nationality the hundred clans that occupied the island: this it did through its special literary language carrying unity of spirit, brotherhood of mind, into all the corners of the country. But all this was gone: the Kerryman was still, perhaps, aware of the tradition, for his work is dainty with purely literary expressions; but the Clareman knew only of one language—that in which bargains were made at the fair and the rent haggled about in the bailiff's office in Ennis.

222

I

It is curious that we know far more of the vagrant Ó Súilleabháin than of the stay-at-home Merriman, of the storm-driven rake than of the family man who kept the homely paths, living on for twenty-two years after the other had burned himself out. It is equally curious that the unsettled, houseless wanderer should have left us, after his thirty-six years of life, as rich, if not a richer, harvest than the settled " teacher of Mathematics," after his fifty-eight. If we did properly discover the true life—that is, the inner life—of the teacher of mathematics, perhaps these two strange facts would lose their mystery: but this true life is at present beyond our ken: such facts of his wayfaring as have been recorded for us can have had but little to do with it: these are, indeed, so external, so commonplace, as well as few, that they scarce tempt us to make even guesses at what droughts and hail-storms it could have been that destroyed the many harvests that must have at least started into growth in that deep and manly soul.

He was born, it is supposed, in 1747, somewhere to the east of Ennis, in the County Clare, the exact spot being still unknown. Neither is it certain what his people were—small farmers, it is likely—nor how nor where he got his education. Perhaps in some hedge-school, or intermittently at the feet of some wandering poet or priest, one bearing with him the relics of a nation's culture, the other the credentials of Louvain or Salamanca. In 1770, in his young manhood, he is found at Feakle, a poor and neglected district in his native county, a district as yet unopened up by a coach-road. Here he is said to have taught school. Some years later he is known as a small farmer, renting twenty acres of land; and in the traditions of the place it is asserted that it was his pupils who raised the firm fences that surrounded the fields. He was middle-aged before he married. After some time he moved into the city of Limerick, living, it is apparent, in a poor way by teaching mathematics. He died there rather suddenly in 1805. Of this we are certain, for the following entry has been found in the *General Advertiser and Limerick Gazette* for Monday, 29th July, 1805:

> *Died.*—On Saturday morning, in Old Clare-street, after a few hours' illness, Mr Bryan Merryman, teacher of Mathematics, etc.

The idea of him that remained among the peasantry was a stout, sturdy, black-haired man.

Such is all we know of Brian Merriman. A life-statement less interesting, balder, more enigmatical—when one considers his poem—it would be hard to come upon in the annals of any literature. No travelling, no adventurings, no disputes with his brother poets—only towards the end the drudgery of daily teaching in a city where English had long since established itself as the current speech: it may be that the teacher of mathematics, walking the streets of Limerick, sometimes, perhaps often, wondered if indeed it was he who, more than a score of years before, had written a striking poem, copies of which had been taken across the Shannon into Sliabh Luachra.

II

He is a poet of one work—*Cúirt an Mheadhon Oidhche (The Midnight Court)*. In addition to it, we have seen only two short lyrics ascribed to him—neither of any importance. For us, then, the whole of him is in this poem of 1,206 lines.

In the opening the poet tells us that, as customary with him, he walked out by the shores of Loch Gréine, a small lake in the north-eastern corner of Clare, and that, being weary, a sleep came to him, and strange visions. He felt the land trembling about him: a storm from the north arose, in the midst of which a vasty, stubborn, bare-boned, angry female, six or seven yards in height, approached him, her mantle trailing a perch behind her in the mire. In her hand she carried her wand of office: she was bailiff to the Midnight Court—the

Court of Aoibheal, queen of the fairies of Thomond, that is, of North Munster. "Arise, O ugly sleeper," she chides, "it is a dark thing for you to be stretched there and the Court sitting, and thousands making towards it." Then the bailiff describes the Court:

Ní cúirt gan acht gan reacht gan riaghail,
Ná cúirt na gcreach mar chleacht tú riamh,
An chúirt seo ghluais ó shluaighte séimhe.
Cúirt na dtruagh na mbuadh is na mbéithe.

It is not a court without law, regulations or rules,
Nor a court of plunder, such as you have always frequented,
This court established by refined people,
But a court of mercies, of virtues, of ladies.

She also relates that it is in pity for the sufferings of the Gael that the Court has been set up; and she reproaches him with being one of those who have not done their part in re-peopling the land when war and death had left it empty of men:

Is folamh 's is tráighte fágadh tíortha,
An cogadh is an bás gan spás dá ndíogadh
Uabhar na righthe 's ar imthigh tar sáile.

Empty and exhausted were left the lands,
War and Death draining them without respite;
(As well as) The pride of kings, and all that went over the sea.

But Aoibheal has consented to forego the delights of fairyland for a while in order to banish slavery from Thomond. Furthermore:

Gheall an mhíonla chaointais chóir seo
Fallsacht dlighe do chlaoidhe go cómhachtach,
Seasamh i dteannta fann is fánlag
Is caithfidh an teann bheith ceannsa tláth libh,
Caithfidh an neart gan cheart do stríocadh
Is caithfidh an ceart 'n-a cheart bheith suidhte.

This gentle and just one has promised to crush down the falseness of law and to aid both the weak and the vanquished, until the stiff-necked are gentle and submissive with ye. Might without right must yield its place, and Right as right be established there.

Having been made to feel that Aoibheal's Court is just and without favour, he is seized upon and swept through the glens into the well-lighted fairy palace where the Court is being held. There in the seat of justice he beholds the Fairy Queen, Aoibheal herself, in the midst of her armed guards. On the witness table he sees a *spéir-bhean*—that is, a beautiful woman —making her complaint in a wild agony of words and tears. What is that complaint? Chiefly that there are hosts of maidens wandering about without protectors—that is, husbands—wandering about like black-robed nuns. A hundred women she is acquainted with are only waiting to be asked! And behold her own case, one of them:

Ar leabhaidh leamhfhuair dár suathadh ag smaointe.	On a bed of insipid coldness, wasted with thought.

If the men make no change in their attitude, why, we must only abduct them! They think of marrying now when no one, except for charity's sake, would go with them. And when one man out of seven does, in the heat of youth, think of taking a wife to himself, whom does he marry but some brown and withered creature who has won him by reason of her money or property. That is what most of all tortures her, to see a gay and dashing youth married to a foolish or withered hag of a woman. This very night such a thing is happening, while she, in all her beauty, both of person and dress, and after trying every spell and charm known to the countryside, is passed over. Moreover:

Táim in achrann dhaingean na mbliadhnta	I am in the strong grip of the years
Ag tarraing go tréan ar laethibh liaithe.	Drawing violently on to the grey days.

She then calls on the presiding queen: Pearl of Paradise, the saving-price of my soul on you! do not loose me as a wanton on the world, without friends, without children, without shelter—a hag on inhospitable hearths, without claim on them, unwelcomed.

An old man starts up to give her answer. He contrasts her laces and flounces with the poverty of her people and her house—those laces and flounces, what paid for them? he wonders. Then he relates the tale of a simple-minded boy whom one such as this lady has captured for herself: only for he has no wish to awake scandal, what might he not tell of her! Surely it is evil for an unwedded man to tie himself to such a one. Not without bitter experience has he come to such knowledge. Before marriage he was prosperous and healthy; a woman, however, wasted both his vigour and his substance; for married and single she made sport; and at last her condition betrayed her: she bore him a son long before her time. Yet, behold, the neighbours recognised all his features in this child that was none of his! Then the wronged father tells how he took the child on his knees, examined it, found it hardy, well-shapen, vigorous: where, then, the necessity for marriage? Marriage with its banns, its feastings, its hired musicians, its drinking and rout!

The old man finishes; and the maiden who had already spoken rises to answer him. In turn *she* relates the story of his marriage, giving the other side of the picture. The young woman would never have married him only that she was in dire want. And having married him, how poor her reward! How blame her if she turned her elsewhere? If she proved unfaithful:

A bhfuil sionnach ar sliabh ná iasc i dtráigh,	Is there a fox on the hill or a fish in the sea,
Ná fiolar le fiadhach ná fiadh le fán	A ravening eagle or a wandering stag
Chomh fada gan chiall le bliadhain ná lá	So senseless as to spend a year, a day!
Do chaitheamh gan biadh 's a bhfiadhach le fagháil?	Lacking for food and prey at hand?

On the other hand, what did he, the husband, lack? If she spent the riches, did he go in want? Is a field the less if a million pass through it? One excuses jealousy in a dashing,

227

vigorous youth, but in a wrinkled, frost-bitten, decrepit ancient!

There then follows a curious passage, in which the angry maiden wonders why it is that the clergy—most of them young, healthy, and with the fat of the land about them—are not permitted to marry. It is an injustice to Ireland!

With that, she places the hard case of all the unwedded women of Erin—(only one man for every three of them)— before the Pearl of Majesty on the seat of justice. Judgment is then given: The maidens are to be given authority to seize on any or every man who has passed his twenty-first year without marrying, to bind him " to the tree that is beside the tomb " and to flay him with cords; while in the case of those still older, the women are to put their wits together and making use of the " true bitterness of fire and steel," to do violence upon them, for death without torment would be too light a penalty for them.

She then announces that she can delay no longer in their midst; but she will return, and woe then to the unmarried! and double woe to those whose faults are the result of their vanity, their desire to boast, and not of the heat of blood or of the outbreaking of passion!

The poet trembles to hear her judgments, and suddenly the huge, terrible bailiff pounces on him and, by the ear, drags him on to the judgment table. The unwedded one instantly bursts out in accusation against him and implores the Pearl of Majesty to condemn him. She does not, however, await the formal sentence. Having called other unwedded ones to her assistance, they all begin to bind the poet's limbs, to use every violence upon him, when he awakes from the pain of his vision.

III

This meagre account of the poem gives but little sense of its tough strength. It comes from County Clare, and it has in it the hardness and, in a way, the bleakness of that upland

county, where hedge-rows are to be searched for and rivers are not. *Cúirt an Mheadhon Oidhche* has no luxuriance in it, nothing flowing, sinuous, gentle or efflorescent. Its accent is, rather, boorish, abrupt, snappy; it is taut and well-articulated. Nevertheless, as must happen in a poem of considerable length, certain portions are more striking than others. The opening lines, the description of the scene, are given a place in every Gaelic anthology—not too wisely, one thinks, for one doubts if they are good. Is there freshness in them? Magic? Any compelling note of emotion? Or is it the one place in the poem where the writer is not himself? The passage, at all events, gives a very false idea both of the poem and poet. . . . .
The short description of the Court has been given already, not for its own sake, but just to indicate how this poem, as, indeed, practically all the Irish poetry of the period, adheres strictly to time and place—the characteristic that marks out the literature as the genuine expression of the nation's soul. In our first chapter the description of the poor man's hut was, it will be remembered, taken also from this poem, again not for its value as a piece of verse. To these quotations let us add the maiden's account of the various charms—*piseógs* is the word still used all over Munster—she practised to win herself a lover:

Níl cleas dá mb'féidir léaghamh
ná trácht air
Le teacht na rae nó tar éis bheith
lán di,
Um Inid ná um Shamhain ná ar
shiubhal na bliadhna
Ná tuigim gur leamhus bheith ag
súil le ciall as.
Níor bh'áil liom codladh go
socair éanuair díobh
Gan lán mo stoca do thorthaibh
fém chluasa,
Is deimhin nár bh'obair liom
troscadh le cráibhtheacht,
Is greim ná blogam ní shlogainn
trí trátha,
In aghaidh an tsrotha do thom-
ainn mo léine,

Every trick one finds to read or
speak about
At the time of new moon or after
she is full,
At Shrovetide or Hallowmass or
in the course of the year,
I understand (now) how foolish
it is to trust in them.
At any of these times I never
sunk into sleep
Without the full of my stocking
of fruit beneath my ear,
It was little trouble to me piously
to fast
For three Canonical Hours with
neither bite nor sup.
In the stream's current I plunged
my shift,

229

Ag súil trím chodladh le cogar
óm chéile,
Is minic do chuaidh mé ag
scuabadh an stáca,
Ingne is gruaig fén luaithghríos
d'fhágainn,
Chuirinn an tsúist fé chúil na
gaibhle,
Chuirinn an ramhan go ciuin fén
adhairt chugham,
Chuirinn an choigíol i gcillín na
háithe,
Chuirinn mo cheirtlín i dteine
aoil Mhic Rághnaill,
Chuirinn an ros ar chorp na
sráide,
Chuirinn san tsop chugham tor
gabáiste.
Níl cleas acu súd dá ndubhras
láithreach
Ná hagrainn congnadh an
deamhain 's a bhráthar,
'Sé fáth mo scéil go léir 's a
bhrígh dhuit
Mar táim gan chéile tar éis mo
dhichill.

Hoping that my lover would
whisper to me in sleep;
Often I swept about the stack
(of hay),
Nails (finger) and hair beneath
the ashes I left,
The flail I placed behind the
hearth,
The spade softly beneath my
pillow,
The distaff in the ' eye ' of the
kiln,
My ball of yarn I put in
MacReynold's lime kiln,
Flax seed strewed in the middle
of the road,
And put a head of cabbage in
the bush.
Through all those tricks I have
mentioned
I invoked the help of the Devil
and his brethren
And, to give the full force of my
tale,
Here am I still unwedded.

This passage is more characteristic of the writer than the
opening; it is not Brian Merriman at his best, but it is Brian
Merriman all through. How downright it is, how clear-cut!
Yet convincing: the lady in the case might certainly have so
spoken; the poet has not gone out of his way to help her out:
each *piseóg,* he has settled, is to get one line and no more.
How impossible it would have been for Eoghan Ruadh Ó
Súilleabháin, lyrist, to write in so determined an order!

Beyond the question of the nature of the verse, one finds the
passage interesting, if only for the assurance it gives us that in
spite of the poverty and hardness of the times human nature
was still very much itself, and virgins were, some of them wise,
and others foolish.

The poet is better in the defence of the ill-born that,
curiously—or is it carelessly?—he puts into the mouth of the
deceived father:

230

Breathain go cruinn é, bíodh
  gurab óg é
Is dearbhtha suidhte an píosa
  feóla é,
Is preabaire i dtoirt i gcorp 's
  i gcnámh é,
Cá bhfuil a locht i gcois ná i
  láimh dhe?
Ní seirgtheach fann ná seandach
  feósach,
Leibide cam ná gandal geói-
  seach,
Meall gan chuma ná sumach gan
  síneadh é
Ach lannsa cumusach buinneamh-
  ach bríoghmhar.
Ní deacair a mheas nach spreas
  gan bhrígh
Bheadh ceangailte ar nasc ar
  teasc ag mnaoi,
Gan chnámh gan chumus gan
  chumadh gan chom,
Gan ghrádh gan chumann gan
  fuinneamh gan fonn,
Do scaipfeadh i mbroinn d'éan-
  mhaighre mná
Le catachus draghain ar groidhre
  breágh
Mar chuireann sé i bhfeidhm gan
  mhoill gan bhréig
Le cumas a bhaill 's le luighe-
  amh a ghéag
Gur crobhaire é crothadh go
  cothrom gan cháime
Le fann na fola is le fothram
  na sláinte.

Judge him fully, although young
He is a right well fashioned piece
  of flesh,
A slasher in bulk, in body as in
  bone,
Find me a fault in hand or foot
  of his!
No weak consumptive this, no
  withered shiverling,
No shapeless lump or stunted
  lubber,
But a forceful active powerful
  blade.
Easy to guess that no vigourless
  weakling
Tied in the grip of duty by a
  woman
Without bone power, without
  force, without figure, without
  waist.
Without love, without courtship,
  without vigour, without desire,
Would bestow in the womb of a
  handsome woman
With reluctant heat this splendid
  fellow.
How without hesitation or falsehood he lets us know
By power of limb and set of
  frame
That he is a hearty lad, proper
  and entire,
Begotten in the heat of blood and
  the violence of health.

Merriman is supposed to have read the English poet, Savage,
and those lines have been compared with his well-known lines
in *The Bastard:*

> Blest be the Bastard's birth—through wondrous ways
> He shines eccentric like a comet's blaze;
> No sickly fruit of tame compliance he,
> He stamped in Nature's mint of ecstasy;
> He lives to build and boast a generous race,
> No tenth transmitter of a foolish face.

231

And, of course, Edmund's speech in *King Lear* comes to mind:

> Why bastard? wherefore base?
> When my dimensions are as well compact,
> My mind as generous and my shape as true,
> As honest madam's issue? Why brand they us
> With base? with baseness? bastardy? base, base?
> Who in the lusty stealth of nature take
> More composition and fierce quality,
> Than doth, within a dull, stale, tired bed
> Go to the creating a whole tribe of fops,
> Got 'tween asleep and wake?

Many other passages from *The Midnight Court* might be quoted; but these will serve. They sufficiently show its character—its downrightness, its integrity, its non-lyric mood. They also indicate why one hastens to discuss how it comes to be so different from the work that was being done on the southern side of the broad riverway.

IV

In a very interesting appreciation of the poet, in the Introduction already referred to, we read:

" In the history of modern Gaelic literature two strikingly original figures stand out—Keating and Merriman—and the latter was the more original of the two. Only by those who have pored over much Gaelic literature can the full extent of that originality be appreciated. Few literatures have been less coloured by the individuality of writers than Gaelic literature. . . . . Its history is a history of schools and forms and movements rather than of men." [1]

And following up these quite accurate observations, he endeavours to have us believe that Brian Merriman broke through the shackles of the schools and stepped forward, an original. Merriman is the exception, the one too strong to submit to rule and drill.

He is certainly different from the poets of Sliabh Luachra.

---

[1] See *Cúirt an Mheadhon Oidhche,* edited by Risteárd Ó Foghludha.

If he were born and had lived amongst them, more especially if he had lived a score of years earlier, then, indeed, one could freely and off-hand describe this poem of his as the work of a rebel. But when one considers how late in the century the poem was written (1780) and that, moreover, it was written in County Clare and not in West Cork or Kerry or in the Barony, near Youghal, then one is not so sure that Merriman rebelled against living institutions. It is too late to talk of " schools " in 1780, no matter what part of Irish Ireland we are dealing with. It is far too late when it is the County Clare we are thinking of. Clare, geographically, is part of Connacht —and it was geographical considerations that had decided where schools were to live on and where they were earlier to fade—and the schools had long before died out in Connacht. Brian Merriman had by heart many a poem written in the schools, but one may question if he himself ever came in touch with a living Court of Poetry. The living influence he came under was the splendid " school " of folk poetry that then flourished all over Connacht. Than any of these folk poets Merriman was less rebellious, inasmuch as his verse is far more regular and far more in accordance with the schools than theirs. One could not classify him as one of them, but he was of the same province; and if, like them, he called a spade a spade it was because he had met with no living men who ever called it anything else. Mr Beaslai says of him:

" He was content to write the everyday speech of the County Clare, a marvellously vigorous and expressive speech, of which he had a royal command."

That speech he was just as much and as little content to use as was any other contemporary of his in Connacht to use his native dialect. And surely the writer quoted discovers this for himself when he notes: " He does not seem to have belonged to any *literary set or clique* like most of the other celebrated Gaelic poets—like, for instance, that hard-drinking school of melodious songsters who flourished on the banks of the Máig a generation before." The question is what literary set he could

233

have belonged to without crossing the Shannon; and even had he crossed it a long search might well have been in vain, unless he could also ferry over that wide river that, as Mr Beaslai admits, divided him from the bright company which drank and chorused in Seán Ó Tuama's hostelry in Croom of the Merriment. It is not, however, the river of years, but the actual river that separates Clare from Munster proper, that accounts for the nature of Merriman's verse. His genius was of Connacht, not of Sliabh Luachra; and considered as such there is no mystery to be solved. He only did what the poets about him were doing, only with more verve, strength, and downrightness.

But what of his ideas? of the curious questions he chose to deal with? Is it too venturesome to assert that the explanation of these is implicit in what already has been written of him? First, however, let us take note of an explanation in the Introduction[1] already drawn upon:

> We have no record to show that Brian ever travelled very far, nor is it necessary to believe that he was ever outside of Thomond. None the less it is curious to find him so closely in contact with the most advanced ideas of the latter half of the eighteenth century. It was in the same year that Brian wrote the " Cúirt " and young Schiller voiced in " Die Räuber " the revolt of youth against human laws and institutions. One feels that Merriman's entrance into the houses of the gentry must have brought him into contact with men who had read Voltaire and Rousseau, and either affected in their talk the mocking scepticism of the one or quoted and discussed the lyric revolt of the other.

It may be true that Brian had entry into the houses of the gentry; and it is certain that people who had read or, at least, gathered in the ideas of Voltaire and Rousseau were, in the shape of officers of the Wild Geese, to be met with in County Clare, as, indeed, along a great extent of the whole western seaboard; it has, moreover, been remarked that the spread of these irreligious ideas may have had some influence on the many rich Catholics who, to save their lands, bartered away,

---

[1] *Cúirt an Mheadhon Oidhche*, ed. R. Ó Foghludha.

at this very time, the faith of their fathers: but is this explanation necessary at all in the present case? The return to nature,
and all that phrase connotes, had surely an import for the
Continent, for England, even for Dublin, very different from
what it had for the backward districts of Munster. To talk
about "Society" and "Institutions" in such surroundings is
to talk bookish theoric. Brian Merriman, to write his defence of
the bastard, needed to hear as little of Rousseau and Voltaire
as Shakespeare had heard when he wrote his; and as for
his protest that age and youth cannot live together, and that
when an old man marries a young wife, he had need watch
her—well, all that is a theme as old as the hills. It is dealt with
in the ballad lore of every people. The folk-poetry in Irish is
rich with it. And had not Eoghan Ruadh Ó Súilleabháin dealt
with it before Merriman, and, to our mind, made better
poetry of it?

There remains the question of the celibacy of the clergy:
where did Brian Merriman strike on the idea that Mr George
Moore, more than a hundred years later, was to make into a
rather amusing short story—the idea that the priests of Ireland
should marry, since being well-off they could afford to rear up
respectable families?

> Bíonn sealbh gach sogha aca ar bhórd na saoithe,
> Earradh agus ór chun óil is aoibhnis.

May he not have come on the idea in any peasant's hut in
Munster? Men and women will love to discuss forbidden ideas
just so long as ginger is hot in the mouth; and if men and
women in general tire of that ancient pastime, the Gaels never
will. In one of the most out-of-the-way corners of Munster, a
piece of land jutting out into an unfrequented sea, I recall
hearing the Irish-speaking peasant fishermen discuss whether
Sleep, Sloth or Pleasure was the highest good! The discussion
was carried on in Irish, but the theme, the phrase itself,
wherever they had come on it, was always quoted in English.
They were not hedonists; they were men worn by wind and
earth and sea, not so defeated in brain, however, that they

235

could no longer enjoy the free working of the mind. The discussing of the absurd as if it were serious and real, is a very Gaelic aptitude, so noticeable that the well-travelled John Synge was likely to think of it as having ousted every other aptitude from that mentality. That such a question as this of celibacy of the clergy might be discussed, and with great apparent seriousness and gravity, in any peasant's hut in Munster will surprise no one who knows these huts and their pastimes.

When Mr Beaslai writes of Merriman: " Brian was essentially a moralist. He attacked the vices and evils which, in his opinion, sprang from the suppression of nature. He did not regard marriage as something lofty and spiritual, a question of affinities, but his view of it was certainly that of a moralist. To him celibacy was something unhealthy and unnatural, which only led to vice "—when he writes thus of Brian Merriman he surely takes the matter somewhat too seriously. The atmosphere of the whole poem is against such a view. What moralist would dare to finish up as Brian does—turning the joke against himself? Your moralist is nothing if not solemn.

Surely this writer is again too serious when he writes: " Brian preaches the return to nature just as the Romantic poets of twenty years later preached it in England. His preaching is not the less effective because it is so artfully concealed. He sees in nature, not something hateful to be suppressed, but something beautiful to be understood and harmonised with the necessities of life. The old man argues against marriage, the young woman for marriage and against celibacy, but both rest their arguments upon the forces and processes of nature. Hence it is that Brian is rather a Greek than a Gael in his attitude towards life. He had the same quick, inquiring mind as the Athenian of old, and the same lack of reverence. His love of the beauty of nature, as all-sufficing, as a moral force in itself, was accompanied by the Greek lack of spirituality." . . . . " In short," the writer concludes, " if one dare use such a simile of a Gaelic poet (and surely one may; for we are all

Greeks, however we deny it), they will feel in it the true spirit of Pan. And that spirit is one that never gets away from the earth and the drossy animal life, but it is still a spirit of health and vigour and mirth that has to be reckoned with by all." It is all very interesting, and true in a sense; but may not one write in much the same terms of all the folk literature of mankind? And one feels that it all applies to Merriman's ideas as they exist in a modern man's mind rather than to them as they existed in the mind of an Irish speaker of the County Clare in the eighteenth century. To argue against them is not necessary if only we keep the poem itself, and not the ideas in it, before our mind. After all, in every society, and more particularly in rustic society, one meets with a class who, lacking sensibility themselves, raise laughter by shocking it in others; and one does not think of *all* of this class as moralists, even though their *forte* is usually a bluntish showing up of things. What Sir Walter Scott said of Sterne may, perhaps, clinch the matter for us: " It cannot be said that the licentious humour of Tristram Shandy is of the kind which applies itself to the passions, or is calculated to corrupt society. But it is a sin against taste, if allowed to be harmless to morals. A handful of mud is neither a firebrand nor a stone; but to fling it about in sport argues coarseness of mind and want of common manners."

V

Even in Eoghan Ruadh Ó Súilleabháin himself—that most lyrical of souls—we came on a certain core of hardness—the hardness of intellect—and noted it as a Gaelic characteristic. But Eoghan Ruadh had many other gifts as well; Brian Merriman had not, and this commonsense, hard-headed wisdom of his, the sort of wisdom that every people crystallises for itself into household words and proverbs, could easily become pedestrian, just as Eoghan Ruadh's lyric strain could easily become an array of tinkling words. In

Merriman, even at his best, there is never a hint of the sense of the incommensurable; and the gifts that were his to lay before us, the intellect relishes and wishes to retain; but it never feels itself overthrown by the might of sheer beauty or dissolved into sympathy through the warmth of charm. The absence of the truly lyrical in himself made him unapt to deal with nature, and, though very frequently quoted, his opening lines, the description of a fine morning by the shores of Loch Gréine, are not, one thinks, really poetic: they are commonplace—nature apprehended by a spirit only slightly raised. His way of seizing nature is blunt, and worlds away from the early Gaelic manner;[1] it is even far away from Eoghan Ruadh's: he could never achieve such lines as:

> An eala go glé ag téacht ar tuinn ann,
> 'San péarla i n-íochtar tráth os comhair,

which flash a scene on us so sweet that the sense may well faint picturing it: nor could he write a line like " Is falainn don aer bhog bhaoth 'na timpal "—where the music is the meaning. If, however, he lacked this charm of the lyrical, he could write lines like:

| Táim in achrann dhaingean na mbliadhnta | I am in the strong grip of the years |
| Ag tarraing go tréan ar laethibh liaithe. | Drawing violently on to the days of greyness. |

In such lines—and he has a number of them—we are conscious of the type of mind that wrote " A Bhean Lán de Stuaim " in the seventeenth century, and " An Cailleach Beara " in the eleventh. This note of devastating bleakness is more truly Gaelic than the soft lyrical tones of Eoghan Ruadh Ó Súilleabháin; in *The Midnight Court,* however, we get no passage of any length sustained in that high style. It exists only meagrely in it; but, then, perhaps, it is the latest Irish poem in which it exists at all.

---

[1] See Kuno Meyer, *Ancient Irish Poetry.*

The poem is otherwise interesting: it is the bridge on which one may pass from the "literary" poets of Munster, south of the Shannon, to the pure folk-poets of Connacht, on the other side. Its versification is vigorous, swift, efficient; but the refinement that came of a living literary tradition is absent. It gives us an insight into its own period, as witness its description of the peasant's hut or the implicit contrast it makes between the fanciful Midnight Court and the court the people had to do business with.

Its author lived for a quarter of a century after he had written it—lived in silence, as far as we know. One does not think of his muse as weak or febrile; yet circumstance, that "unspiritual god," as Byron called it, somehow defeated his spirit. Was it the poet's moving into Limerick City caused the havoc? Did he really think to make fame or fortune there as teacher of mathematics? Or did he nurse the hope of returning to his native places among the Gaels to ease his much-enlightened soul of melodies; putting off that return, however, not noticing how strong is the grip of the years, how violently they drag one on to the days of greyness? There is surely, after all, more tragedy in his life than in that of Eoghan Ruadh Ó Súilleabháin: tragedy less flamboyant, certainly, yet, perhaps, as surely springing from some central weakness in himself.

CHAPTER X

THE MINOR POETS

The three poets, Ó Rathaille, Ó Súilleabháin and Merriman, whom we have just surveyed, bring us from the end of the seventeenth century into the opening years of the nineteenth. Besides these there were, of course, many others, some of them only a little less great, yet all, however much less, full of interest. Sometimes one of them will open up a new district for us, a new school, with notes of its own, we may be sure, if only we knew it through and through; at other times we find them grouping into engaging fellowships, bantering one another, freely, brightly, with the missiles at hand, as it were, very vividly renewing for us the stir and fret and humours of their own countrysides and their own day; while at other times, again, it is some trick of personality, some strength of character in one of them, that makes us eager to know more of him, his songs, and his little world. Now, however, there is not room for more than simple notes on the more memorable of them.

I

SEÁN CLÁRACH MAC DOMHNAILL
(JOHN CLÁRACH MACDONNELL)

One thinks of Seán Clárach Mac Domhnaill as a sort of gentleman farmer; but then he lived in the first half of the eighteenth century, dying in 1754, aged 63 years, before the Gaels had become utterly destitute. He lived long enough, however, to learn that the Pretender's attempt to rouse these islands had hardened the authorities everywhere against all men and ventures of a Gaelic nature. He was the chief poet of the school that assembled, twice yearly, it is probable, either in Rath Luirc (Charleville) or in Bruree. In Rath Luirc the " Court " held sessions at the *lios* of Kiltoohig, situated in his own farm, while their meeting-place in Bruree was more historic still: Bruree, in Irish Brugh-Righ, means King's Palace, and certain remains of ancient forts, remnants, it is said, of the *brugh* of Oilioll Olum, the most famous of the pre-Christian kings of Munster, are still to be seen in the district. Quickened by the memory of ancient royalty, the Gaels tended the flame of their native learning. To those Courts gathered in the poets of Limerick, of East Cork, and North Cork, with, perhaps, occasionally one from Kerry or Tipperary. Mac Domhnaill's importance for us is that he presided over their deliberations.

He was learned, it is said, in Greek, Latin and Irish, and proposed to translate Homer into his native tongue. He was one of the few poets who made any translations from English, his Irish version of *My Laddie can fight and my Laddie can sing* being both musical and spirited; and, generally, seems to have been among those who, perhaps unfortunately, in the middle years of the century, thought Jacobitism almost the only theme worth singing. In one of those Jacobite songs of his we hear the kettle-drums rolling:

> 'Sé mo rogha é thoghas dam féin,
> Is maith an domhan go dtabharfainn é,
> D'fhonn bheith ar bórd ar long gan baoghal,
> Do bhárr na gcnoc 's i n-imigcéin.

But his most famous song is a satire written on the death of the tyrant of the local fields, Colonel Dawson of Aherlow. It was so fierce that the poet would surely have swung for it if caught. The first verse runs:

> Taiscighidh, a chlocha, fá choigilt i gcoimeád chriaidh
> An feallaire fola 'san stollaire Dauson liath,
> A ghaisce níor bh'fhollus i gcogadh ná gcath lá ghliagh,
> Ach ag creachadh 's ag crochadh 's ag coscairt na mbochtán riamh.

And this Dr. Douglas Hyde has translated in its own metre:

Squeeze down his bones, O ye stones, in your hall of clay,
Yon reeking, gore-sprinkled boar, old Dawson the grey.
Sheathed was his sword when the foeman called to the fray,
But he cheated and sold, and slowly slaughtered his prey.

But perhaps a more literal translation of the last two lines will better bring out the sting in them:

His valour was not noticeable in war nor in strife on a day of sword-play,
But (was ever noticeable) at wounding and hanging and hacking the poor.

Two other lines contain a striking image:

In Eatharla fhosaigh, i n-oscuil idir dhá shliabh
Gur cheangail an gorta don phobul dá gcur fá riaghail.

In fortified Aherlow, in a gap between two hills,
He hitched Hunger to the people forcing them to obey.

And two other lines very vividly paint the tyrant who was above the Law:

Dá dtarraingid brosna nó scoilb nó scatháin fiar
Do bhainfeadh na srothanna fola as a slinneáin siar.

If they drew away wood-strippings or twigs or crooked branches
He would whip streams of blood down from their quarters.

It is certain that he wrote a great deal now lost; and if this poem were missing we would find in him a dainty versifier, given to experimenting, rather than a poet, nor could we understand why it is that the poems made to his memory, if gathered together, would bulk much larger than what we have from his own hand. This fierce satire, we may be sure, was greedily seized on by the Galtee people: it relieved their hearts; the poet, it is easy to understand, had to fly from the district. It is said he found a hiding-place in London.

.   .   .   .   .   .

Eamonn de Bháll (Edward Wall) was a poet who lived in

Dungourney, a little place about half-way between Cork and Youghal. It is said that he came to Mac Domhnaill's home town—Rath Luirc—and found there a messenger to carry this verse to the town's poet:

Innis do Sheaghán gheal Clárach
  úr uasal,
File 'gus fáidh nár ghnáthaigh
  gnúis ghruamdha,
Gur mise an Bhállach fáth-ghlic
  ó Dhún Guairne,
'S go mb'annamh mo thrácht
  'san Ráth i rúm uaigneach.

Inform noble, vigorous, bright
  John Clárach,
Poet and scholar whose face is
  seldom gloomy,
That I am Wall the poet of Dun
  Gourney,
Not often found in Rath Luirc
  in a lonely room!

Seán Clárach answered that to find so learned a poet in a lonely room was to him a cause of heavy grief. They came together, and the night passed for them as did that ancient night in France when Ronsard and du Bellay met haphazardly at an inn for the first time.

As poets, as members of the one institute, did Seán Clárach and Eamonn de Bháll meet. It is said that in the Middle Ages a craftsman, on arriving in a strange town, would go straight to the Guild Hall of his own craft; nowhere else was he more sure of welcome, for there his own half-secret learning would be best understood and most valued. In Ireland, the " beds of the poets " had long been destroyed, yet, even so, there were still in such places as Rath Luirc poets' hearths, and poets' voices to welcome fellow-craftsmen in to them out of the lonely nights.

Seán Clárach is buried near Rath Luirc, and this is the inscription on the stone above him:

I.H.S.
Johannes Mac Donald cogno
minatus Clárag vir vere
Catholicus et tribus linguis
ornatus nempe Graeca Latina
et Hybernica non vulgaris
Ingenii poeta tumulatur
ad hunc cippum obiit aetatis.
Anno 63. Salutis 1754.
Requiescat in pace.

DONNCHADH RUADH MAC CON MARA
(DENIS MACNAMARA THE RED)

In journeying through the Hidden Land we have already come upon three schools—Sliabh Luachra, with Aodhagán Ó Rathaille and Eoghan Ruadh Ó Súilleabháin to speak to us of its virtues; the Blarney School, with Diarmuid Mac Cárthaigh to pilot it into new and humbler ways; and that at Rath Luirc, with Seán Clárach Mac Domhnaill presiding over its sittings. We have, besides, met with a poet who stood in the doorway of no school at all; that is, Brian Merriman of the County Clare. With another Clareman, now, we are to speak, Donnchadh Ruadh Mac Con Mara, or Denis MacNamara— schoolless also?—No, but the brightest ornament of one of the most famous of them all—a school, however, that lay far away from his native county, hidden in the Comeragh mountain mass that rises up mid-way between Clonmel and Dungarvan. We may call it the Sliabh gCua (Gua) School.

He was already 32 years old when Brian Merriman was born; and yet, he was to outlive him by five years (1715-1810). Of that long life we catch only haphazard glimpses; and only that those somewhat startling appearances are fixed in his verses the memory of them, too, was doubtless long since as deeply swallowed in the general gloom as those of which he made no song. It is said that in his early manhood he was sent to Rome to study for the priesthood, that he was expelled from the college there, that he landed in Waterford, and found his way to the famous school at Sliabh gCua, which ever afterwards remained the anchorage to which he always returned. Another theory has, however, been lately used to account for his being in County Waterford, so far from his native place. Sliabh gCua is in the Power country. Certain of these Waterford Powers were transplanted to Clare under Cromwell—" close to the country of the MacNamaras, with which family the transplanted Waterford gentry formed alliances by marriage and otherwise. Some Powers were restored under Charles II, and it is conceivable that MacNamara came in their train to Waterford."[1]

It is a reasonable explanation. A second question comes to us: Did our poet really make that voyage he describes so picturesquely in his famous poem? Whether we answer yes or no, it is certain that every line of it illuminates both his period and his adopted countryside—illuminates them as by flashes of the most careless, yet the most searching of rays: " In January, 1784, the Catholics of Newfoundland petitioned to have as their superior the Rev Francis MacDonnell, a Franciscan of Waterford, pleading that seven-eighths of the population of St John's were emigrants from that town, and that it was essential that their superior should be able to preach in Irish as English."[2] And Young tells us what he had noticed in Waterford eight years before: " The number of people who go as passengers in the Newfoundland ships is amazing: from sixty to eighty ships, and from three thousand to five thousand annually. They come from most parts of Ireland, from Cork, Kerry, etc."[3]

It is this trafficking between Waterford and Newfoundland —the " Land of Fish," as the Gaels called it—that Donnchadh Ruadh's long poem commemorates; and the question whether or not he had actually ever made the voyage he describes is interesting, yet not really material; later he was, indeed, to make many voyages, his greatest lyric, the well-known *Bán Chnoic Éireann Óigh' (The Fair Hills of Holy Ireland)* having been written, it is said, in Hamburg. Still, his trade was neither fishing nor sailoring, but one even emptier still— schoolmastering. And even as schoolmaster his story has something new for us: " Though relaxed in vigour, the Penal Laws were still on the Statute Book. By these laws the craft of the schoolmaster was felony. The law on the matter was, however, allowed to become practically a dead letter because no one

---

[1] Rev P. Power, M.R.I.A., *Donnchadh Ruadh MacNamara*.
[2] Ward, *The Dawn of the Catholic Revival in England (1781-1803)*.
[3] *A Tour in Ireland* (1776).

could be found to lodge informations. Donnchadh, dismissed from his school, and smarting under the indignity and its practical consequences, made formal report—so, at any rate, it is stated—against the teacher appointed in his stead."[1]

That is a startling vision of him, yet it may all have been little more than a reckless joke; for, in his prime, he was a careless, roystering, turbulent man of the hills, a " spoiled priest " in reputation, a frequenter of the company of squireens, a traveller on the seas, familiar with the haunts of sailormen in Waterford and Dungarvan. He wrote a " pass " for one of his pupils, and he nicknames the famous teachers in the district:—Christopher Mac Heavy-bottom, Giddyhead O'Hackett, Coxcomb O'Boland, Tatter O'Flanagan, dirty, puffy John O'Mulrooney, Blear-eyed O'Cullenan and Giggler O'Mulcahy.

It is this reckless creature we again discover in the next episode: he, a Catholic, applies for and obtains the parish-clerkship of the Protestant Church of Rossmire! " Abjuration of the errors of Rome was a condition *sine qua non* for the post, and with the condition Donnchadh determined to comply. . . . . Together with an out-at-elbows squireen of the hard-drinking, hard-swearing and dare-devil variety, William Power of Ballyvoile, to wit, Donnchadh read his recantation in the Protestant Church of Mothel, or Carrick-on-Suir."[2] Two other poets, Andrias Mac Craith and Piaras Mac Gearailt, did much the same—" abjured the errors of Rome "—and all three, it is likely, spent only about the same short term in the new faith. Mac Craith was such another as Donnchadh Ruadh; both laughed, it is clear, at the foolery; with Mac Gearailt, however, it was otherwise, as we shall see.

After this, lest we should forget that we are journeying in an unlighted land, we come on a gap of thirty years in the annals of our poet's life. When he again lifts his voice he is eighty years of age; but his friend, his brother poet, one of the

---

[1] Power, *op. cit.*

[2] Power, *op. cit.*

same school, too, Tadhg Gaedhealach Ó Súilleabháin, is dead, and he must bewail him: this is his utterance:

Thaddeus hic situs est, oculos huc flecte viator,
Illustrem vatem parvula terra tegit!
Heu! Jacet exanimis, fatum irrevocabile vicit
Spiritus e terra sidera summa petit!
Quis canet Erinidum laudes, quis facta virorum?
Gadelico extincto, Scotica musa tacet.
Processit numeris doctis pia carmina cantans
Evadens victor munera certa tulit.
Laudando Dominum praeclara poëmata fecit
Et suaves hymnos fervidus ille canet.
Plangite, Pierides! vester decessit alumnus,
Eochades non est cunctaque rura silent,
Pacem optavit pace igitur versatur in alto,
Ad superi tendit regna beata Patris.

Translation by Dr Sigerson:

This is the grave of a Poet. O Wanderer, glance here in sorrow:
Famous he was and beloved, weeds shade him now and grey dust,
Woe! he is gone, he is conquered by Fate's invincible arrow—
Yet, hath his spirit, from earth, soared to the stars, 'mid the Just.
Who sings the glory of Eirinn? Who the heroic achievement?
Lost is our silver-voiced Tadhg, broken the Harp of our Land!
Singing his musical numbers he left us, to mourn in bereavement,
Victor, in triumph, he fled, bearing his gifts in his hand.
Often, in praise of the Lord, did his song rise, flow'r-like and vernal,
Sweet now the hymns that he sings, standing 'mid angels above.
Weep, O ye Muses! your nursling has gone to the regions supernal—
Dead, our MacEochad is dead! Silent are woodland and grove.
Peace he desired, while on earth; peace henceforth awaits him eternal,
Far in the Father's high home, 'mid the fair Kingdom of Love.

In silence he lives on another fifteen years, in poverty, one fears, depending for his bread on the charity of simple people; and then, finishing all, we discover this in the *Freeman's Journal:*—

October 6th, 1810, at Newtown, near Kilmacthomas, in the 95th year of his age, Denis MacNamara, commonly known by the name Ruadh, or Red-haired, the most celebrated of the modern bards. His compositions will be received and read until the end of time with rapturous admiration and enthusiastic applause.

His life, when we thus catch glimpses of it, with long dark-
nesses between them—the roving " spoiled priest," the schoolmaster finding shelter here and there in the farmers' houses,
the pensive voyager, the grinning parish-clerk; then the old
man, a blind beggar about the roads, according to one
account; and, last of all, a stooped and venerable figure,
eighty years of age, raising his voice above the corpse of his
friend—thus haphazardly spied upon, his life seems tragi-
comedy from end to end. He was wild and reckless, reckless
both of this world and the next; but then, over against this
idea of him, one recalls his *Bán Chnoic Éireann Óigh'*, that
lyric which has so easily found entrance into every anthology
of Gaelic poetry put together in our time—so poignant in
feeling, so deep in colour, so simple, yet withal so rich:

An áit úd 'nar bh'aoibhinn binn-
    ghuth éan
	Pleasant in that place the sweet
	    voice of birds

Mar shámh-chruit chaoin ag
    caoineadh Gaedheal—
	As a soft and gentle harp bewail-
	    ing the Gael—

'Sé mo chás bheith míle míle i
    gcéin
	My fate is to be a thousand
	    miles away

Ó bhán-chnuic Éireann Óigh '.	From the Fair Hills of Holy Ireland.

No matter how often the words break in on one, the old
charm remains golden and soft within them, no vocable
jarring on us, no tint misplaced.

One thinks also of the quiet mastery of style in his piece of
burlesque—*Eachtra Shéamuis Grae*—of the earnestness which
breaks to the surface in it when poets and poetry need
defence. See how the Philistine speaks (she is really a Surly
Dame who refuses the Poor Scholar, Séamus Grae, a lodging):

An mhuintir ag ar gnáthach	Such people as shelter
Scoláirdhe as sagairt fós	(Poor) Scholars and priests
Do chidhimse nach fearrde	I do not see that their rye
Thig gráinne don t-seagal dóibh.	Bears better grain for it.

No emphasis, just right; and she then asserts that if she had as
large a brood as the *dreóilín*—the wren—she wouldn't think

of sending one of them to school—that is, of course, to such schools as then obtained. How does the Poor Scholar reply?—

" An té dhéanfas," ar an Scoláire,
" Beidh sásadh ó Dhia aige,
Beidh an rath air de láthair
'S beidh na grása 'ge 'na dhiaidh sin:

" But he who does," said the (Poor) Scholar,
" Knows he fulfils God's ways,
He is blessed here at present
And is afterwards filled with grace.

" Ní bhfaghair-se dul i g-caithis
Leis an aicme gheibh eolus
'S dom dhóigh ní dhéanfainn malairt
Ar do chuid seagail ná eornan!"

" It is useless for you to contend
With those who are learned;
And for all your rye or barley,
My thought is: I'd not exchange."

And further, he tells her:

" Is lucht eoluis," ar an Scoláire,
" Atá ' cumhdach do thighe ort
Ag déanamh scáth ' do Shliocht Lóbuis
Do tóghbhadh as an aoileach!"

" 'Tis the learned," said the Scholar,
" Protect your house for you,
Sheltering Clan Lóbuis (the plebeians)
That were raised from the dung!"

The Poor Scholars and Poor Poets sheltering, as of their charity, Clan Lóbuis, Surly Dames and all! Even in those lines of it where only is fun and scolding there is the same quiet mastery of style.

Then, again, one thinks of the Keating-like directness and strength in certain stanzas of his *Duain na hAithrighe*—his *Song of Repentance*—the thoroughly Gaelic bleakness of it; or of his Latin epitaph; and when to these that we have named—*Bán Chnoic Éireann Óigh', Séamus Grae, Duain na hAithrighe,* the *Epitaph*—one adds his long narrative poem, so bright, so swift, so carelessly strong, one beholds in him a many-sided genius, wanting neither in depth nor in wit, nor in music, nor in strength, as reckless of his power, of his only riches, as he was of everything else, temporal and spiritual.

That longest poem of his, *Eachtra Ghiolla an Amaráin (The Adventures of a Luckless Fellow),* is truly his, every note

249

of it, every gesture. It is also, as we have said, the living voice of his time and place.

To give some idea of it: A sense of his wretchedness swoops upon him as he lies in bed: to mend his fortunes he thinks of voyaging to America. He leaps up lightly at morning and bids his friends farewell:

Do chuir mé slán lem' cháirdibh in aenfheacht,
'S ag cuid nír fhágbhas slán le foiréigion.

Farewell I bid my friends when leaving,
To some, I own, with no great grieving.

He catalogues all the "slops" he had to gather for the journey:

Do thug an pobul i bhfochair a chéile
Chum mo chothuighthe i g-cogadh nó i spéirlinn—
Stór nach g-caillfeadh suim de laethibh,
As cófra doimhin a d-toillfinn féin ann;
Do bhí seacht bh-fichid ubh circe 'gus eunla ann
Le h-aghaidh a n-ithte chomh minic 's badh mhéin liom—
Cróca ime do dingeadh le saothar
As spólla soille ba throimhe 'ná déarfainn,
Bhí tuilleadh as naoi g-clocha de mhin choirce ghlain-chréitheartha ann
Re dríodar na loisde 's iad croithte le chéile,
Lán an bharaille do b'fhearra bhí in Éirinn
De phrátaoibh dearga air eagla geur-bhruid'—
Do thugas cag leanna ann do lasfadh le séideadh
'S do chuirfeadh na mairbh 'na mbeatha dá mb'fhéidir—
Do bhí agam jackets chomh gasta le h-aen-neach
Agus léinteacha breaca go barraibh mo mheura,

The people gave me open-handed
To carry me o'er the sea till landed—
A store for a month—to me right pleasing!
A great deep chest I'd rest at ease in—
Of eggs seven score it held, no boasting,
For frying or boiling, poaching, roasting—
A crock of butter packed full tightly,
A piece of bacon fine and sightly,
Nine stone of oatmeal clean-sifted,

No joke of a load for him who lifted—
A barrel there was of the best then growing
Of new potatoes, Munster's sowing,
A keg of good ale—all hail who brew so!
'Twould liven the dead, if aught could do so—
The neatest of jackets I had in plenty,
Of new check shirts I owned full twenty—

250

Leaba 'gus clúda i g-ciumhais a chéile	Good bedding, the best that Cork afforded,
Ceangailte ar dhrom mo thrúnc le teudaibh—	On the top of my trunk securely corded—
Bhí bróga istigh ann, bhí wig as béabhar	I had shoes and wig and brand-new beaver,
Agus stór mar sin anois nach ndéarfad!	With money go leor—I'm no deceiver ! [1]

The lines give point to Young's remark: " A great point for them is to be able to carry out (to Newfoundland) all their slops, for everything there is exceedingly dear, one or two hundred per cent dearer than they can get them at home."[2]

In this passage we find the note of the whole poem, a swift slap-dash vision of life, alert at every point, unforced, rich in invention. His sketch of the innkeeper's daughter is as fresh as when written:

Do bhí sí fáilteach fáinneach, tréitheach,	Her ringlets fair, her face still fairer,
Ba chaoin, deas, sásta an *drawer* le glaodhach í,	Pleasant she smiled when of liquor the bearer,
Gach sórt d'á d-tagadh a bhlaiseadh ní sheunfadh,	To sip she ne'er was loth, invited,
D'inneósadh eachtra, startha 'gus sceul duit,	And many a tale for me recited,
Ní ghlacfadh sí fala ná fearg go h-éug leat	Offence at jest she ne'er took gravely,
Fad bhraithfeadh sí airgead agat ar aon chor!	At least while I was spending bravely!

In four lines, of great swiftness, the ship is far on the sea:

Scaoiltear seolta ar nóin do Phœbus,	At eve to Phœbus the sails are spread,
Do bhí Æólus leó agus Tétis,	Æolus and Thetis sweep ahead,
Scinnid de phreab amach san treun-mhuir	In a leap the midst of the sea is won
Go ndruidid abhfad i d-teas na gréine.	And they move into the heat of the sun!

In a passage full of life he gives us the names of his fellow-

---

[1] See *Eachtra Ghiolla an Amaráin*, edited by Tomás Ó Flannghaile, for the whole poem and translation, of which this is a sample.

[2] *A Tour in Ireland* (1776), by Arthur Young.

voyagers, all real people, we may be certain, and describes their horrible sea-sickness: they are all pell-mell on top of one another; making an end by slyly adding that he himself—let it be on his soul if he were any better, stretched out like an ox, like a sack, without a whistle or groan in him!

And so the Luckless Fellow makes his voyage until they meet a Frenchman:

" *Helm-a-lee!*" 's ba bhínn an sceul liom,
Dubhairt Captaoin *Allen* go feargach faobhrach—
" *Gunner, give fire! we'll fight the negroes,*
We'll conquer or die, my Irish heroes!
All hands aloft!" do phreab mé am' léine
'S do bhí *cutlass* am' ghlaic as faobhar air—
Gunna 'gus piostal in ionad a chéile.
Torann as tintreach gach uile thaobh dhínn—
Do bhíomar bórd re bórd ag reubadh
Ag gabháil de ghunnaidhibh i mullaighibh a chéile,
Ráig as gorraidhe as buillidhe treuna,
Fuaim as geoin as gleo agus caorthainn,
Gártha 'gus troid as gol as béiceach—
Do chualaidh Corcach 's nir bhfogus d'á chéile
Fuaim an chogaidh so as torann an lae sin!
Frigéad mear Francach, lom, glan, gleusta
Do chuir sinn i b-ponc 's i scann-radh ár n-daothain
Fá dhá-fhichid glan-ghunnadh d'a léigion gach féile
Ba rogha linn casadh chomh gasta 's dob' fhéidir
'Sa long badh mheasa chum reatha bíodh fae dhé!

" Helm-a-lee!" (to me how pleasing!)
Cried Captain Allen, all fears appeasing—
" Gunner, give fire! we'll fight the negroes,
We'll conquer or die, my Irish heroes!
All hands aloft!" he roared, and quickly
I leaped from my bed, no longer sickly,
Musket and pistol I plied untiring,
Thunder and lightning the guns' dread firing—
And soon we closed, and I saw but dimly
Each sweeping the deck of his foeman grimly—
Frenzy and fury and blows resounding,
Clamour and cries from all surrounding,
Smiting and fighting and slaying and groaning,
The roar reach'd Cork — I've heard men owning
That never before had there been such a rattle
There known as the thunder of that day's battle!
A swift French frigate, well-rigg'd and bearing
Two score bright guns, had given this scaring—
And being o'ermatched in the fight quite fairly
To trust to our speed was our need now clearly!

252

And the end of his voyaging is:

Ar loing fad mhairfead ní rachad
   má fhéudaim
Muna rachainn le stracadh nó
   ceangailte le teudaibh!

Never again on a ship they'll
   find me
Unless by force they should take
   and bind me!

But no, that is not the end. The poem, we must keep in mind, was written in the mediæval Irish Munster of the eighteenth century. This is the final cadence:

Mar bharra ar gach ní le Chríost
   bíodh buidheachas—
A Chara bí am'dhíon, a Rí ná
   tréig sinn—
A Rí na bhflaitheas do cheannuigh go daor sinn,
Sgaoil ár nglasa ó'n bpeacadh
   san t-saoghal so,
Tóg-sa t'fhearg dínn, neartuigh
   agus saor sinn,
As fóir ar ár n-anam—sin agaibh
   mo sceul-sa!

To crown all things, to Christ be thanks—O Friend, protect me, O King, abandon us not—O King of Heaven, Who has dearly redeemed us, loosen our bonds of sin in this world, take off Thy anger from us, strengthen and free us, and help our souls— there ye have my story!

What an ending for such a poem! Read the Irish aloud, and it reads well, noticing how it rises up and up, strengthening to the *dash* in the last line; and then: " there ye have my story!" So, in the Irish-speaking districts, when a traditional singer has lifted us high on the viewless wings of poesy he, suddenly, in the last cadence, breaks the spell, and brings us back to earth. How does he do it? By suddenly dropping the music out of the song, *speaking* the last few words, and in the most casual, conversational tone, too, instead of singing them. One thinks it wrong of him, yet, listening to it, one certainly becomes wonderfully aware of the strength of those wings that have been bearing us aloft; and again, so casual is the tone, one interprets the sudden change as saying: " After all, 'tis a poor thing, and you have had enough of it, and I am not a great singer "! Delightfully human! And whatever else Donnchadh Ruadh was, he was delightfully human!—a luck-less fellow, hard-pressed, strong neither in faith nor will; yet, we may assume, it often was his happy lot to fling out this bright and rattling song to his mountainy audience, every one of them well-fitted to relish all its quips and cranks, its hundred allusions—as well as to appreciate critically its swiftness and its jocund music. And so he may not have been so luckless a fellow after all!

SEÁN Ó TUAMA AN GHRINN
(JOHN O'TWOMEY OF THE MERRIMENT)
(1706-1775)

" October 5th (1776). Passed through a very unentertaining country (except for a few miles on the bank of the Shannon) to Altavilla, but Mr Bateman being from home, I was disappointed in getting an account of the Palatines settled in his neighbourhood. Kept the road to Adair, where Mrs Quin, with a politeness equalled only by her understanding, procured me every intelligence I wished for."[1] Then the traveller, Arthur Young, goes on to tell us all that he had learned about the Palatines—how Lord Southwell had settled them in that part of Limerick some seventy years before, how they had kept up the custom of having a burgomaster, how their language was dying away. He did not enquire of Mrs Quin— she was Lord Dartry's sister—if she had ever heard of one John O'Twomey, who had died just a year before his visit. Had he done so, he might have learned that she had had a servant of that name, who looked after her hens—unless O'Curry's information on the matter is not to be trusted. That servant is already known to us as one who had once—it was when Seán Clárach Mac Domhnaill died—an unforgettable vision of the Muses:

| Naoi soillse is naoi lóchrainn 'na lámha | Nine Brightnesses with nine lanterns in their hands. |

[1] Arthur Young, *A Tour in Ireland.*

254

But Mrs Quin would have better remembered him, perhaps, as the writer of a half-humorous, half-bitter poem on this servitude of his, in which she is called the Dame of the Slender Wattle—Bean na Cleithe Caoile. It is certain that no other hen-keeper in the wide world, and to search all its ages, ever eased his heart of bitterness in such a strain. Eoghan Ruadh Ó Súilleabháin, we recollect, used, in his forlorn moods, to recall that his blood had come down to him from the ancient kings of Cashel. Seán Ó Tuama, in his desolate days, keeper of hens to one who was hard and proud and not of his religion, could recall only that once he had spent his days on the " track of poems " in the company of gentlemen of the faith of Jesus; that in those days he used to have money without stint in his grasp, however little respect this Dame of the Slender Wattle now used towards him:

> Do chaitheas-sa seal fá rath ar leirg laoithe,
> I gcaidreamh fear is flaith ar chreideamh Íosa,
> Airgead geal im ghlaic gan deireannaighe ar bith,
> Cé dealbh mo mheas ag bean na cleithe caoile.

It is likely that, afterwards, he was, in the traditional way, to sup on still harder fare and to chew still bitterer thoughts. Those brighter moments he had known, it was when he kept his tavern at Mungret Gate, towards the Fair Green, in Croom. Again, in the wide world, was ever an inn-keeper's sign inscribed as his:

Ní'l fánach gan fagháltas ar uaisle Gaoidheal,
Bráthair den dáimh ghlic ná suairc-fhear groidhe,
I gcás go mbeadh láithreach gan luach na dighe
Ná fuil fáilte ag Seán geal Ua Tuama roimhe.

No landless wanderer of the noble Gael,
No brother bard, no doughty heart and game,
Though presently he lack the price of ale,
But John O'Twomey welcomes all the same.

It is not hard to understand how such an inn-keeper came down at last to the shepherding of hens!

255

While in Croom, Croom of the Pleasuring, as he himself was Seán Ó Tuama an Ghrinn—John O'Twomey of the Merriment—news came to him in 1754 that Seán Clárach Mac Domhnaill was dead. He recollected how, in an evil day, Seán Clárach had stood by him, calling him, when rumour had belied him, a bright laughing scion with no hardness in his heart; he recollected, too, how often they had wrestled with each other in wit, in poetry—and so sat him down and made an elegy for his friend. But another thought, as well as this sense of personal loss, came to him with the fateful news— that on his shoulders lay henceforth the burden of keeping Irish learning alive in all that countryside. Those other poets we have been lingering with, their names are linked with places where even still Irish is freely spoken—Sliabh Luachra, Sliabh gCua, Ballymacoda. Not so with Seán Ó Tuama's name. His countryside to-day is purely English-speaking; and this great change he saw taking place before his eyes. With no delay he set about his task. He sent out a *gairmscoile*, or school-call, to the poets of the district on the 23rd September, 1754, inviting them to gather in Croom on the 21st of the following month, in memory of Seán Clárach Mac Domhnaill, to keep alive, as he was wont to do, the Irish customs of their forefathers. The little that still lives of the language will soon become nothing, he says, unless some way is found to foster it. . . . We must, therefore, remember him as the man who inherited Seán Clárach Mac Domhnaill's leadership; and that the nature of the battle-field—soft, rich grazing lands—was all against him. There were no cold-looking and threatening mountain ranges in it to keep off the traffickers and the land-grabbers.

No singer of that period so often in his lines makes reference to poets and poetry and their schools. At the same time, there is, perhaps, no poet in whose songs we are so keenly aware of how meagre the tradition had become, how much it needed the sustenance of fresh ideas and visions. Yet he was a genuine poet, full of striking lines, musical, swift, and strong. His song describing Croom Fair must have bestowed upon its charms, at least for his contemporaries, some share of that light that was never on sea or land. In his only *Aisling* we find this description of the *Spéir-bhean's* hair:

A craobh-fholt cas mar ór síos 'N-a thóirsidhe go troighthe ag fás.	Her ringleted luxuriant locks like gold Went down, torch-like, to her feet.

And here is a verse that shows what ease of style the old tradition had achieved:

> 'Bé chífeadh uaidh gach ruathar bróin,
> Gach daoirse chruaidh gach cruadhtan fós,
> Gach sceimhle fuair ár n-uaisle rómhainn,
> Budh líonta a ghruadh le duartan deor.

And note how that sense of style is destroyed in the translation —Mangan's—on which that stanza is usually judged:

> Oh! who can well refrain from tears
> Who sees the hosts of a thousand years
> Expelled from this their own green isle,
> And bondsmen to the Base and Vile?

The Base and Vile! A literal translation might run: " He who would make himself a vision of every sorrowful rout, every dire enslavement, every hardship, every flaying that our nobility have suffered in the years gone, his cheeks would fill with a flood of tears."

An incident that fell out in his time fixes very clearly for us the place he held, as by poet-right, in the people's mind. " When a Dominican friar, named Denis Hedderman, went over to the Protestant fold and became a minister of the reformed religion, no less than three poets—one from so distant a place as Castle Lyons—addressed poetical epistles to Ó Tuama giving vigorous expression to their indignation and indulging in gloomy anticipations of future disasters. This incident serves to emphasise strongly the commanding position

Ó Tuama held amongst his brother bards. He was but a lay-man, a mere tavern-keeper, a married man with a family, yet is he appealed to in these poetical epistles as the representative Irishman and Catholic of his day, at least in that part of the country. Ó Tuama's reply to one of these epistles is, perhaps, the most vigorous thing he has written."[1]

The series of poems mentioned might be used to illustrate, if one more example were needed, how the poets of a country-side would gather to a theme; a pleasanter choice, however, of this same characteristic of theirs is the group of poems on Fr Nicholas O'Donnell's horse, "Preabaire," which, "overlooked by a spirit," vanished from this earth. The good friar lightly, though in excellent "chain" verse, bewails his "translated" garran. The others comfort him. The friar takes up his pen again, rounding the series to a close, and in his last poem we find this verse:

> Dá dtagadh an cúigear úd go maiseach ar clár,
> Ag canadh 's ag scrúdadh na n-ughdar do cheapadar dáimh,
> Dob aite, dar liom, a gclú a n-ainm 's a gcáil,
> Ná flaitheas na Mumhan a bpúint 's a nglagaireacht smáil.

Making poor prose of which we get:

> " If those five (the poets who had taken part in the contention) were festively to gather round a table, singing and scrutinising the poets' songs, their name and their renown would be pleasanter, in my opinion, than the principality of Munster, their wealth and their vicious chattering."

And in the last verse this he follows up by saying that were they thus to gather in to Seán's "Dún"—that is, Seán Ó Tuama's tavern—even his grief for his bewitched garran would scatter away from him: Seán, therefore, was not wanting in the ' simple worship of a day ": when he died, it was

---

[1] An t-Athair Pádraig Ó Duinnín, *Filídhe na Máighe.*

only fitting that a great many poets should lament one who was not only earnest, but jovial. He is buried in the graveyard at Croom.

ANDRIAS MAC CRAITH
(ANDREW MACGRATH)

Mac Craith was known as An Mangaire Súgach, The Merry Pedlar, though his trade was schoolmastering, like so many others, and not peddling. His name is coupled with Ó Tuama's, in death as in life, just as du Bellay's is coupled with Ronsard's. They loved each other: and yet we find Mac Craith calling his friend a spy; but then Ó Tuama had written him down a wandering old bard, an incompetent bard, and one who did not truly understand how ignorant he was! The Merry Pedlar's reply is swift and fierce as a splash of water in the eyes: it is a *tour de force,* wonderful for its wordcraft and energy:

> Iarsma íogair gan oideas,
> Iarmhar daorscuir le daille,
> Gan chiall gan chuimhne gan chruinneas,
> Gan mhian gan mhíne gan bhinneas.

Translation is of no avail; and what a snarling threat in:

> Gach breillice brillsce breall-bháird,
> Nó giolla gan ghaois do ghabhann páirt
> Libh-se ná tuigeadh go leigfeam fá líg
> Go rithfidh ar baois 'n-a labhrán.

Of course, it is only a matter of "words, words, words," as both parties to the bout well understood; but what amazing dexterity!

Mac Craith is said to have been the wildest of all the bards of that wild time. He made no secret of it himself, frequently

259

so describing himself in his verses. Yet he was a genuine poet, greater than Seán Ó Tuama, greater than Seán Clárach Mac Domhnaill, the greatest poet of that Cork-Limerick country-side. His drinking song is worthy of Burns at his best. I have no idea of the tune to which it was sung, but the last line of each chorus invites a wild roar:

> Is maith an bheart i n-aon
> Do chaith a choróinn 's a réal,
> 'S a liacht scramaire gan chéill
> Do mealladh ris an saoghal,
> Atá anois ag dreoghadh san chré,
> Fir ag a mnáibh dá n-éis,
> Is iad-san fá líg san teampull.

Which might be, loosely, rendered:

> A good thing 'tis for one
> To spend his crown, his sixpence,
> Considering how vast a crowd
> That the world wheedled to its way
> Now rot within the clay;
> Their wives with new men play
> And they within the church, a tombstone under!

There are seventy-five lines in it, every one of them full of headlong energy and sound. Like Donnchadh Ruadh, he went for a while with the Protestants, for a little while only, the minister throwing him out. Where was he then?—neither Catholic nor Protestant! But he didn't take it seriously; made, instead, a merry song of it all:

" O dear friend (Seán Ó Tuama, doubtless, who replied to the verses), are you distressed to find me cast out, a wanderer, neither Protestant nor Papist!"

Then he gives the two pictures of his poor self, the minister's, the priest's, both equally contemptuous and hard. What can he do but take up with neither side? And, slyly, he has his revenge:

Cé fada do bhí Magdalen is
    Dáibhí an king
Ar mearbhall 's an t-apstal do
    chuir cách i mbruid,
Do glacadh iad nuair chasadar i
    gcáil 's i gcion
Is ceachtar díobh níor Phrotes-
    tan ná Pápaire.

Although for long were Magdalen
    and David the King
Astray as also that Apostle who
    wrought destruction to all,
When they changed back again,
    in affection and esteem they
    were received,
Though neither of them was
    either Protestant or Papist!

He then goes on: Since he has ceased to be either Protestant
or Papist, he must needs become either a Calvinist or an
Arian; and then:

'Bé aca san den aicme-si a
    dtráchtaim-se,
Nár dhearmaid na haitheanta is
    atá gan choir,
Caitheadh liom a gharbh-leac go
    hábalta,
Cibé aca san mé Protestan nó
    Pápaire.

Whoever of this company I
    speak of has not yet
Forgotten the Commandments
    and is free of guilt
Let him fling at me mercilessly
    a massy stone,
Whether I be Protestant or
    Papist!

There is strength and ease in everything we have of his;
but in his most famous poem there is more: there is fine feeling; two at least of the stanzas are priceless: he has been
driven from Croom of the Merriment into loneliness:

Is fánach faon mé is fraochmhar
    fuar,
Is támh-lag tréith 's taomach
    truagh,
I mbárr an tsléibhe gan aon,
    monuar,
Im pháirt, ach fraoch is gaoth
    adtuaidh.

A wanderer and languid am I,
furious and cold, weak, prostrate,
disease-smitten, wretched on the
mountain-top, with none, alas!
to befriend me—except heather
and the north wind!

Don tsráid nuair théidhim mar
    éan ar cuaird
Ní háil leó mé is ní réidhid lem
    chluain,
Bíd mná le chéile ag pléidhe dá
    luadhadh,
Cá háit, cia hé, cá taobh 'n-ar
    ghluais?

When as a bird in its questing
I enter the village, there's no
welcome for me, they are cold
to my jesting, and the women,
gathered together, question one
another: Who is he? Where is
he from? Where is he going?

The heart stirs to it; and, again, we may notice in it that easy perfection of style the old tradition had arrived at. He outlived his friend Ó Tuama, who loved him more, he tells us, than anyone else. Then he wanders away into the darkness, as did Villon. We do not know when he died, nor where; but his weary limbs, it is supposed, are stretched out somewhere in the graveyard at Kilmallock.

PIARAS MAC GEARAILT
(PIERCE FITZGERALD)
(1700-1791)

It would not be easy to find a quieter, more hidden, more forgotten countryside than that which stretches slowly along the sea between Cork Harbour and Youghal Harbour. It lies well south of the roadway that unites Cork, Midleton and Youghal, and is familiar, therefore, only to those who dwell in it. To the western half of this dead land—the Cork Harbour side—came, in 1734, the gentle Berkeley; and here he was to stay almost until he died. His wings were clipped: he had had his dreams of the New World, of the Old, broken: Utopia was neither in the Old nor in the New: and the Utopia he now found himself in was a land stricken with famine and many plagues.

In the eastern half—the Youghal Harbour district—at the same time lived a young man who used to sign himself Áird-Shirriam Leithe Mogha, which, literally turned, gives us, High-Sheriff of Mogh's Half—that is, of the South of Ireland. The real message of the phrase is: Chief Poet of Munster!

Ag seo fá'm láimh is fá'm shéala go daingean, diongmhalta	Herewith under my hand and seal, firmly and securely,
PIARAS MAC GEARAILT	PIERCE FITZGERALD
Áird-Shirriam Leatha Mogha.	*High-Sheriff of Mogh's Half.*

One wonders if those two men, Berkeley and Fitzgerald, ever came to meet, or ever came even to know of each other. Of those famines and plagues, and of the misgovernment under which they flourished, Berkeley wrote wisely and with feeling, yet as of evils he looked upon from a vantage point; but Piaras Mac Gearailt felt them both in body and soul.

I

Mac Gearailt's father made his will in 1722, and the witnesses were Thomas Garde, Peter Carey, John Power—names still common in that countryside. Note, now, that not one of them is a Gaelic name; and, indeed, even to this day Gaelic names are not so frequent as outland names in any of its parishes. It was Norman country for a long while; later it was Sir Walter Raleigh's country; Mogeely, a little place not far away, is mentioned in his will; then it was the Earl of Cork's country—another Elizabethan—in general, a thoroughly " planted " district, therefore, and not one but many language struggles have had their rise and fall within its bounds; until to-day we find it speaking Irish with a richness, a fluency, that is excelled only in one or two other hidden places in the whole of Munster.

When in 1722 the poet's father made his will, the poet's self was a boy of thirteen years of age; he was at home in Ballymacoda, about four miles across the bay from the town of Youghal. But his three brothers were at school in Spain! When we read of the Flight of the Wild Geese, after Limerick, we seldom dwell upon its consequences in after years, on the constant traffic that went on between the Continent and quiet places in Munster, where to-day the mention of Spain or France or Austria is as infrequent as reference to Alaska or Japan.

Long before Piaras had grown to manhood and come into possession of Ballykineally he knew that only for the fortunes of war Ballykineally, instead of being the whole of his possession, would have been merely the home farm of a huge region. To lose Ballykineally now would, therefore, be to lose even the very name of property. In that was the sorrow of his life, for a moment came when he had not the strength to say: Let Ballykineally go with the rest. To retain it, he must take the hilly road to Kilcreddan Church, to enter it as a Protestant, to become, in his own words, "an innocent child of the Reformed Church."

The people had become accustomed to such strange and heartless doings; and, therefore, we are not surprised to find only one poet mentioned as having upbraided him for his weakness. To this poet, Barry of Clonmel, Mac Gearailt replies in a poem one shrinks from reading, so full of confusion of mind, of bitter pain, it is:

A chogair, a charaid, 's a Bhar-
    raigh is múinte méinn,
Is doilbh liom ceangal le Calbhin
    is Liútar claon,
Ach golfhairt mo leanbh, 's a
    gcreachadh gan triúch, gan
    tréad
Thug srothanna óm dhearcaibh
    'na gcaisibh is túirlint déar.

O gossip, O friend, O Barry,
    most cultured in behaviour,
'Tis sad for me to cleave to Cal-
    vin or perverse Luther,
But the weeping of my children,
    the spoiling them of flocks
    and land,
Brought streaming floods from
    my eyes and descent of tears.

And he tells us that it was his own interest in worldly things that drew down this war upon his soul, that he could not bear to see his child and all that belonged to him "sucked down into the clay!"

Nár thoil liom mo leanbh 's a maireann bheith súighte i gcré,
Seoch cogadh do tharraint ar m'anam le dúil 'sa tsaoghal.

The poem is full of uncertainty, full of distress; and reading it, even to-day, one hopes the sufferer was granted his prayer:

Braon beag ded' Naomhthacht, a
    Rígh na nGrás,
Léig orm, réidh liom, is feidhil
    mé óm' námhaid.

A little drop of Thy Holiness, O
    King of the Graces,
Let fall on me, calm me, and
    guard me from my enemy.

It need not be said that his "going to Church," as the phrase then ran, had no likeness to Donnchadh Ruadh's or the Merry Pedlar's. With those two it was one of many wild and reckless flings; both of them wastrels, they collared from their "conversion" a few shillings or pounds for a night's entertainment; they had no fields to retain or lose.

Mac Gearailt was a sober-minded man, simple in soul, and to the day of his death lamented his moment of weakness. The simplicity of his character we find best revealed, perhaps, in his curious poem on the *Characteristics of the Blessed Virgin*. He begins and ends with a note in prose: "There is a part of the Saxon Lutheran religion which, though not for choice, I have accepted that I do not like—that never a petition is addressed to Mary, the Mother of Christ, nor honour nor privileges nor prayers, and yet it is my opinion that it is Mary who is . . . ." And then follows a litany full of striking and beautful expressions instinct with Gaeldom:

Crann soillse is criostal na Críostaidheachta.	Tree of lights and crystal of Christianity.
Lonnradh is lóchrann lóghmhar na spéire.	The glow and precious lantern of the sky.

· · · · ·

Grianán na Glóire!	The sunny chamber in the House of Glory!

And how Gaelic the ending!—indeed, it almost takes one's breath away:

Tuile na ngrás, agus Tonn Chliodna na Trócaire.	Flood of graces, and Cleena's Wave of Mercy!

The prose note at the close is surely very naïve. It may be translated:

265

Indeed, it was at Mary's request that Christ wrought His first miracle, changing water into wine, and, on the head of that, earnestly from my heart I pray every Protestant to be of one thought in disposition, opinion, mind, and intelligence with

PIERCE FITZGERALD *High-Sheriff of Mogh's Half.*

It is certain that he went to Kilcreddan Church only just on such occasions as were necessary, and that, once the officiousness had died away, he went no more.

This, then, is one aspect of the man, his holding on, for the sake of his children, to the remaining handful of the Fitzgerald property, his never-ceasing flood of tears in consequence.

II

As chief poet, his way was to gather the singers from both sides of the Blackwater to his house in Ballykineally twice in the year; and for fifty years he is thought to have presided over these meetings, his staff of office—*Bata na Bachaille*— in his right hand (the actual staff is said to be seen still in some farmer's house in the district). One thinks that no other "Sheriff" of that time in all Munster ruled those "arch poets," as an old Irish-English folk-song names them, with greater dignity and sense of tradition. He lived in a nest of singing birds: and among others it may be that Seán Clárach Mac Domhnaill, Tadhg Gaedhealach Ó Súilleabháin, Donnchadh Ruadh, Moran, Eamonn de Bháll (Wall), Liam Ruadh Mac Coitir, Eamonn Ó Fláithbheartaigh, and Seán Ó Cuinneagáin at one time or another brightened the threshold of his house for him. But the story of his school has not yet been told with any fulness.

III

Further, there is the Jacobite poet to be considered. Five of his poems are *Aisling* poems, and it is certain that this is but a handful of the many of them he scattered from him. His best-known poem is not an *Aisling*; it is for all that a Jacobite song, and is said to have been written about 1750. It is known as *The Munster War Song*. It is so agile, so decorative in manner, that one might easily attribute it to Seán Clárach Mac Domhnaill. In the refrain one hears the beating of the waves against the onward-driving ships that are bringing the Pretender and his forces to the shore:

I

D'aithnígheas féin gan bhréag ar fhuacht
'S ar anfhaithe Thétis taobh le cuan,
Ar chanadh na n-éan go seiseach suairc,
Go gcasfadh mo Sheasar glé gan ghruaim.

Measaim gur subhach do'n Mhumhain an fhuaim
'S d'á maireann go dubhach de chrú na mbuadh
Torann na dtonn le sleasaibh na long
Ag tarraint go teann 'n-ár gceann ar cuaird.

I

I knew it well by storm and cold,
The waves which lash the shore foretold,
The birds' sweet notes in forests tell
Our Prince comes over ocean's swell.

'Tis time for Munster now to cheer,
'Twill glad our wasting clans to hear
The dash of the wave 'gainst the ships of the brave,
And gallant hearts that are drawing near.

II

Tá lasadh 'san ngréin gach lae go neóin;
Ní taise do'n rae, ní théidheann fé neóil;
Tá barra na gcraobh ag déanamh sceóil,
Nach fada bheidh Gaedhil i ngéibheann bróin.

Measaim gur subhach do'n Mhumhain an ceól
'S d'á maireann go dubhach de chrú na dtreón
Torann na dtonn le sleasaibh na long
Ag tarraint go teann 'n-ár gceann fé sheól.

II

The sun's full splendour shines each day,
No cloud obscures the pale moon's ray,
The slender branches sigh the tale—
The mist shall soon rise from the Gael.

'Tis time for Munster now to cheer,
'Twill glad the sons of chiefs to hear
The dash of the wave 'gainst the ships of the brave,
And gallant hearts that are drawing near.

III

Tá Aoibhill ar mire agus Áine
    óg
Agus Cliodna an bhruinneal is
    áilne snódh;
Táid milte agus tuilleadh de'n
    dtáin seo fós
D'a shuidheadh le buile gur
    tháinig an Leoghan.
    Measaim gur subhach do'n
      Mhumhain an ceól
    'S d'á maireann go dubhach
      de chrú na dtreón
    Torann na dtonn le sleasaibh
      na long
    Ag tarraint anall 'nár gceann
      fé sheól.

III

High triumph have Aoibheall
    and Aine at last,
Eana's fair virgins' gloom is
    past;
A thousand and more of this
    joyous train
Now herald our hero with fairy
    strain.
    'Tis time for Munster now to
      cheer,
    'Twill glad our drooping tribes
      to hear
    The dash of the wave 'gainst
      the ships of the brave,
    And gallant hearts now draw-
      ing near.

IV

Is annamh dam maidean ar
    amharc an laoi
Ná bainim chum reatha go
    fairrge síos,
Mo dhearca do leathadh ag faire
    de shíor
Ar bharcaibh an fharaire ag
    gearradh na slíghe.
    Measaim gur subhach do'n
      Mhumhain 's gur binn
    'S d'á maireann go dubhach
      de chrú na ríogh
    Torann na long ag scoilteadh
      na dtonn
    Ag tarraint go teann 'n-ár
      gceann gan moill.

IV

In storm or calm, at peep of
    day,
With eager steps I seek the
    bay,
And strain my eyes in hopes
    to greet
The first glance of our Prince's
    fleet.
    Oh! joyful in Munster the
      music rings;
    And joyful to all who mourn
      their kings;
    The dash of the wave 'gainst
      the ships of the brave,
    And gallant band the future
      brings.

V

Cruinnigheadh gach duine d'fhuil
    Mhileadh thréin
Go ritheann 'n-a chuisle de'n
    bhfíor-fhuil braon,
Do milleadh le dlighthe 's do
    cradhadh le claon,
Go mbuailfidh sé buille le báire
    an tséin.
    Measaim gur subhach do'n
      Mhumhain i gcéin

V

All ye whose hearts beat warm
    and fast
With Gaelic blood, the die is
    cast;
Rise up, rise out, like chiefs of
    old,
And smite the foe whose doom
    is told.
    Oh! sweet in Munster, sweet
      abroad,

'S d'á maireann go dubhach
   de chrú na dtréan
Torann an dtonn le sleasaibh
   na long
Ag tarraint go teann 'n-ár
   gceann le faobhar.

To the saddest race of each
   proud lord
Is the dash of the wave 'gainst
   the ships of the brave,
Who come to join us with the
   sword.

This translation—it is by Dr Robert Dwyer Joyce—is certainly very spirited; here and there it lacks the ease, the force, the full sound of the original. The slight change in each refrain will be observed: the effect in the original is stronger, for the rhyme is changed every time: the change is, therefore, more various, yet more patterned, than in the English version. Only a people trained in literature, skilled in decoration as such, would value such dainty variations as are brought in; and this poem, so spirited, so bright, so finely decorative in feeling, should, as well as any, teach us how far removed from mere folk-poets, careful only of the message, never of the manner, those Munster poets were, whether of the school of Sliabh Luachra or that of Ballykineally.

IV

There is still another side of him to be dwelt upon. In 1769 he had to keep the bed with illness. When convalescent, he gave his time to writing out a book of poetry, some of it his own, for a young girl—a Miss Creagh—who lived near Mallow. The manuscript, consisting of seventy pages, is still to be seen in Maynooth. For a week he bent earnestly upon it; then finishing it, he writes a little note offering "the simple, miserable little gift I promised" to the young lady, and this he follows up with some gallant verses—he was sixty-nine years of age—ending with:

Finished by Pierce, the son of Michael Fitzgerald, the eighteenth
   day of September in the year of our Lord 1769.

And then he rounds all to a close with the surprising words:

Sic transit gloria mundi.

One thinks that some sudden thought, some vision of his own aged self, flashed across his brain as the impulse which prompted the whole endeavour died down into the coldness of achievement.

Yet, he was destined to live on for more than a score of years after this illness: in his last year, 1791, on the 4th July, he lays down his Staff of Office, his *Bata na Bachaille*, handing it and all his powers, his authority, his sway, unequivocally over to Edward Flaherty:

Gach ceannas, gach réim, gach tréineacht daingean gan spás,
Fá thearmann Éamuinn Shéimh Uí Fhlaithbheartaigh an áigh.

For seventy years he had been writing poetry: and whatever of power or authority or sway sat within his eyes was his simply because of this high gift.

He seems to have become quite poor in his old age, dying in the house of his married daughter in Clashmore, on the other side of the river. But they brought him home; and he now lies on the hillside, a few fields away from the house in which he suffered so much.

MÍCHEÁL COIMÍN
(MICHAEL COMYN)
(1688-1760)

I

Of the poets of the century the life of none is more enigmatical than that of Mícheál Coimín.

We have already, in the notes on Seán Ó Tuama, come on

that group of poems which had for theme the fate of Fr Nicholas O'Donnell's little nag, *Preabaire (The Sprightly One)*. "True brown, truly handsome," she was overlooked by a fairy from the hills in the south. Mícheál Coimín of County Clare was one of the poets who comforted him with verse:

Preabaire ar lár san ár gan tapa san uaigh, Is mo shagart breagh sámh gan láir ag taisteal na gcuan.	Preabaire slain in the slaughter, stilled in the grave, And my fine gentle priest horseless travelling the harbours' mouths.

Unable to forget the story of Ireland since the disastrous Union, one trusts that it is quite certain that it was Coimín who wrote this pleasant little poem. It would teach us how well Catholic and Protestant (for Coimín was a Protestant) got on together, even in the Penal times, when both shared the one culture—the one language and national tradition.

"The family of Mícheál Coimín was long settled in Clare," writes Professor T. F. O'Rahilly, "but they claimed to be descended from the Comyns who were Earls of Buchan in the thirteenth century. Having lost his ancestral estate in Cromwellian confiscations, Patrick Comyn obtained, in 1675, a farm of land from the Earl of Thomond at Kilcorcoran, in the parish of Kilfarboy (north of Miltown Malbay); and here his son Mícheál was born. In 1702 the poet married Elizabeth Creagh, niece of Sir Michael Creagh, a former Lord Mayor of Dublin. Mícheál Coimín was a Protestant, and it is not surprising to find him living in more comfortable circumstances than the other poets of the time; but his sympathies were wholly with Ireland and against her oppressor."

If one who has been reading the reckless memoirs, the gay biographies, the flashy recollections (Sir Jonah Barrington's, for instance), which light up for us the life of Anglo-Ireland in that century, close them and move on into the literature— poems, songs, notes, anecdotes—of the contemporary Gaels, what surprises him is how sober it all is, how much it lacks

271

the note of melodrama. Their "crimes" were, perhaps, confined; and in either case they were too over-burdened for such flauntings: they had neither the wherewithal nor the leisure nor the freedom. But Mícheál Coimín shared, it seemed, in some of the flashy doings of the squireens; and hearing of these incidents, we would be perplexed if we did not know of his different station in life: though a Gael, he could afford to have his fling, even to the breaking of the law. We are told that he abducted a young lady, Harriet Stackpoole, from her father's house (it was a favourite recreation with the bloods of the time); we learn also that of the very small harvest of songs, eight or nine all told, that remain to us from his hand, three of them deal with this escapade of his. Sharing thus both in the recklessness of the Anglo-Irishman and in the traditions of the Gael, he is a most interesting figure; and one regrets the want of fuller information.

He died in 1760—that is, fifteen years after the '45—in a period when everything Gaelic was decried as savouring of rebellion. Protestants, naturally, were more conscious of the anti-Gaelic atmosphere than Catholics; Coimín's son, Edward, who seems to have been of the reckless type of Anglo-Irishman, breathed in this after-war bitterness, and, ashamed of being the son of a Gaelic poet, went and burned all the manuscripts he could find in his father's house! In this way is explained why so small a bulk of poetry remains after Mícheál Coimín.

The poet is buried in Kilfarboy churchyard.

II

His memory is dear to us because he set down in dainty verse the ancient legend of Oisín's journey to Tír na n-Óg— the Land of the Ever Young. When he did this the story was, it is likely, already in the possession of every Gaelic mind in

Ireland: in some minds handsome and full, in others meagre and flat: Mícheál Coimín, then, in putting it into Ossianic verse, did a thing that thousands, perhaps unknown to themselves, desired to have done. He used such a language as needed for its following only the slightest acquaintance with the literature: between one thing and the other, one understands why numerous copies began at once to be made of it. Those copies passed from hand to hand, crossed the Shannon into Kerry, crossed Galway Bay into Connacht; travelled north and south along the seaboard, and found their way even to the Hebrides.

What sweet music it is; how gracious and gentle!

Ag seilg dúinn ar maidin cheógh-
    aigh
In imiol-bhórdaibh Locha Léin,
Mar a raibh crainn ba chumhra
    bláth
As ceól gach tráth go binn ag
    éin.
	'Twas a summer's morn and a
	    mist hung o'er
	The winding shore of sweet Loch
	    Lein,
	Where fragrant trees perfume the
	    breeze
	And birds e'er please with a
	    joyous strain.

The very metre, of which the translation gives an idea, is in itself attractive, with its woven rhymes. In the Irish, with its numerous l's, n's and m's, the verse is a sweet mouthful. The thousands of dwellers along the western seaboard had now one other lay in which to lose count of their miseries. Neatly packed in verse, they could now easily memorise that story and carry it with them out to sea in their curraghs, or to the ploughing or the shearing, or on those slow pack-horse journeys of theirs along those bleak, treeless upland roads of Coimín's own countryside. It was their custom to sing such verses; and it is certain that they had scores of other lays in the self-same metre to test it by. O'Curry, who was himself a Clareman, tells us: " In Ireland, I have heard my father sing these Ossianic poems, and remember distinctly the air and the manner of their singing." Then he gives account of a teacher named O'Brien, " who spent much of his time in my father's house, and who was the best singer of Oisín's poems that his contemporaries had ever heard. He had a rich and powerful voice; and often on a calm summer's day, he would go with a party into a boat on the lower Shannon, at my native place, where the river is eight miles wide; and having rowed to the middle of the river, they used to lie on the oars . . . . on which occasions O'Brien was always prepared to sing his choicest pieces, among which were no greater favourites than Oisín's poems. So powerful was the singer's voice that it often reached the shores at either side of the boat in Clare and Kerry, and often called the labouring men and women from the neighbouring fields at both sides down to the water's edge to enjoy the strains of the music."

If O'Brien sang this Lay of Oisín in Tír na n-Óg— " Comyn's Lay," as it was called—those happy ones in the boat, at the water's edge, had surely one magical hour at least to look back upon. Yet if they compared this lay with the many others that relate the loves and adventurings of the Fenian heroes—Finn, the guileful poet; Oisín, his son; Goll Mac Mórna, with his one eye; Conán Maol, with his loose lips, and Diarmuid Ó Duibhne, with his great hour of love and his great woe—if they compared this new lay with some of the others—some of them reaching back almost a thousand years—it was just in this quality of magic that it fell short. For all that, what a gift that Protestant landed gentleman of Kilcorcoran made over on his Catholic peasant neighbours for the easing of their bitter woes!

Besides the famous Lay, he also made for them a story that is only a little less famous—*Torolbh Mac Stairn*. Towards the end of his life he sat him down to write this strange wonder-tale of Torolbh Mac Stairn, nephew of Aralt Mac Canúit, King of the Danes; and our wonder at the tale itself is scarcely less than the wonders related in it gravely by that old man, in whom passion, it must be, had well-nigh died away. How much of the tale is his own, how much of it his people's, it would not be easy to say; but everywhere in it are the magic and the sudden stab that at once make folk-lore so aloof, so surprising and yet so intimate in the reading:

Do bhí sé ag siúbhal le hais an chuain gur shroich doire dluith diamhair coille do bhí ar bhruach na haille, agus do chonnaic ann triúr ban ag siúbhal re céile, gan aon ag feithiomh ortha.

He was walking by the harbour's side until he reached a close mysterious wood that was on the edge of the cliff, and there he saw three women walking together with none attending on them.

To the most beautiful of them he gives his heart. The next day he makes to the same ground, hoping to see her again; but she is not there. He learns that she is gone away to her own country. "He went to his bed, and was in danger of death." The physician names his illness: "the love of a woman." The young man arises, takes ship, sails far and wide, and fails to discover his beloved in any land until finally he reaches the great assembly at Tara. And the passage in which his finding of her is told will, as well as any other, give us to feel the charm of the tale:

D'éirigh Torolbh ina sheasamh agus do ghluais d'ionnsuidhe na bantrachta, agus bu mhaith an mhaise sin dóibh. Ar an gcéad amharc thug ortha do chonnaic ar a lár istigh Fionnabharthach, do chinn ar a raibh ann i ndeilbh agus i ndéanamh, i sgéimh agus i ndreach; agus ar a feicsin dó níor fhan lúth, tapa ná urlabhra ann, ach mar bu chloch nó crann é. Dála Fhionnabharthaigh d'aithin ar an gcéad amharc é, agus do bhán sí mar shneachta na haon oidhche, agus an dara feacht dhearg sí mar an rós, agus d'éirigh n-a seasamh agus do ghluais roimpe tríd an mbantracht dá ionnsuidhe, agus adubhairt de ghuth árd mhór sholus-ghlan, i gcomhchlos dá

Torolbh arose and approached the womenfolk, and that they took well. At his first glance he saw Fionnabharthach (his beloved) in their midst, above all that were there in shapeliness, in build, in beauty and in complexion; and beholding her, he became as a stone or tree without strength, motion or speech. As for Fionnabharthach, she knew him at the first glance; and she grew white as the snow of one night; and at the second look she reddened like the rose, and she stood up and went through the womenfolk towards him, and in the hearing of all present she said in a distinct, clear, loud voice: "A truly-gentle welcome before you to this country, O

275

raibh i láthair: "Fior-chaoin fáilte romhat don tír so, a oighre Ríogh Lochlann! Is fada do chuaird agus is maith do cheannuigh tú mise, agus ní thréigfinn-se thú i gcríoch Lochlann ach dá fhéachuin an raibh cumann nó comghioll ceart agad dam, agus anois ó chím go bhfuil, an luach saothair is fearr ar mo chumas do thabhairt duit do gheobhair é, isé sin mé féin," ar sí, ag síneadh a láimhe chuige, "agus admhuighim gur tú amháin m'aon togha agus m'aon rogha d'fhearaibh an domhain uile."

Do rug Torolbh ar an rioghain idir a dhá láimh agus do phóg sé agus dfháisg le n-a chroidhe í, agus dob fhearr leis a seilbh an uair sin na ceannus Éireann agus Lochlann le chéile.

heir of Denmark's King! Long has been your voyaging and dearly have you purchased me; and in Denmark I would not have deserted you only that I wished to know whether your love and pledge to me were true; and now since I know they are, the best reward I can give you you will receive, that is, myself," and giving him her hand, "and I confess that you only are my one choice and selection of all men in the world."

Torolbh took the lady between his two hands and kissed her and pressed her to his heart, and what he then had in his possession was more to him than the chieftainship of Ireland and Denmark together.

The accents remind one of *Aucassin and Nicolette;* and if we turn to the end of the story we come full on the spirit that informs so much of the art of the Middle Ages. After a world of adventures, Torolbh sickens of his life of slaughter, for it was a little thing for him to slay one hundred in one day's fighting, and he flies to the waste places. There he finds a Jew. An angel tells them they are to die, the two of them, on the third day; and making ready for that, they go and dig themselves a grave:

D'ullmhuigheadar iad féin go hachmuir agus ina dhiaidh sin do chuireadar cóir adhluicthe ortha féin agus do thochladar fá chuas carraige ar thaoibh an ghleanna feart nó uaigh fhairsing ghlan, agus bhí dias aingeal ag tabhairt conganta dhóibh; ionnus an obair nach déanfadh cúig céad fear go

Soon they made themselves ready, and after that they put grave clothes upon them and they digged a clean, spacious grave in the hollow of a rock on the side of the valley; and two angels assisted them, so that by the third day they had as much work done as five hundred

276

raibh déanta ag an dias sin an treas lá. Do bhí an uaigh sin fada doimhin glan agus do chuireadar caonach fír-mhín gorm-uaine deagh-bholaidhtheach agus luibheanna cúmhartha, noch dfhás ar leagadh na súl tré mhíorbhuilighibh Dé, ar an taoibh istigh den uaigh sin.

An uair tháinic an treas lá do ghluais an dias grádhmhar so go doras na huaighe agus do chuireadar a nguidhe chum Dé neimhe agus talmhan. D'éirgheadar 'na gceartsheasamh taréis a n-urnuighthe do rádh agus do chuadar láimh ar láimh go bun na huaighe agus do shíneadar annsin taobh ar thaoibh le n-a chéile ar an leaba chúmhartha chaonaigh sin agus do thuit a gcodladh ortha araon agus d'éaluigh an t-anam ón gcolainn acu.

men could not have done. That grave was clean and deep and long, and they lined it with sweet-scented herbs and pleasant-smelling blue-green tiny mosses, which, through a miracle of God, grew in the twinkling of an eye on the inside of the grave.

When the third day came the loving pair went to the door of the grave and they sent up their prayers to the God of Heaven and Earth. Having done so, they stood erect, and went hand in hand to the bottom of the grave and stretched themselves there side by side together on that perfumed mossy bed, and sleep fell on them and their souls escaped from their bodies.

The whole story is an array of striking pictures like that, with that great secret power of the Middle Ages informing them: magic and intimacy achieved, apparently, without trouble. It is a story that cries out for an efficient illustrator.

These, then, were Mícheál Coimín's gifts to his people. Now, note how different his work is from that of his contemporaries. Reading his, we are in a place apart, a palace of art. Reading theirs, we are in the midst of all the bitterness in which they moved. Yet, theirs is the more living and the braver. Coimín's Protestantism, I believe, accounts for this avoidance of his own time and the themes it suggested. His work enables us to understand a great deal of literary work done in Ireland since his day by very worthy men who have stood, perhaps, just a little too far off from the storms that in their time have harried and worsted their people.

SEÁN Ó COILEÁIN
(JOHN COLLINS)
(1754-1817)

Seán Ó Coileáin is for us at present the poet of two lyrics
—one the famous keen for Timoleague's ruined abbey,
the other a song about the Pretender. It is the first that makes
him a memorable figure, for it is one of the unique things of
modern Irish literature: it is found in every anthology.
Before referring further to it, the very uncertain facts of his
life may be set down.

He was born, it is said, at Kilmeen, some miles north of
Clonakilty, a farmer's son. His mother dying, he was reared
up by her people, in what place is not known—not far, it is
likely, from his birthplace. Again, it is not known to what
college in Spain he was sent to study for the priesthood. He
never became a priest, however. In his early twenties he is
found opening a school in Myross, a jut of land that looks
southwards over the sea between Castlehaven and Glandore
harbour. It is one of the most secret places in Ireland, without
traffic, almost without the pulse of life. He lived as riotously,
it seems, as a poor schoolmaster could, his haunts being
Union Hall, a fishing village; Skibbereen; and Roscarberry.
When four children—two sons, two daughters—had been
born to his wife, jealousy is said to have arisen between
herself and her sister. At last his wife turned her back on
him and went to her people. The poet, however, did not
remain companionless. When his wife died, a "sort of
marriage," so the legend runneth, was arranged between him
and her sister, who was already a mother. Wilder and wilder
grew his habits; and in the end this second wife of his, taking
advantage one day of his being from home, burnt down his
house and his treasures—books and manuscripts. It is a strange
history; but it may all be no more than a folk idea of one
who was very likely quite unlike the quiet people among
whom he lived and died.

Miserably, in poverty, he died in Skibbereen, and was buried in Kilmeen graveyard, a short distance only from that famous abbey which he keened. In his time, there in West Cork, he was known as the Silver Tongue of Munster.

.   .   .   .

It is not certain that he wrote the Lament for Timoleague. The Jacobite song, *An Buachaill Bán*, is a quite typical *Aisling*; indeed, one of the most perfect, if in these we look chiefly for music and decoration:

> Maidean laoi ghil fá dhuille craínn ghluis
> Dhoire am aonar cois imeall trágha
> I bhfís trém' néaltaibh do dhearcas spéirbhean
> Ag teacht ó thaobh dheas na mara am dháil;
> Ba chirte a braoithe ná buille rínnchuirr
> Tanaidhe caoil-phinn buailte ar phár,
> 'Sé dubhairt le díograis, "Och, uaill mo chroidhe-se
> Nó an bhfeicfead choidhche mo Bhuachaill Bán?"

The verse has been translated by " Eireannach ":

> With crimson gleaming the dawn rose, beaming
> On branching oaks nigh the golden shore,
> Above me rustled their leaves, and dreaming,
> Methought a nymph rose the blue waves o'er;
> Her brow was brighter than stars that light our
> Dim, dewy earth ere the summer dawn,
> But she spoke in mourning; "My heart of sorrow
> Ne'er brings a morrow, mo Bhuachaill Bán."

The translator may have worked from a different version, for his fifth and sixth lines are to be found in the second stanza; not in the first. It will be seen that such a poem gives us little help in determining whether its author wrote the Lament, with which it has nothing in common. But it helps us to understand why certain scholars hold that the Lament is, at the one time, both too good and yet not good enough to be the work of Seán Ó Coileáin. He was known to be a traditionalist: he is said to have written a history of Ireland and to have translated certain books of Homer into Irish; his *Aisling* is, as we have said, quite typical. Yet, it is just in this traditional knowledge that the Lament is found wanting. Seán Ó Coileáin would have known the history of the abbey, its connection with the MacCarthys—and such learning is native to Irish poetry; yet, not a touch of it is found in the lyric. It is said to have been written in 1815, when Seán was on old man, and yet it is written in one of the dead bardic metres: it can have been, then, only obviously an exercise. And the chosen metre is not worked out perfectly —the faults, again, being such as a good traditionalist would not have made. The blemishes, it will be understood, are found only in the unessentials. The essentials are not only right, but are perfectly right according to the best modes of Irish poetry. In every line of it there are at the one time both homeliness and intensity—the double test-stone which I find never to fail in estimating Gaelic poetry: by the same test-stone may all pre-Renaissance art-work be recognised and understood. It was a Gael who wrote this poem, a Gael whose mind was nurtured in Gaeldom: that is all that we at present may with certainty hold. It seems to us that Seán Ó Coileáin could have written it; and that he or any other poet of the time would fall just into such errors as are to be found in it. One thing is clear: no pedant ever wrote it. It offends the surface-laws of Irish metrics. But the hidden canons of Irish art, those that the soul rather than the mind seeks and intimately apprehends—these it obeys.

The poem runs: In a night of great stillness the poet wanders by the sea, meditating on the cruel changes incident to life, when, forgetful of his steps he suddenly finds himself looking at the gateway of the ruined abbey:

Bhí foradh fiar ar a thaoibh—
Is cian ó cuireadh i gcló—
Ar a suidheadh saoithe is cliar
As taistealaigh trialltha an róid.

" By its side was a crooked bench—long since it was fashioned!—where learned men and clerics used to sit, as well as wayfarers passing the road."

Thereon he sits and weeps, his meditations on the mutability of things vividly reinforced:

Do bhí aimsear ann 'na raibh
An teach so go soilbh, subhach!

"A time there was when this house was prosperous and happy!"

A touch of that natural simplicity which distinguishes Goethe's lyrics from those of lesser men. Then the poet pictures what he sees, with that precision that is ever the handmaiden of intensity:

Och, ní fhionnaim anois fád'iadh
Ach carnán criadhta cnámh!

"Woe, within your shelter now I find only heaps of earth and bones!"

He then turns to himself. He, too, has changed: "the hunt of the world went in his face," and now his only use is to weep. His heart is a withered kernel:

Dá bhfóirfeadh orm an bás
Badh dhearbh m'fháilte fá n-a
chómhair!

"If death come to me with relief a true welcome I'd give it."

There is an account of a priest reading Gray's elegy to this Seán Ó Coileáin, requesting him to make such a poem. It may be so; and the poem made is just as Irish as Gray's is English.

CONCLUSION

As a last note to this book, there are certain points I should wish to underline.

I

Entering a gallery of the sculptures of ancient Greece for the first time, one is struck with the absence of what we are pleased to call "individuality" in the artists who wrought them. Gods, demi-gods, creatures of the shades, the woods, the streams, mortals, too—all of them flaunt before us the same round and perfect limbs, the same serene brows. We are not urged to re-speak ourselves the thoughts that still or inflame their breasts. Had they none? we ask ourselves. And had their creators nothing to say from their own hearts, warm, urgent? To all of them did Life present the self-same countenance, shapely, yet expressionless; the self-same limbs, peerless, unworn by the storms within the spirit? And how much stronger would this feeling of ours be if the Renaissance had never happened, it, after all, being but a gigantic accident and not duly in the nature of things—if national-Christian sculpture had blossomed on and on right down the centuries, so that here and now it and no other were our tradition in the cutting of stone? Yet, it does not require much trafficking with these bright marbles to know how vain is such questioning; and, indeed, our wonder afterwards is that ever such misapprehensions should have chilled our welcome to such gracious presences. How foolish and dull we were to have indulged, even for a day, the thought that all those ancient sculptures must have been wrought by the same hand, in the same place, and at the same time!

When we are newly-arrived at a strange palace of art, what we are most conscious of is not the essentials, but the traditional moulds in which these essentials are embodied. Of such city beautiful we are not yet freemen: it is not yet ours. To be free of a tradition, really to know it, is to be unconscious of the moulds it is accustomed to use.

So with one who, educated into English culture, strikes on Irish literature. What he is most aware of in it is what he most likely speaks of as *clichés*: he is like the new visitor to the Greek sculptures, who cannot rid himself of those self-same straight noses, benignant brows, and rounded limbs. Those *clichés* continue to haunt him until he has seen them so often that he can see them no more: then only he begins to feel what the artists foolishly dreamt could never escape his notice.

Traditional moulds in Irish poetry are as self-contained, as rigid, as unmistakable, as the traditional moulds in Greek sculpture. Those moulds in themselves are worthy of remark; but one hopes that the time is at hand, at least in Ireland, when all that can be said of them will have been so often said that the essentials will at last be considered worthy of discussion.

II

In studying those Irish poets, one becomes more and more conscious of the great lack of long-established, adequate, and native moulds in modern literatures; and one also becomes very sceptical of the honour paid to "individuality." One begins to think that that saying of the style being the man has done untold harm; one wonders if it has not been wrongly interpreted. And one fears that, because of this fetish, if England or, indeed, almost any "modern" people had to live through what Ireland had to live through in the seventeenth and eighteenth centuries, no literature worthy of the name would remain afterwards to tell of the agony.

III

In such study one also becomes aware of the violence, the annihilating violence, such moulds inflict on what we so glibly name "individuality." And perhaps this explains why these moulds are necessary, for such sort of individuality as they destroy is not really the man: it consists usually of merely assumed characteristics, worthy of nothing except annihilation.

If we take Mícheál Coimín's two longest works, his *Lay* and his story, *Torolbh Mac Stairn,* and know nothing of him except as he exists in them, we should never dream that he lived, at least in part, the life of Anglo-Irish Ireland in the eighteenth century. There they stand, rich in Mediæval qualities, the very qualities which, of all others, were most flouted in the Dublin, and, indeed, the world, of that day.

Or take those lines:

> How entertaining Amaryllis finds
> A method to revive our drooping minds,
> And surveys sylvan groves in pleasing hours
> Amongst the stately trees and shady bowers.
> The feathered choir melodious notes do move
> With tunes attending to the heavens above.

If one ask what weary Fleet-street scribbler or harmless country parson wrote them, how strange to be answered: Neither. It was Seán Ó Tuama an Ghrinn wrote them! How inflexible a thing, then, is a literary mode! How it imposes its will on one! And how learn as much if one cannot get clear outside such of these moulds as are second nature to us?

IV

On reading the biographical notes we have of those poets of ours, the prudent reader will recollect Browning's *How It Strikes a Contemporary*. What we know of those poets is really only such an image of them as our peasant folk-mind created for itself. These traditional accounts have not yet been sifted or examined with care: we should accept them only with great caution. And we should also keep in mind the spirited defence that Dr. Sigerson has put up for one of those men, Ó Cearbhalláin. " He had one failing: at a time when all were convivial he was convivial: in the case of stupid persons who have endowed the world with nothing this failing is passed over; in the case of any man whose genius has made him a benefactor it affords a welcome theme for censure to that respectable class—the men of no genius."

.   .   .   .   .   .

Here, then, my tribute, humble, halting, inept, unlearned, to a body of men who for long were almost entirely forgotten and who as yet are only most clumsily apprehended—their lives, their works, their genius. Of all our forgotten dead, of whom these words following have been written, those poets, it seems to me, most terribly upbraid us: " To them has been meted out the second death—the lot feared beyond all else by men of honour. They have been buried by the false hands of strangers in the deep pit of contempt, reproach and forget-fulness—an unmerited grave of silence and shame."[1]

---

[1] Alice Stopford Green, *The Making of Ireland and its Undoing.*